AF540514

CHANCE AND PROBABILITY

By the same Author

- Violence and Religion: Cross Cultural Opinions and Consequences
- Social Behaviour of Children
- Contemporary Social Science Research: An Evaluation of National and Non-National Contributions
- Spirituality and Well-being

About the Author

Ralph Tanner has a B.Sc. and Diploma in Social Anthropology from Oxford University and a D. Phil in Law from Stokholm University. He has done fieldwork in Thailand, the Philippines, Guyana, Zambia, Zimbabwe, Tanzania, Uganda and Kenya as well as in Britain and Eire. He was Chairman of the East African Institute of Social Research and Lecturer in Comparative Religion in the University of London. He has published books on Murder in Uganda. Witchcraft killings and religions and successful change and a cross cultural study of the Roman Catholic Mass. He has co-authored books on the social ecology of religion and the environment. He has written numerous articles on the social aspects of religious change, translation and language use in religion, as well as on behavioural theories in the *Journal of Modern African Studies, Africa, Journal of the Social Sciences, Nordic Journal of African Studies, Antropos, Studia Missionalia and others.* He is currently working on studies of religious behaviour as a working misunderstanding and the commonplace nature of religious experiences

Chance and Probability

The Limitations of the Social Sciences

R.E.S. Tanner

CONCEPT PUBLISHING COMPANY PVT. LTD.
NEW DELHI-110059

ISBN: 13-978-81-8069-729-6

First Published 2011

Published and Printed by

Concept Publishing Company Pvt. Ltd.
Regd. Office:
A/15-16, Commercial Block, Mohan Garden
New Delhi-110059 (India)
Phones : 25351460, 25351794, *Fax* : 091-11-25357109
Email: publishing@conceptpub.com
Website: www.conceptpub.com

Editorial Office:
H-13, Bali Nagar, New Delhi-110 015, India.

Cataloging in Publication Data--*Courtesy:* D.K. Agencies (P) Ltd. <docinfo@dkagencies.com>

Tanner, R. E. S. (Ralph E. S.), 1921-
Chance and probability : the limitations of the social sciences / R.E.S. Tanner.
p. cm.
Includes bibliographical references (p.) and index.
ISBN 9788180697296

1. Chance. 2. Probabilities. 3. Social sciences—Research. I. Title.

DDC 300.72 22

Dedication

Father J. Laishley, S.J.
as an acknowledgement of his intellectual stimulus to my understandings over the years.

Preface

Social scientists aim professionally at scientifically acceptable research and results based on pragmatically obtained and coordinated information. It is more reasonable to see our research as no more than attempts to make as pragmatic as possible the collection of data on behaviour which is subject to constant change and influenced by factors which are either unknown or impossible to ascertain. We are the recorders of recent history

So it would seem that the efforts of the social sciences to estimate the future beyond some of the common sense immediacies in applied work is unlikely to be more than professionalized guesswork with little hope of accurate fulfilments.

Further social scientists in their research work are usually intruders into social environments over which they have little hope of unobtrusive immersion. Their access to information about more than everyday affairs available to guests and tourists, is largely a matter of chance.

Even if social science researchers attain and maintain long-term involvement within their areas of study, their outsiders status remains. They provide valuable qualified insights as to the nature of particular behaviours but there are always factors involving probability, the very long odds on some particular processes occurring in which the factors relating to chance in their own behaviour as well as to what they may be able to see and hear. Inevitably issues of probability and chance must predominate in the professional work of social scientists.

Acknowledgements

In many years of field work in human behaviour the chance association with certain men became key figures who enabled my understandings to be humanized through the asset of bilingualism. These men Dashi Yaw of the Kodaung,Myanmar, Ntemi Kapongo of Nassa, Nfumo Kabadi of Nyegezi and Juma Ndamulo of Mwanza provided the openings for the operation of chance for which I remain grateful to their memory; may they rest in peace.

More immediately I am grateful to Sharon Cure, the Librarian of Trinity College, Oxford as well as to the staff of the Tadley branch of the Hampshire County Library for a constant flow of off-prints who have enabled valuable explorations into the unknown.

Contents

PART—C
PROBABILITY—PROFESSIONALIZED GUESSING

Part—A
Social Science and Human Behaviour

1

Introduction

Uncertainty is a permanent feature of both human social life and human psychological understandings. Substantial amounts of time and effort are spent everywhere in estimating the probability of future events through what are considered to be scientific methods. In addition there are contemporary social and religious ways of finding out and controlling the unknowable future. Sociology and psychology think that as social sciences they have the potential and in some cases the real ability to produce conclusions about their work and future probabilities which have parallel accuracy to the productions of the hard sciences. In this they have two constant difficulties which they have been unable and indeed will never be able to overcome. At the same time all contemporary societies and individuals have developed their own secular and religious systems for attempting to keep the future under institutional and personal control.

Firstly, whatever mastery social scientists manage to achieve over the complexities of human behaviour and the possible enduring patterns which they may be able to identify, there will always be the inevitability of chance events disrupting whatever evenness societies may achieve or endeavour to establish.

Chance events are constantly and irregularly occurring in all societies, institutions and to individuals. Some may be expected as part of the inevitability of life but others erupt into the lives of almost everyone without any warning; being bitten by a rabid dog or poisonous snake in India, the deaths from stampedes in crowded conditions which have occurred often enough at sporting events as well as at Mecca during the Hajj. There have been many thousands more deaths in natural disasters often more predominantly housebound women as men were away fishing when the recent 'tsunami' tidal waves or earthquakes struck Indonesia, Thailand, Kashmir and Sri Lanka.

So probability assessments will always be subject to a wide range of accidents for which history provides endless examples such as the nuclear leak at Chernobyl, Russia which can have been expected to happen in some nuclear plants somewhere some time but from events for which we have no advance preconceptions at all such as the emergence of new diseases of which the AIDS epidemic is the best known and the monstrous acts of mass terrorism such as the destruction of the World Trade Centre in New York and the Mumbai attacks. There is the long drain of proportionately more destructive persistent terrorism in Northern Ireland and Iraq. Recent research emphasizes the inadequacy of considering either genetic or environmental effects during one period of development outside the context of preceding and subsequent influences (Clarke and Clarke, 1984). "When in non-human populations both genotype and environment are held constant 'chance' variation in the lifespan of individuals in a population is still quite large" (Rea *et al.*, 2005). There is no reason to exclude human beings from the inevitabilities of both biological and social chance.

Even if we examine the statistics from medical institutions we will always see that the actions of physicians and surgeons of undoubted competence and with adequate professional support, based on their assessments of probability will always show significant inaccuracies from chance, misadventure and error. The unexpected will always cloud medical actions because they are dealing with human variability and not just the hard facts available from clinical laboratory evaluation of inorganic chemistry.

We will see that the methodologies of the social sciences to collect information about human behaviour seem to lack much of the sophistication of medicine. From this fact alone we must expect greater inaccuracies when they quantify their conclusions about human behaviour rather than making them from more general qualitative assessments and less exact probabilities.

Estimating the future probability of events with which we have no personal connection other than a professional commitment will depend on our range of knowledge. This may increase or diminish the range of alternatives and the degree to which we are dispassionate about the data, a difficult requirement in itself.

Intuition (Myers, 2002) is often a feature of personal relationships for which there are clues provided by the situation. Judges, psychiatrists and police officers are intuitively poor at detecting liars, not much better than chance but federal agents perhaps with more training and experience were still only 64 per cent correct (Ekman and O'Sullivan, 1991).

There is ample evidence that we are biased towards events and people with whom we are familiar (Moreland and Beach, 1990). It has also been suggested that instinctive evolutionary needs (Zajonc, 1998) have required us to avoid the unfamiliar. Of course, professional training and practical experience can make individuals whether diviners or diagnosticians more competent in assessing data and presumably basing their behaviour on what they have worked out as conforming to the appropriate probabilities.

Any disaster, however large or small, will always be a major turning point in the lives of those involved as individuals because as Stalin is reported to have remarked that mass deaths are only statistics but a single death is always a tragedy. In a stampede at a Zimbabwe football match there were twelve deaths; this event will have been a turning point in the lives of their relatives and in-laws and probably just as traumatic for the public workers who had to disentangle the bodies (Madzimbamuto and Madamumbe, 2004).

The second factor which prevents the social sciences from taking on the professional characteristics of the hard sciences and thus from being able to make positive and scientifically acceptable statements about the anticipated consequences of events, is the scientific weakness of the data on which they base their conclusions. We cannot know whether the statements of informants or the contents of documents are exact and indeed the extent of this inexactness. The only scientifically acceptable fact is that such a person made such a statement at a certain time and place but what they actually said requires verification. The witnesses of an event cannot be considered as producing scientifically acceptable facts. The legal systems of non-literate societies start with the assumption that all witnesses are biased and that to require the swearing of an oath to tell the truth is no more than optimistic stupidity.

The standards of proof maintained by the social sciences are usually less than what would be required by a Western court of law to establish that something had occurred beyond reasonable doubt. The murder of children are horrifying events for all those involved but as comparison of the official evidence on child homicides in the United States showed there was little uniformity except for the ethnicity and gender of the victims (Lyman *et al.*, 2004).

Social scientists consider themselves to be reliable witnesses in matters which they are researching but these are occasions which are complex at whatever level they are studied. These professional men and women are no different to others who have been found to be poor observers particularly when they have to cope with coincidental multiple variables. A research project showed that with an American sample their accuracy on dealing with a five-way interaction was no better than chance and that three or four variables were the limit to the human processing capacity (Halford *et al.*, 2005).

So we will see that the standards of social science which go towards statements of probability are almost invariably evidentially weak so that they could be classed as professionally committed guesswork. We can do no more than quote Karl Popper's general comment about anthropology as a pseudo-science 'The triumph of social anthropology is the triumph of a pseudo-observational, pseudo-descriptive and pseudo-inductive generalising methodology and above all marks the triumph of a pretended objectivity and hence an imitation of the methods of natural science' (Popper, 1964).

We perhaps know but would rather not admit that relying on assessments of probability as to what may or may not happen in the future regarding specific events or general eventualities on which to base our actions, is often neither logical or accurate. What is given as what may happen in the future is rarely exact enough on which to base actions and retrospectively have more often than not been wide of the mark. Nevertheless schooling, marriages and farming are all based on estimates of future success. Probabilities as much as anything are based on hopes of avoiding misfortune rather than on their inevitability.

Much would depend on the amount of hard data available on which to make predictions such as the weather and disease identified by laboratory testing. When the data are weak and depend as much as anything on qualified opinions, probabilities become less exact. Norwegian psychiatrists were asked to predict the one-year outcome for 88 schizophrenic patients and they made reasonably accurate predictions which were better than chance (Atakan *et al.*, 1990) but the adjective reasonable allows for wide interpretations and perhaps their relatives could have guessed at much the same level of success given the optimism of many relationships.

Humans have been preoccupied as far back as historical records go with concerns about how and to what extent they can base their activities on an assumed knowledge of the future. It is indeed possible to act on the assumption that the future will happen as planned but the planning does not take into account all the factors that may be involved to some usually unknowable extent. We know well enough that chance events are likely to disrupt and destroy even the simplest and most immediate of plans. Even a day ahead involves probabilities; trains run late, the car will not start, cows break out of their field and wild animals get in, white ants can cause a house to suddenly collapse, just as storms can disrupt holidays, house repairs and harvesting.

Going beyond the immediate future involves so many imponderables which may or may not occur that probability is no more than informed guess-work in which the Hindu diviner, economic estimator, scientifically trained physician and one's grandmother are probably equally competent in making longer term forecasts. Most informed opinions are based on the assumption that previous patterns will be more or less repeated; uncertainty cannot be factually allowed for because we do not know and indeed can never know what the future might be.

As far back as historical records go persistent and professionalized efforts have been made to guess-estimate the future in all societies and in all known social contexts and these forms of what might well be called divination have formed part of every culture. Prayers for a successful marriage and the hopes of medical probabilities have much in common. Unreliable as they may have been statistically, all these traditional and quasi-traditional modern professionals will have made their estimates on the probabilities involved based on certain accessible factors; an acquired knowledge of the people who are wanting to know the probable future and the situations in which they are involved. In the same way the modern political and economic planner knows the issues which are at stake of which one will certainly be their own reputation in providing satisfactory probabilities about the future often in ambiguous terms or covered by a list of the possible adverse eventualities. Economic forecasters have a poor record once they go beyond the relative simplicities of market research evaluations.

There is the famous conversation recorded by the early African explorer and Christian missionary David Livingstone and a rain-maker in which the latter remarked that he hoped Europeans were not so stupid as to believe that the rituals he performed made rain (Livingstone, 1857, 23-5). It is not so much the professional guessing the future on which to base personal actions but a way of organising behaviour to fit in with possibilities which have been authenticated by socially useful processes. These have slowly developed whether they are the prayers at a Christian shrine, the divination procedures in a Taiwanese temple or through the rituals of a doctor's consulting room. A visit to any reputable Chinese, Japanese or Indian temple will show that the estimating of probabilities is a major preoccupation of people in their thousands. Moreover, they find it useful to do so. The rationalist in his concentration on the provable is certainly right but it fails to provide how we should cope with the alternative 'blanks' left behind.

So we need to examine the circumstances in which statements of probability are made by whom and for whom and what have been the reactions to successful as well as unsuccessful estimates. This is not a situation in which there can be any sustainable division between less developed and more developed societies and between people with different levels of education, intellect or status. Working out the probabilities about what concerns their future are equally the concern of the Masai cattle herder in Tanzania as well as the Mumbai businessman, the insurance actuary and the Taoist diviner specialising in *feng-shui*; they are all as it were in the same business for the same reasons.

Probability is a consistent preoccupation of humans in all social environments as they are always concerned if not worried about their futures. Once we leave the exactnesses of hard science, we are always in environments affected by multitudinous undefined and indefinable variables complicated by chance. The assessment of probabilities is a very personal matter and only in a minority of cases a professional one affecting a small range of affairs. But intuition has little part in this study of social science probability assessments coming from data which they may or may not have collected themselves. The whole range of probability production has to be assessed in a culturally global perspective and to avoid such an approach must be biasing. The Western scientifically guided production of probabilities covers only a small proportion of its social existence and its success is a questionable or as acceptable as the results of Zambian Ndembu or Chinese Taoist divinations; restrict the definition and the resulting statistics and social understandings are similarly restricted.

The future is a matter of concern to all people whether as individuals or in the various social collectivities from families to whole societies. Since this future is inaccessible not only because of chance but also because we have repeatedly shown little ability to foresee what science will discover often by accident, it remains a source of anxiety.

We thus put enormous intellectual and personal effort into trying to foresee and control the future. We do this in a minority of situations by using available scientific methods often based on inexact data as well as by more personal, private and secular rituals in attempts to foresee and control luck and fate.

Since these scientific and personal efforts to foresee and control the future are closely intermingled, it is impossible to separate them except through the biases inherent in the dominances of the scientific mind. Thus it is prudent to start any study of chance and probability by illustrating the weaknesses in quantifying human behaviour and the extent to which the social sciences have probably not gone much beyond what would have happened by chance anyway. Hence many ways in which contemporary varieties of divination may serve parallel purposes to the social sciences in providing a more humanly acceptable form of coping with probabilities for men, women and indeed children.

2

Social Sciences and Human Behaviour

Once we have established that scientifically accurate conclusions about human behaviour are difficult to obtain beyond a limited range of simple primary correlations because any human activity is variable, unstable and related to innumerable factors which are difficult to define, there are two consequences. Firstly, that probability as to what might happen in the future becomes more an exercise in excluding possible influences than in involving incontrovertible factors; and secondly, the intrusion of chance as a fundamental feature in all the factors involved in reaching conclusions from research.

THE DELUSION OF FINDING EXACTNESS

The social sciences are a group of modern academic disciplines principally sociology and psychology that are concerned with human behaviour. They are theoretically midway between the presumed longstanding exactness of the hard sciences and the imaginative thinking of the arts and humanities. Social scientists use combination of quantitative and qualitative methods in their attempts to accurately describe and predict human behaviour.

The social sciences exercise much theoretical thought and research energy in trying to find universal laws for human behaviour so that the apparent similarity of all human beings as a single species can lead to keys to behaviour which would be equally applicable in the riverside communities of the Amazon as to the canal-side ones in Amsterdam. They attempt this in the same way as the 'hard' sciences which have achieved this in the laws of physics and other conclusions which have withstood the test of time even if we admit that there are fashions in scientific thinking (Kuhn, 1962). The results of these efforts lead to a conclusion that 'as for predictive theory the study of human affairs that of an eternal beginning. In essence we have only specific cases and context dependent learning' (Flyvbjerg, 2007). It is a useless quest as individuals and the circumstances in which they live are too varied to allow for the finding of any universal laws covering behaviour.

In this work the social sciences tend to be seen as 'soft' in contrast to the inescapable realities of the 'hard' sciences if only because individual and collective human behaviour is always in the processes of predictable and unpredictable change. Nevertheless its research on human behaviour is linked to every aspect of human life and indeed no human activities can escape a range of correlations to the harsher unstable realities of economics, medicine and geography.

It is one of the delusions of social scientists researching human behaviour that exactness, the 'truth' if not immediately available is out there waiting to be found. Apart from the philosophical nature of any such assumption it is exceedingly doubtful that this can exist even for the hard sciences (Kuhn, 1962). Human behaviour internally and externally is constantly changing from one minute to the next. This is the situation facing researchers despite the continuing consequences of the European Enlightenment, the determinist followers of Comte, the fashions in scientific thought and the tremendous advances in scientific exactness. Permanency in the form of behavioural laws has continued to elude researchers. Accuracy if it exists at all has always been found to be narrowly circumstantial.

The first difficulty is that human beings are individually different and it seems likely that any found similarities are the result of excluding many psychological, physiological and social factors from such assessments. This disguises the fact that these calculated averages are difficult if not impossible to apply to individuals. Moreover, these individuals are in the constant processes of biological and psychological change. The human being as an identifiable single unit is basically unstable.

Secondly, the social theatre in which the individual performs has very little stability and it is one in which the social environment, the audience before whom the individual performs is itself similarly unstable. There is a constant process of change initiated by individuals and social groups apart from those which are totally outside the control of either individuals or societies in the environment, global economics and political movements. This means that whatever is being currently researched is in the process of becoming out-of-reach history.

Finally, the social science researchers themselves are not and can never be detached systematic machine-like observers of human behaviour; they are creatures of their own socializations. Just as those whom they observe do not conform to averages, there are no typical researchers. Each one is different so that all that they see and assess is filtered through and becomes in part the result of a changing individual process. It is safe to conclude that instability is the dominant feature of all human behaviour and as such chance is a constant factor in what is encountered and recorded.

As the nature of scientific enquiry and the understanding of human behaviour has become increasingly interdisciplinary with blurred boundaries between specializations, the importance of what the social sciences may and indeed can contribute has grown and with this an imbalance between intrinsically variable social factors and the growth of 'hard' scientific assumptions.

So on the one hand social scientists feel that their profession ought to have the same standing as the natural sciences. The 'hard' scientists conclude that this cannot be so because of its inability to meet their standards of fact and methodology required for any activity to be classified as scientific. There have been a number of comments by prominent scientists and thinkers as to the validity of the social sciences to be classified as a science. Apart from Popper, Ernest Rutherford, the Nobel Prize winner for nuclear physics, said that 'knowledge that one cannot measure numerically is a poor sort of knowledge' but also that 'in science there is only physics, all the rest is stamp collecting' (Birks, 1962). While the expressed feelings of 'hard' scientists may have become less exclusive and more aware of the unexplained and perhaps inexplicable and limited aspects of their understandings, there still remains a general view that social science research cannot produce results which can be confirmed by others who have a less personal involvement in their validity.

THE ORIGINS OF SOCIAL SCIENCE

Centralized states have frequently counted people and property from as far back as written historical records are available certainly from several millennia before the Christian era. This has always been carried out for severely practical reasons related to politics and revenue. There was never any accumulation of numerical data for the acquisition of knowledge isolated from immediate political and economic needs.

The founders of the social sciences may have been firstly the Persian Al Biruni who died in CE1048, a mathematician who wrote widely on scientific subjects with a general interest in the behavioural aspects of all that he came across. He could certainly have taken a quantitative approach should he have seen that this could be a reasonable way of recording data. He was critical of hearsay and stated that eyewitnesses could only provide short-term information. Perhaps more specifically the Tunisian Ibn Khaldun who died in CE1406 could be called the forefather of sociology with his three volume *Muqaddimah,* an introduction to history (Khaldun, 1967). Both these scholars among a number of similar Muslim intellectuals were certainly polymaths from the breadth of their knowledge probably without any parallels in Western culture at that time. They were qualitative in their approach to the accumulation of knowledge about human behaviour.

So throughout history until the European Enlightenment, people and property continued to be counted for short-term rational reasons rather than for any abstract pursuit and accumulation of knowledge. With this came not so much the understanding that human behaviour could be quantified which had been known for some millennia but the idea that all human activities could be accurately recorded in much the same way as inanimate materials. There was an almost overwhelming move towards mathematical models culminating in the work of the still influential Auguste Comte. He stated that ideas passed through the sequential stages of theology, philosophy and science as the founding father of modern sociology allied to the works of Leibniz, Marx, Darwin and Mendel. So from then on the social sciences under professional pressure to be scientific rather than social has usually tried to quantify the results of its research.

Science consists of statements about objects and their relationships which start from precise definitions. That indeed is a hard standard to follow unless what is involved is inanimate and has some long-term consistency. Conclusions about the collision of two pieces of granite are likely to survive the lives of the scientists who made these calculations. Such facts are expressed in numbers. Blood pressure can be expressed accurately enough in numbers but the reasons which may or may not account for high or low rates cannot be defined with the accuracy required by science as all the behavioural factors are individually and environmentally fluid.

Numbers are reflections of exactness unless there have been errors in the preceding calculations. They are not symbols which can have a fan of personal and institutionally provided meanings. They have no parallels to a religious icon, a cross, a *swastika,* a national flag or a picture, although there can be numbers which have magical connotations. The number 7 is exact and obviously enough it cannot have the same equivalences as 6.99 or 7.01.

The difficulty is over what this numerical exactness represents and human characteristics and human behaviour do not fit easily if at all into what individuals are and do. Since we are all discretely different in our behaviour even to our identical twin numbers can be used to describe such individualism in isolation. It is questionable if in fact the person can ever be socially isolated but numeracy becomes increasingly inaccurate when it is used to describe what individuals do in association with others.

When numbers are used to describe human characteristics and behaviour this is made possible by either restricting the data to a limited range of knowable and partially definable factors, such as age, education, locality and marital status. This is a distortion by restriction or by creating a statistical reality out of the many thousand possibilities. Almost every social science report restricts from the nature of the hypotheses tested and what it excludes. A study of American high school dropouts (Pagani *et al.,* 2008) found that this was tied to single parent mothers who themselves had not finished high school and pupils who had had to repeat primary school grades. It is not that these conclusions are wrong or possibly rather obvious but that they exclude a whole range of other possible reasons; the absence or presence of a supportive extended family, social welfare help, local role models, part-time work opportunities for the mother and her health to name just a few active factors. In addition there will be the existence of bias which come from single factors or a combination of factors. Design faults in the research project, data errors, personal influences over conduct of the project, its analysis and the ways in which the conclusions are presented.

It is not that social scientists are deliberately providing false or at least falsifiable data but that numerical exactness in relation to human behaviour and characteristics is just not a scientific possibility except under the conditions which we have suggested. Numbers do not fit easily into the constantly changing ephemeral and indefinable nature of human behaviour; they can indicate trends better than actualities.

THE RESTRICTION OF FACTORS CONSIDERED IN RESEARCH

Let us look first at the ways in which social science researchers reach their conclusions by restricting the numbers of factors that are considered in order to make the material manageable. To relate the epidemiology of a particular disease to a single act or type of act is certainly making an easy correlation. However to relate this to ten variable factors and there is a loss of manageability and progressively more so for whatever additional factors are brought in for consideration.

There must be hundreds of factors which are possibly related to HIV infections as an event affecting single individuals and none can be ruled out from the start as too insignificant to be worth considering in its singular involvements. The ruling in and ruling out of factors must diminish the value of conclusions or correlations of what is considered. A comparative study of mental illness among Christians and Muslims in the Lebanon (Katchadourian, 1974) is an extreme case in which the only factors considered were sex and religious affiliation and yet the conclusions are made to the numerical accuracy of one decimal point. Surely the social tightness of their communities and extended families must have been factors as would have been the prolonged periodic violent political instability of that country.

Another study comparing the death rates of legitimate and illegitimate children in North Carolina was tied only to the factors of white and non-white (Scurletis *et al.*, 1969) was similarly shown to this level of numerical accuracy. It did not consider that skin colour except in its obvious extremes is both a physical and social classification.

Educational level is frequently recorded as a dominant factor related to examination levels passed, or numbers of years spent in the educational system. However, the tests are not standardized nor are they related to the personal or environmental factors by which individual children are processed. Being educated is an individual process involving both formal and informal elements. Their records of achievement are largely the statistical creations of use to planners which may be of limited value in explaining the subsequent behaviour and abilities of individuals.

Whether the individual is married or not is often listed but marriage in most circumstances is a legal rather than a definable social state. There are no static factors involved which can be used either as the result of self-evaluation or from observation since any relationship can change overnight. Although the Tanzanian Sukuma are predominantly pastoral subsistence farmers when asked whether a couple are married on a certain date tend to reply that they are more or less married than they were at a comparative date; this surely is a comment that approaches to social reality rather than as a binary enumeration. The legal status of marriage may not even include sexual intercourse which is absent from a proportion of Western marriages and may not occur in the inheritance of widows under Tanzanian Shashi customary law or the pre-pubertal Hindu arranged marriages between children.

It is safe to conclude that no human characteristic or behaviour can be numerically reduced to conclusions drawn from many simplistic primary categories, and the exclusion from consideration of the assumed unessential derivative factors. Whatever may be the cumulative significance of averages we may be certain that they do not fit any individual with any social realism.

THE CREATION OF STATISTICALLY VALID PSEUDO-REALITIES

A high proportion of social science publications involve tables of statistics which we are assured have all been checked for internal validity. There can be little doubt that this is so and that the authors cannot be faulted on their mathematics. Any study of social behaviour which puts its conclusions into numbers will be as accurate or inaccurate as the socially acquired data on which they are based.

Let us take almost at random the results of social science research on religion and old hospitalized patients (Koenig *et al.*, 2003) in which tables of exact numbers give figures for such categories as intrinsic religiosity, observer related religiosity, self-related spirituality, daily religious experiences, use of religious television and wireless and organizational and non-organizational affiliations and so on. These are all quite valid areas in which there may be correlations with the use of health services during hospitalization. But how can daily spiritual experiences be expressed as numbers with any anticipation of accuracy? What is a spiritual experience and in what ways can we be sure that these persons have had the experiences which they claim to have had? How can an observer rate the religiosity of other persons whose religious ideas and practices may be in the mind and for whom they may not have any long-term close relationship? Social science observers are predominantly agnostic and would not give the benefit of the doubt to older patients over seemingly 'primitive' ritualisms. What reliability can be put on their statements about the use of religious television and wireless when we can have no assumption that they have remained awake during the claimed times. Quantitatively expressed data in social science records have to be statistically suspect because they are usually based on definitions which have none of the hard accuracy required for numerical expression.

In practice there can be no assumption that any of the numbers used to illustrate the conclusions of these researchers have any such exact validity beyond the fact that the data was recorded numerically and that the tables are arithmetically correct. This is not to suggest that they are wrong but only that their statistical expression gives a false backing to possibly useful and valuable factors. These might just as well have been found out by qualitative and seemingly impressionistic methods.

A study of the grief reactions of widows in the first year of their bereavement in Boston and Sydney (Maddison and Viola, 1968) included several behavioural changes which can only have come from self-reporting; increased smoking and alcohol intake, general nervousness, depression, persistent fears, repeated peculiar thoughts, nightmares and insomnia for which figures are given in the illustrative tables. These are all factors which can have no consistency between one person's interpretation and another even if they shared an understanding of the language used by the researcher or written in the questionnaire. We do not know the extent to which these answers provided by the widows conform to what those cultures consider to be the appropriate behaviour for such people. We have no confirmatory data for what they have stated to have occurred and this may have occurred anyway for reasons which may have had little to do with bereavement. The consequences of bereavement may be economic deprivation rather than sentimental and relief from unsatisfactory and tiring relationship involving either care or abuse.

A study of women's health in Goa, India (Qadeer, 2006) contains a number of tabulated numerical conclusions. These tables include income levels, age, causes of death, incidence of acute and untreated ailments. All of these would be either self-reported or supplied by medical institutions. We have no data as to the extent of this professional coverage and whether these diagnoses were made by doctors with laboratory confirmations. Medical diagnoses unless confirmed by laboratory analyses cannot have an assumed record of accuracy when multiple morbidities are present and when medical rituals alone may have a short-term placebo effect.

A recent study of the assessments of intelligence testing done mainly through various versions of the Wechsler Intelligence Scale for Children (Flynn, 2007) comparing numerically expressed results from different societies over a time sequence appeared to show that in European societies intelligence was rising by about 0.3 per year. This appeared to have occurred for as far back as tests were available. As Flynn points out that if such results were worked out retrospectively whole Western populations would have to have been classified as mentally retarded.

The results of intelligence tests have always been expressed numerically and have been given considerable political and educational attention. The point is not only that expressing such results numerically is creating a largely fictional value to such widely accepted mass testing, but that it must have missed out factors which vitiated the whole process. This probably tested social progress in a society but not intelligence.

Any study of social science research which expresses its results statistically are perhaps handicapping the value of their work by suggesting that its accuracy conforms to scientific standards. It probably does no more than conform to the statistical requirements of this form of professionalism. However, there is no reason to suppose that such conclusions are in themselves useless as they may well provide indicators of likely behaviour round about that time and in the stated communities and localities.

FAULTY PROCEDURES IN SOCIAL SCIENCE RESEARCH

Social science data cannot result with any accuracy from its collection under laboratory conditions because people can only be restricted physically for limited research periods. This cannot parallel laboratory experiments with animals and inorganic materials. There can be no boundaries imposed on where and when their thoughts and habits may have arisen and the extent to which these invade the experimental situation. We can never be completely sure what participants are bringing with them into the research situation. The researchers into human behaviour can only impose hypothetical boundaries on participants and none at all on their thoughts. Some scientists from outside the social sciences referring to medical research have gone so far as to claim that most published research findings are false in some respects (Ioannidis, 2005) because of procedural failings. Such conclusions apply even more to the results of social science research when it imitates the procedures and indeed the professional ambitions of 'hard' science.

A particular design failure may be the use of scales in which respondents are asked to give their involvements in an issue or the researcher involved does with the material with which they have been provided. This is done in a numbered scale or by the use of such terms as very often to never. This is plainly not a way that any individual ever grades their own behaviour and if this is done by respondents personally a high standard of literacy and intellectual competence is required.

Many questionnaires provide respondents with clues as to the type of answers required. To start a questionnaire on superstition (Rudski, 2003) with the heading 'many people think that James is superstitious as he believes in ghosts etc., will not produce results in terms of superstition. A person who sees a ghost is not thinking that she has seen one, she has had a real experience and this may have little to do with superstition.

A study of cross-cultural universals (Osgood *et al.*, 1975) using more than twenty different scales in covering a number of widely divergent societies cannot assume that any uniformities exist. No less than 121 different scales in English have been used to study religious meanings and behaviour (Hill and Hood, 1999), each of which will involve different understandings not only from their creators but in those to whom each was has been applied. There are few grounds for concluding that such scaling exercises have any validity outside those of the researches own creation.

The questions asked may be ones which most people will not have considered in their everyday lives and could be asked satisfactorily to a very small proportion of any Eastern or Western literate community. In a legal sense they are leading questions suggesting the framework within which they should be graded. The questions asked which have to be scaled may require a relatively uncommon linguistic ability from the early uses of such a methodology such statements as 'I think the church seeks to impose a lot of worn out dogmas and mediaeval superstitions' and 'the church represents shallowness, hypocrisy and prejudice' (Thurstone, 1928) are not commonplace conversational issues in any community then or now except in university seminars. All such questions might have been more usefully posed to suggest alternative and binary opposed ideas or as open ended questions.

Such studies as that of religion and HIV infected military personnel (Jenkins, 1995) involved scoring the data on a three-point scale; self-directed coping relying on self rather than God, relying on God to cope and collaboration between self and God. These follow a long line of similar scaling studies to that originally proposed by Thurstone and the Guttman (Guttman, 1944), Likert (Likert, 1932) and Bogardus (Bogardus, 1933) scaling systems. It would seem that every branch of the social sciences has produced and repeatedly used their own sets of scales. It does not seem that there has ever been any extensive testing of the relationship between scaling and individual understandings as to what may have been involved in such compulsorily abbreviated expressions of complex ideas. The English poet Robert Browning wrote in a sonnet 'How do I love thee? Let me count the ways'; an unusual way of expressing emotion, but no one except social scientists would scale their own behaviour.

Just as questionnaires are not a 'normal' way of obtaining

information but a bureaucratic imposition, so requiring people to scale their behaviour or ideas is even further outside normal ways of understanding. Nevertheless there are numerous scales in use in every branch of the social sciences including the evaluation of depression and severity of illness. These scales require respondents to state that their own particular pattern of behaviour or thinking has one of five alternatives from very strong to very weak. Some scales are more complex and indeed more difficult to attribute to them any high degree of validity such as the Stapel scale which has ten grades used in market research in which respondents are asked to put a numerical value to words or phrases describing an object.

The primary concern with the scaling of acts is that they do not adequately correspond to the complexity of any act such as interpersonal violence and it tells us nothing of the contexts in which violence occurs. Violence in sexual relationships and those resulting from anger have many similarities but scaling tells us nothing about how social signals may have been misread in the early stages of any physical relationship where much violence is recorded as having occurred among students (Foshee *et al.*, 2007).

In practice does anyone of whatever intellectual quality actually scale their own behaviour or type of thinking and if they are required to do so by some social outsider what are the grounds for assuming that their replies have any validity beyond the plain fact that they have chosen one point on the scale rather than another for unknown reasons. We do not know whether there is any understanding of such a grading in that culture. In some cultures such as that of the Sukuma there may even be a cultural distaste for any such open grading of human capacities as socially divisive. What validity will their replies have outside the immediate or distant social environment in which they are made at that particular time? This is almost always unknown and testing and retesting would have to be done in identical circumstances. Respondents may well remember what they did in such a strange activity. Both literates and non-literates may have clear memories of such unusual events as being tested by an outsider. There would seem to be a consistent series of difficulties for accepting the validity of scaled replies since they are artificially induced (Campbell and Fiske, 1959).

Although extremes may be valid and more easily classified

most people most of the time are in the predominantly grey areas of indecision in which researchers would not be able to find anything which would slot into the arbitrary divisions of a five-point scale. So it comes down to the same difficulties that will occur in any attempts to categorize. Social science researchers have only to attempt to apply such scaling to their own feelings and behaviour and to admit that there is a certain underlying absurdity in scaling itself and the arbitrary divisions which it entails.

THE POSSIBILITIES OF SCIENTIFIC MISCONDUCT

There are no reasons to suppose and indeed to conclude that social scientists are morally distinct from the generality of mankind and are, therefore, less likely to be involved in professional misconduct over their research. There may be reasons to suspect that such misconduct is relatively frequent.

The 'hard' sciences base their conclusions on well defined data which are then available for checking by others in the same specialization. Moreover many aspects of such research results touch directly on human interests as in medical work on particular treatments for laboratory confirmed diseases so there are constant reality checks coming from the use of research results on human beings. Adverse consequences whether they have occurred because of misconduct or mistakes can be expected to be spotted quite quickly as with the conclusions of Woo-Suk Hwang about his work on human cloning (Kennedy, 2006). The practical concerns related to 'hard' science research involve very many people outside their professional exclusivities and the pharmaceutical industry has been involved in some questionable research practices. A review of 74 clinical trials of anti-depressants found that 37 positive studies were published but 36 negative studies were either not published or published in a form that conveyed a positive outcome (Turner E.H. *et al.*, 2008). Of the 170 contributors to the most recent edition of the American Psychiatric Association's Diagnostic and Statistical Manual of Mental Disorders, 95 had financial ties to drug companies including all of the contributors to the section on mood disorders and schizophrenia (Angell, 2009). The review of every placebo controlled trials submitted to the United States for such anti-depressants such as Prozac found the differences between such drugs to be so small that it was unlikely to be of any clinical significance (Kiasch *et al.*, 2002). Such results should warn us to be suspicious of all research results in the social sciences as a matter of common prudence.

On the other hand the social sciences have no wide-ranging numbers of people interested in checking their results. A wide-ranging report on Ugandan secondary schools presented to the Ministry of Education contained substantial mispagination but no recipient reacted to this. A table of statistics related to genetics published by a British professor had been printed in reverse but no one referred this back to the author.

Social science research is written largely for and within a closed professional community in which it may be easier to falsify research data. It is very much a career driven discipline based on 'publish or perish' and there is thus an incentive to introduce information in support of a fact which the researchers may believe in good faith to be true or wish it to be so.

There is also the fact that the social sciences are inexact professions in which it is usually difficult to reproduce data accurately when there are so many additional time related hidden factors. These may well have affected results with or without the knowledge of the researchers themselves which they might subsequently claim to have contributed to what might have appeared as inaccurate (Goodstein, 2002) so that it will be difficult to make accusations stick. Freeman assessed Margaret Mead's conclusions about Samoan adolescent sexuality to be mistaken using data obtained from high status older men forty years later who might have had similar reasons for not wishing to disclose their own behaviour to intrusive outsiders (Freeman, 1983).

Where researchers work with others it is more difficult to alter results as 'hard' science requires the collaboration of subordinates and laboratory technicians. Social science experiments always have social frameworks which involve many others inside and outside the experimental situation. There would be a range of evidence available which could be used to discredit the validity of what has been reported.

More importantly most fieldwork provides no evidence at all in support of what the researchers conclude other than their own field notes however regularly and accurately they seem to have been kept. The private diaries of Malinowski provide little evidence in support of his theories and if anything their pedestrian nature makes his major theoretical works seem to be more attributable to his imagination than might have been the case if there had been no such diary (Malinowski, 1967). Oscar Lewis's mammoth work on the lives of a Mexican extended family has little substantive backing and could be read as a fact based novel and no less valuable nevertheless (Lewis, 1979). Casteneda's writings about his relationship with a Yaqui mystic appear to have been an imaginative creation of a relationship with a fictional character (Casteneda, 1968). All these works have been found valuable by others who may or may not have had personal reasons for their enthusiasm.

For many fieldworkers who have carried out their research under lengthy conditions of more or less total social isolation from their own societies, it would be difficult to establish the dividing line between fact and fiction. We are perhaps inclined to give the benefit of the doubt to comprehensive studies of 'strange' behaviour which intellectually hold together and make exciting reading in that context such as Leinhardt's work on the Dinka (Leinhardt, 1961) and Evans-Pritchard's on the Nuer (Evans-Pritchard, 1967). Such authors present complex ideas but obtained under what circumstances when they have had a limited knowledge of the natal languages used for these ideas or who may have used interpreters of very doubtful linguistic and intellectual capacity.

There is always the difficult issue for professionals as to who raises these issues of professional misconduct as there is little popular support for anyone raising the question of the truthfulness of another professional's conclusions. Their own professional position may be damaged and the legal issues of slander and libel can become involved as with Casteneda suing his ex-wife. Universities are also reluctant to raise issues of academic dishonesty by members of their own staff as it raises the questions involving its general status and often have only taken action after there has been media attention stopping the action when the person concerned has resigned or died (Martin, 1992).

It is certainly correct that the data from much fieldwork is evidentially unsupported and such researchers would find it difficult to prove their conclusions in any legal or scientific sense. That their results are not questioned more often is that the issues and the researcher involved are not important enough to merit such an attack in the contemporary climate of public and professional opinion.

It would seem that much data from past research could be classed as recorded but unsubstantiated gossip. We similarly tend to believe our fellow professionals although we may suspect that much published research has been initiated along the lines of the conclusions being established first and the supporting data sought for and invariably found.

Finally, there are errors in the data used in quantified conclusions. In 'hard' science data can be checked by subsequent researchers under virtually identical conditions and in this way errors and fraudulent claims can be discovered. The only variable will be the new researcher as the data comes from predefined basic definitions. Social science research is based on definitions which have none of the exactnesses of hard science and even for such very general issues as religion there are almost as many definitions as social scientists making them. This method of checking cannot be applied to social science research because the behavioural situation cannot be replicated as the social environment and the participants have all changed. Freeman's rather personal attack (Freeman, 1983) on Margaret Mead's interpretation of Samoan adolescence (Mead, 1928) may or may not have elements of inaccuracy, but he relied on the views of contemporary informants about what may or may not have happened more than fifty years previously; in such a long period of almost revolutionary change accurate connections with the past may well be extremely tenuous. This approach can be just as methodologically criticized as the original fieldwork.

The detection of deliberate or accidental fraud in the social sciences must always have existed but is not likely to be detected unless the research has resulted in the publication of so unusual results that it attracts the attention of other researchers but this will usually happen too late for any serious questioning of these results. The role of interpreters has never been investigated to assess the information that they have provided and yet these men and women who are presumed to have an intellectual capacity is some ways paralleling that of their employers. They are probably of very limited education in the language used by the researcher and a vocabulary that is unlikely to exceed a thousand words and a limited understanding of grammatical alternatives have given instant translations which have been taken to hold very sophisticated information.

We know that errors must occur because the information recorded has not been cross-checked or subjected to the requirements for acceptance as evidence in legal systems based on Anglo-American legal principles. Even in this there are often considerable inter-cultural linguistic difficulties. A murder case occurred in Tanganyika before an English judge, American accused, Jamaican prosecutor, Tanganyikan police officers, a Kenyan of Greek extraction and an imported American as defense lawyers. The witnesses whose natal language was kiSukuma and who would have given their evidence in kiSwahili through an interpreter. It is difficult if not impossible to check the reliability of information because the researchers may not have the time and the funds to check what they are told except by the unreliability of their own on the spot intuitions. In this matter the case file was stolen after the acquittal so that nothing could be checked. Also there may just not be the information which can support many statements; age is rarely recorded by birth certificates and indeed there may be no supporting data at all to testify to an individual's passage through life. Informants can produce fictional life histories just as readily as accurate ones if indeed such a thing exists.

Overall there is perhaps a tendency to assume that information provided is correct unless subsequent data suggests otherwise rather than to start from the somewhat more realistic viewpoint that all data is in some way questionable until its reliability is confirmed. Informants will always be putting forward their own views whether they are subsistence farmers in Bengal or university staff from a French university. The researchers themselves are not necessarily good informants with their own theoretical commitments and personal abilities recording as they must, one aspect of an event at a time.

Few social scientists allow for the fact that they are participant observers and that whether they like it or not there must be doubtful assumptions of professional detachment, as they are part of what they are researching. The idea that they can be detached from what they are working on is something in the nature of a professional delusion. Few social scientists are fully aware of the extent to which their own socialization, sex and age bias their viewpoints and their arrangements of the data which they themselves have collected. An American researcher working on the dreams of adolescent Ugandan Karamajong found herself represented; an extreme example perhaps but any researcher is an influence on the data they conclude whether they like it or not.

THE HANDICAP OF PRAGMATISM IN SOCIAL SCIENCE UNDERSTANDINGS

The majority of social scientists have been trained in understandings and procedures which have developed from the European Enlightenment and the academic conceits which have led to these being imposed globally in higher education without too much attention being paid to the circumstances in which this pragmatism was created and is applied.

One of the most extraordinary aspects of cross-cultural understandings has not been the reasonable evaluation of parallel process as in agriculture over the use of certain methods with cereals and soils and their susceptibility to infections and parasites but in the consequences and misunderstandings which come from the narrowness of this culture based pragmatism; the problems and understandings start and finish with primary factors.

The Sukuma of Tanzania plant their crops at intervals so increasing the chances of catching the sporadic rather than general rainfall in the cultivating season using cattle manure as a fertilizer when the distance between cattle byres and their fields makes this effort worthwhile. Agricultural advisers advocate larger plantings with mechanical aids and fertilizer, basing their suggestions on short-term annual quantifiable data. The Sukuma have based their traditional system not so much on intuitive guesswork but their experience over many generations which would stand up very well as an early form of time and motion work study evaluation balancing out the chances of profit and loss.

Any inter-cultural comparison is reasonable enough except for the scientific presumption that literate quantified pragmatism must be superior from the start to the time-tested non-literate conclusions of subsistence farmers used to the realities of farming on mainly poor laterite soils with an uncertain rainfall. However, even these two ways of looking at the methods of these subsistence farmers are inadequate for the Sukuma base their practices on their assessments of and control over chance. It is possible in the rainy season to be standing on a hill in sunshine and seeing heavy rain falling on another area less than two miles away. For the Sukuma this is not only chance but involves the problems of controlling probability.

However, when such metaphysical factors are involved the Western minded or trained pragmatists regard these ways of coping with chance and deducing probability as being of limited importance because they cannot be defined or quantified. We thus come up against the differences between scientific methodologies to which the social sciences aspire from their self-defining title and what has been called 'naive' observational methodology (Milstein, 2005). This requires testing theories with observational evidence, defining what is involved conceptually and operationally, using unbiased evidence in making truthful claims and reconciling theory and observation.

Most of the world's populations do not see their lives as quite so clearly attached to such simple binary oppositions between a fact and a non-fact. The Kachins of northern Myanmar in any rice cultivation and the Ilongot of northern Luzon with their mountainside tiered rice fields are obviously enough sophisticated farmers. Both cultures attempt to control the probabilities of annual success by allocating named spirits to the control of each set of fields however small and for whom they build overlooking spirit shrines. To their ways of thinking such practices are just as pragmatic as the use of fertilizers since both ways of cultivating are tied to chance and the probabilities of anticipated local disasters.

Social scientists have been warned against trying to force the pragmatically unusual or scientifically unacceptable behaviour of those they research into categories, but this is what they repeatedly do when they formalize behaviour into orderly ways and categories (D'Andrade and Romney, 1964). Perhaps social scientists who usually do more than tend to see behaviour in quantifiable terms cannot avoid this process of categorization which they can then analyze into the formal structures required by their professionalism.

THE RELUCTANCE TO ACCEPT METHODOLOGICAL LIMITATIONS

The whole time social scientists are faced with the plain fact that only in very general non-specific terms do the people in any community or in any activity behave in similar ways. Some seventy million people are estimated to have attended the last Kumbha Mela on the Ganges but who they were and what they did would have been not only varied in the sense of physical activities but will also have had very different psychological experience for all those who came there about the same time.

Even to suggest that some activity is the 'normal' way that people conduct their lives is always contradicted by what actually happens to individuals. Of course, they cultivate on an annual cycle but how individual farmers fit into this cycle will follow personal social and physical environmental factors. Even factory workers on a conveyor belt are only having a similar experience by cutting out their mental processes from any conclusions; some may be dozing as automatons but others will be thinking of beer, football and the evening food. An eight-hour shift will have many different mental experiences between the first and last hours as would be the case with all the long Coptic services in Ethiopia.

It is as if there was a professional need to create order out of apparent disorder in situations in which in fact there is no order in any mechanical sense nor any chaos which would destroy the continuing existence of communities and groups. Social scientists distrust generalizations but often use methodological processes which do just that in describing group behaviour numerically.

While this is obvious enough in sociological research, psychology also tends to take individual out of their social environments and to subject them as individuals to tests and the scaling of the results. This would appear to put the people being investigated into special socially isolated environments which might well provoke special behaviour. Tests in the sense accepted by Western educationalists and psychologists are no part of 'normal' social life neither is the consultation in which the individual is isolated with a socially distant professional. The so-called tests in tribal societies as in the movement between age grades and in the initiation ceremonies to special groups are social processes which do no more than insure that almost everyone does in fact pass; it is only a grading process in a very loose sense of insuring social cohesion and is not the discriminating system of examinations. Any examination introduces pervasive social discriminations. This is as obvious in a Croatian primary school which graduates its pupils in status related coloured costumes as in the graduation ceremonies English and Philippine universities.

This then becomes the major difficulty in understanding cultures within an overstressed and overstretched paradigm of pragmatism. Even when social scientists come up against the metaphysical and ultimately non-pragmatic they are always reluctant to accord it any over-prominence in the lives of 'other' people and 'other' cultures which they nevertheless accept for their own lives. Few would admit even in private that they chose their partners on purely pragmatic grounds 'I married her for her money' or that their choice of television viewing, literature and household decoration were illustrations of pragmatism.

Professor Evans-Pritchard has stated the difficulties of any such social science approach in the introduction to his study of Nuer religion (Evans-Pritchard, 1967: viii). 'So strong has been the rationalist influence in anthropology that religious practices are often discussed under the general heading of ritual together with a medley of rites of quite a different kind, all having in common only that the writer regards them as irrational, while religious thought tends to be inserted into general discussion of values.' Other researchers (Jules-Rosetts, 1978) have written that 'by describing divination as a misguided form of social analyzing, the anthropologists idealize their own form of enquiry and hide behind a veil of objectivity'. Another social scientist (Zeltlyn, 1990) wrote 'anthropologists proclaim diviners, clients and themselves as 'imputing' meanings in order to make sense of behaviour that is assumed to be connected to a hidden state of affairs.' So we often have a situation in which metaphysical issues are an essential part of many people's thinking according to their generally accepted cognitive understandings which are quite coherent and logical to them for which there are pragmatic procedures and consequences. Gorer in his study of the English (Gorer, 1957) described them collectively as a superstitious people and that conclusion came after his comprehensive study of the Sikkimese Lepchas (Gorer,1938).

In social science research and its attempts to understand human behaviour there is the constant methodological problem of the metaphysical paralleling the pragmatic aspects of social and psychological actions. These attempts are often handicapped by labelling these metaphysical understandings and related behaviour as superstitious as if there were no substantial similarities in developed societies.

There can be no clear cut binary opposition between pragmatism and 'superstition' however defined. The Oxford English dictionary's definition is unreason, fear of the unknown, mysterious or imaginary, an irrational religious system or unfounded belief in general. This does seem to be a definition from a very particular and indeed narrow cultural point of view as it leaves undecided what beliefs are irrational and unfounded. Much the same approach has occurred in the English-Swahili dictionary in which superstition is exemplified by divination, magic, amulets, casting lots, good and bad omens, evil and ancestor spirits for all of which the Swahili speakers themselves can provide their own rational foundations for these practices and beliefs and their accepted social usefulness. Whatever may be the reasoning behind these activities in a wide range of cultures irrationality cannot be one in any binary sense and no definition can discard the understandings of whole Eastern cultures.

On the other hand Jahoda (Jahoda, 1968) divides superstition into those practices that form part of a cosmology or coherent world-view, socially shared superstitions involving luck and divination systems, the occult experiences of individuals and finally idiosyncratic beliefs and rituals. These definitions come from his long experience of research in Ghana.

At the other extreme there are the professional rationalists of which Dawkins is currently the prime example (Dawkins, 2006). These people have any number of private devotions for which there can be pragmatic but not necessarily rational explanations; indeed if there were it would destroy their own claims to individuality and perhaps reduce their overall intellectual status to that of rather highly developed primates. Superstition is a pejorative word which most people would apply to the thinking and behaviour of people from whom they are socially distant.

So there is a category of the non-scientific at the extreme edge of which there are patterns of thinking and behaviour whether in Banaras, Birmingham or Bamako which can be classified by professional outsiders as superstitious but this does not exclude them from being an almost essential part of rational individual and collective social behaviour which social science researchers have to accept as realities with as much possible importance as pragmatic factors. The importance of non-pragmatic realities has to be accepted.

THE ABSENCE OF ADMITTED FAILURE

Social science researchers invest time and their resources in their work and it seems likely that their results are based on the data which they have obtained by the onward process of logical sequential connections. It is more likely that the results or rather the conclusions come quite early in the research process and then the data is sorted into supporting these results. If the approach is qualitative, then such an approach is reasonable as the researchers are working on their sense of what is going on from a detailed understanding of all the factors which might be involved, as Samuel Goldwyn, the famous American film director remarked 'I'll give you a definite may be'. However if the approach is quantitative then the possibility of error is far greater as they are using numerical exactnesses to illustrate statements for which the only connection may be the researchers own conclusions and their creation of illusory stability.

In whatever approaches are attempted, the researchers are certainly more likely to anticipate success in what they have planned to do so that there is a theme of optimism that they will be able to make their sense of what they are observing perhaps rather more than observing the sense that others make of their lives. So the conclusions which we read are details of success within the confines of professional and academic requirements and rarely detailing the failure to succeed in the proposed research or more likely the impossibility of achieving reliable data on what they had hoped to do.

For whatever reason a large number of research projects fail but little is known about the reasons beyond the more obvious ones of ill-health, domestic problems and political blockings. When businesses go bankrupt, the reasons are usually matters of public record but the equivalents in the social sciences are not similarly recorded. In the 1960s, 30 per cent of post graduate researchers affiliated to the East African Institute of Social Research in Kampala failed to produce any results in return for their grants and their fieldwork.

Overall there has been a professional reluctance to illustrate the limited importance which should be given to quantitative expressions of social behaviour. Few social scientists detail the many and various reasons for the unreliability of any human activity being expressed numerically and their own failure to be able to turn their own data into such a static form of expression.

THE DOMINANCE OF PRAGMATISM IN UNDERSTANDINGS

It is not just that social scientists are almost all agnostics and are unlikely to give any particular credence to private spirituality and public religious activities, but their approach is a linear form of pragmatism which shutters out influences which such an approach considers are not relevant. Whether social scientists see what certain individuals and communities do as superstitious or illogical is really irrelevant. These people whether they come from a Barotse community of subsistence farmers or are semi-skilled factory workers in Britain with an interest in football, they experience their private and public beliefs and practices at any time as a coherent and to them logically connected whole. The fact that this is constantly changing demographically and because of minor chance factors is not how they see their lives unless there are major upsets involving divorce, death, crop failure and redundancy.

It is hardly likely that anyone taking Communion according to the beliefs of the Roman Catholic Church as the Body and Blood of Christ sees this in either rational or irrational but just as part of their self-functioning set of beliefs, a religious job specification. The same approach dominates the Hindu belief in *Karma* and the Sukuma belief in the ability of dissatisfied ancestors to upset their social lives once it has been diagnosed by a reputable diviner. These ideas are pragmatic in their social environments and Western linear pragmatism is not relevant.

These people have a bounded rationality by which they know exactly how many cows they have and what is their bank balance and these totals are accepted by in-laws and accountants. But once we leave the limited range of mutually accepted 'hard' facts which must always be a relatively small proportion of total life activities, we are in the realm of beliefs which must cover the vast majority of human understandings and linked activities. The belief in the Taoist Goddess of Mercy is not irrational in the understandings of the Chinese who make offerings to her.

Rather than see some sort of binary opposition between the rational and the non-pragmatic, we have to accept that metaphysical factors cannot be compared to *modern* agricultural understandings in Bali which have replaced their system which combined religion and the control of water flows to their wet rice fields leading to ecological collapse, lowered yields and the growth of plant disease (Lansing, 1987,1991). In this case a pragmatic assessment had led to the neglect of essential factor holding the whole system in time tested togetherness. Social scientists working over the Balinese connection between religion and rice cultivation are (un)able to discuss certain symbolic connections between water sources, sacred places and gardens (Geertz, 1972).

Thus there is the overall problem of social scientists 'having the notion of a non-normal mode of cognition according to their thinking, not only reinforcing positivist philosophy but also undermines two prevalent aspects of African divination; participation in seances and trans-cultural divination. Defining divination as a non-normal mode of cognition based on the practitioner's liminality, goes against its frequently described dialogic nature which actively involves the clients (Myhre, 2006).

We are looking at the question of so-called science in relation to human behaviour and so-called superstition as if it was a clear cut binary opposition. This is a theoretical hypothesis of very limited validity except that there is a category of the non-scientific at the extreme edge of which there are overwhelmingly popular patterns of thinking and behaviour and which can be classed as superstition by those who are predisposed by training and personality to see such behaviour as irrational in these terms. Such a definition would apply to the writers on astrology reported to out produce in publications those who write professionally or popularly on psychology in the United States as well as the interpreters of Tarot cards in Chicago or divination sticks in contemporary Chinese Taoist temples as well as the Ndembu diviner working from bones. These practitioners of superstitions know how much money they have in the bank or their number of livestock and both are certainly practicing the logic of tax avoidance.

Scientists from their many and obvious successes in the research which they have conducted, assume that this can be repeated indefinitely as it has in the past and can be expected to do in the future. But this is a faulty assumption that the light at the end of the tunnel based on facts and figures can be reached and that it will lead progressively to the extinction of the illogical and superstition. It is certainly correct that hard science will increasingly produce astonishing results which will have little effect on the thinking of ordinary people who have their own very different problems to surmount. It is not only the aggressive rationalism of those with a Dawkin's like approach but the placid and no doubt kindly meant rationalism of others (Wolpert, 2006) which can provide limited help for those experiencing the inevitable difficulties of living whether in Mumbai or Manchester.

But with these intellectual successes comes the growth of elitism and the failure to recognize that the expansion of science has not resulted in any parallel reduction of anxiety or any increase in successful solicitude. The curing of disease has led to the lengthening handicaps of old age, and economic stability remains no more than a political slogan. Modern men and women are just as subject as their ancestors to new diseases, tsunami disasters and innumerable personal distresses. These are as inevitable a part of life and as common as they have always been, but may have been augmented by what can be experienced as the destructive ideology of scientific conceit.

THE WEAKNESSES IN SOCIAL SCIENCE PRAGMATISM

The social scientists want their research to produce results which have some universal applicability and they have so far failed to be able to do this even within a single society or culture. This is not a question of debating the moral aspects of their endeavours but of listing the factors in human behaviour which make it impossible to produce or even to think of the possibility of producing universal rules paralleling the long-term ones that have been produced by the 'hard' sciences. Any universal rule has to start from similar situations having similar results and there can be none in human behaviour.

If chimpanzees can be identified by their individualities it would seem more than obvious that human beings will similarly vary whatever their genetic composition not so much in how they originate but in how they develop. The identification of DNA compositions can only be the start of any descriptions. The nature *versus* nurture is an old controversy but even identical twins who have many identifiable similarities have different social experiences; looking at yourself across the room for years on end is an experience of nurture rather than nature. A sample of one hundred reputedly similar individuals used in sampling can be no such thing as it is just a collection of one hundred different people made to appear similar by a bureaucratic process of excluding variable factors.

The most important point which social scientists usually overlook is that social behaviour is always changing even as they look at what is going on. One day can only be very crudely similar to the following one; the individual is older and the social environment in which he or she lives is always changing just as rapidly. A fact of behaviour is relevant to that time and place; tables of data recording what might have been the situation in one year has little likelihood of being equally accurate for the following twelve months. The whole behavioural world in which humans operate is constantly moving in every part and it has only the illusion of stability largely created by the social scientists' quantifications for professional reasons.

Everyone experiences their lives in unitary terms so that all their activities cannot be divided up except by losing this important psycho-social wholeness. A Kung Bushman going hunting or his wife looking for wild fruits do not divide up these activities into starts and finishes. Time certainly exists but to divide up life according to the calendar is associated with literacy and bureaucracy and has no ethological basis. It would seem that modern society divides activities into categories by stopping and starting points. To put any social activity into a slice of life situation is to avoid its natural wholeness; getting up, washing, eating, going to work and working is a single process. Dividing up any activity is more for the professional convenience of the social scientists and the needs of industry than an aid to the understanding of the wholeness of human behaviour.

If 'truth' can be obtained by social science research, it probably has to come from the study of single individuals and any such accuracy from such intensive study would be diminished in proportion to the number of individuals studied. The accuracy of descriptions of a social relationship defined as marriage by that society would become infinitesimal when it is based on the experiences of a hundred couples; there would be a long list of one hundred variations.

No social scientist is able to deal accurately and equally with more than half a dozen informants. She knows that the community which she is studying consists of several hundred perhaps thousands of permanent and transient members. So she takes a sample either by the use of random numbers presupposing that there is a list as in a school, hospital or prison or by some idiosyncratic process forced on her by the 'disorderly' way in which they live. In the end much probably comes down to convenience combined with the time and money available and the accidents of encountering one person rather than another. It is a matter of chance who is selected and there is little likelihood that those chosen are similar. Indeed the whole process of sampling is probably going to miss the unusual people who act as role models for others and hold important positions or who have outstanding personal characteristics. Sampling is a process for the convenience of the researchers. It is an artificial grouping of crudely similar people into averages to which no one member of the sample or the surrounding social grouping or community will conform. Its conclusions might well be guessed at by a qualitative assessment with equal accuracy.

Statistics whatever their source are often, perhaps inevitably, seen as having a high degree of accuracy and researchers and their supervisors and employers are often mesmerized by the seeming stability of print. Apart from the official reasons for the recording of any information, it has to be recognized that they also have a defensive role for the people and organizations that produce them; they show the justification for an organization's existence and just how usefully busy they have been. Where local government positions depend on the size of the populations to be governed, people may be borrowed at census time just as cattle may be moved out of a locality when there is compulsory destocking because of over-grazing. The reputation of the police depends on their success rates in detecting crime; professional criminals often have a long-term relationship with their local police force and in a number of cases when they are going to plead guilty anyway, they confess to other crimes to oblige the police who then have a higher clean up rate. In one year in Kenya the annual reports of two departments did not agree on the number of criminals who had been judicially executed in the past year. Whether a couple is married or not depends on who is being asked, the man or the woman. The membership of a Christian denomination may depend on the health and educational advantages of membership. The list of the inaccuracies that have been and can be expected to be found in statistics in even the most bureaucratized states is certainly endless and censuses are notorious for the number of people who avoid being counted. This situation is made more difficult by the fact that statistics are usually if not inevitably historical documents and are thus beyond any verification from parallel sources; the details of traffic accidents which are confirmed independently by hospital and insurance company records for instance.

Events which are recorded numerically are indeed history by the time they come into print so that they have a very short life as possibly accurate information. Medical information has a similar short life not only because the scientific side of what has been recorded becomes replaced but also because the human behavioural component has inevitably changed so that any follow up sample cannot be a replication of the original one. A study of systematic reviews of clinical medical information found that a quarter need updating within two years of publication but more importantly 7 per cent were out of date by the time they were published (Shojania *et al.*, 2007). We have to accept that any quantification of human behaviour is going to be out of date much quicker and to a much greater extent than scientific information in isolation.

How can a social event be adequately covered so that the description parallels what has happened? Even photography and sound recordings are biased in their accuracies since they are pointed in one direction and behaviour in its realities is circular. The more people involved in an activity, the more complex becomes the creation of accuracy because the researchers have to choose what to observe and indeed what they are led to see; in prison research a disturbance in one area attracting the researcher's attention, may well be a distraction for something happening in the opposite direction. A Hindu temple ceremony may go on for a week with rotations of performers but only one researcher who is physically limited in what he or she can do. What is chosen to be recorded is often the follow-up of what the researchers consider to be important for their purposes. In a Sukuma ancestor propitiation ceremony there are the main performers who attract attention but there will be a fringe of affines married into the sufferer's family who are attending who stand passively at the back. In their own way they have their own importance but this tends to be ignored by the patrilineal preconceptions of most social scientists.

So what is taken to be the taxonomy of a social situation is more likely to be enabled by the psychological and physiological abilities of the researchers and their biased preconceptions of what ought to be recorded. What is seen as exciting and interesting is more likely to be recorded that the monotonies of water carrying, washing clothes, cooking, excreting and walking to work.

The quantitative element of the social sciences wants to create exactness in support of its research results but what is produced can only be historical quantifications to illustrate situations which are now of no more than historical interest and are accurate in so far as they are defined by the researchers themselves rather than by the situations which they are used for. Legal systems try to categorize crime but then have to alter the penalties to fit the variations in which guilt has been defined and in these decisions non-literate assessors have perhaps greater perspicuity. Their definitions of crime are never exact and vary between their ideas of public and private delicts in which urinating when drunk in a water source is a matter of communal concern while murder is a private matter. The homicide files of the Uganda police give the reasons which often state no more than that there was a quarrel and they see no point in attempting more sophisticated analyses.

The turn-style nature of much reporting of attendance at social activities records numerical equivalences as if they were social equivalences. It is only at the simplest of levels that people attending an activity can be recorded as equal even if it is to a football match. Attendance in the sense of whole-hearted participation in any social activity lacks any adequate definition and will vary with age, intelligence, ability to see and hear and the particularized elements in any particular moment; someone with Down's Syndrome and a doctor of philosophy may well show similar but definably different signs of enjoyment. In the same way that sexual ecstasy and anger share physiological expression but to divide them socially requires a wide range of complex definitions. Traditional peoples with a limited sense of time are less concerned with the start and finish of activities and in this sense may be less demanding on such concepts. Participation in lengthy Coptic ceremonies may involve lying down and sleeping but they are not woken up for more conscious participation. In Sukuma propitiation ceremonies people drift in and out along a range of visual rather than audible involvement.

Prayer is an activity seemingly common to all people in all cultures at some time or another and its physical form may be stereotyped in many religious systems. The prayer books of committed Roman Catholics might contain the total of ceremonies which they have attended in the year but we can have no idea of what was involved for such persons. Double-blind tests carried out to assess the medical consequences of prayer which have shown small percentages of biological influence, can only be taken on trust, we have no means of knowing that those involved have prayed at a constant level of intensity, whatever that may mean, at the required times. It would seem unlikely that any human behaviour can be categorized with any narrow accuracy paralleling the demands of the 'hard' sciences and if divided up to illustrate its diversity into smaller and smaller categories, the point of quantification would seem to be lost in the process.

There is also the problem of units of measurement which are imposed on human behaviour. Evans-Pritchard has pointed out that in the understandings of the Nuer, time goes more quickly in the wet than in the dry season (Evans-Pritchard, 1939). Much the same would apply to all subsistence farmers who find that only in the dry season do they have time to sit around to gossip, building up their social networks. It seems likely that in urban-industrial communities holidays go quicker than working weeks.

Orthodox Christianity and Islam have become timed religions for their formal ceremonies starting at clock times. Traditional ceremonies start when 'enough' people have arrived to validate the expressed intentions of those involved. The Manus islanders who reorganized their communal life in what they understood to be a modern way of living, and timed the start and end of work periods by the ringing of a bell (Mead, 1956). Most subsistence farmers start their work by sun-time which will vary with cloud cover so that there is a slower start for work in rainy weather. Age may start with the time of known conception or only start when the child is socially recognized as a social being. In some societies there is a prolonged state of being half dead and then really dead after a further ceremony quite distinct from what goes on for the necessarily quick disposal of the body in tropical climates.

Pastoralists may see their cattle in terms of their characteristics rather than in their numbers and replying to the question of how many children, cows or containers of maize or rice an individual may have, would be seen as both pushing themselves forward communally or unwisely making spirits from one side of a family actively hostile to their side's success. Times and distances are usually seen in terms of social needs, experience and neighbours who are not related may be seen as living a long way off while being within sight.

Age which is persistently recorded for the participants in any survey is often not known with any exactness and reluctantly stated even when it is known; a person's social position is often dictated by what he or she does or has done and whether they are married or not. The dividing line between age blocks makes for artificial divisions. Somthing that Westerners may know exactly because of legal requirements and their efficient national bureaucracies.

Causality is a constant preoccupation in social science. Respondents either answer with the statement that this is what we have always done or is thought of in far more distant chains of relationship than the simplicity of primary causes; of course, it is obvious that the man broke his leg because the tree fell on him but most people would work out far more complex reasons for him being there at that particular time since they have neither the concept of luck nor that of the natural inevitability of statistical accidents. Linear and proximate causation may be scientifically adequate but in any sense of social understandings it is clearly inadequate. Even if there is an hereditary explanation for some physical fact the majority of people do not accept that there is any such inevitability about their misfortunes and that it is either God's will or the malevolence of ancestors, neighbours or unrelated spirits.

Just as symbols will have fans of meanings, any social activity will have a fan of factors which will have gone to its particular expression which will always be difficult to disentangle and will vary with every occasion which even the most repetitious of behaviour illustrates. Explanations that any individual may give for her, his or their behaviour can only be partial if only because many of the factors in motivation and decision-making are hidden from the actors. Reasons are social as much as scientific and we know from conflicting evidence of single events that no one sees anything in the same way as other participants.

In all research involving human behaviour we should accept that the collection of data in forms of inter-personal confrontation is not some system for mirroring events which the researchers hope will be unbiased. Far from being a simple recording of facts, it is a confrontational experience which is inevitably filled with biases of both form and method as the question and answer intrudes into or comes from the privacies which most people feel to be a form of private property.

Social scientists seek for stabilities in human behaviour and it seems likely that if any are found they are as likely as not created by the processes of data collection and analyses. It is not only that human behaviour is constantly on the move by its very nature; it is an ant-heap of two-legged anthropoids. More importantly everyone is constantly being pushed in or off their planned behavioural courses by chance events of which some could have been anticipated but not to happen that week. They are always knocked off any regularity by events which they could not anticipate in any realistic sense except by wide-ranging insurance policies which are beyond the means of most people. Chance will affect them almost everyday as to who they meet and the consequences of what happens in the environment when even Britain has earthquakes and everyone becomes affected by international affairs whether as farmers or fighting men or because of the movement of disease over international borders.

THE PRESUMPTION OF ORDER

One of the fundamentals of research is the finding and presentation of order to those who read and evaluate the results of what has been done. A messy collection of information is an affront to the logical thinking of those intellectuals who perhaps presuppose that human behaviour and how it is integrated into society has to be basically orderly even if this is not readily apparent; somewhere there is an orderliness which it is the obligation of the social scientist to discover.

We accept that there is disorder which the social scientists define as deviance but we are not sure whether such behaviour should not be defined as a different form of order as in the polygynist Christian cults in the United States, terrorist cells in Western Europe and among those who accept the paintings of Paul Klee as art, the works of James Joyce such as Finnegan's Wake as literature and the 'ramblings' of Gertrude Stein as poetry. In all societies there are breaks from the predominant veneer of orderliness which are interpreted as a different form of this same orderliness rather than just extreme forms of the inevitable differences between the multiplicities of any individual human behaviour. All societies have these extreme breaks in orderliness which can be seen as the basic dialectic initiating change.

Since researchers who see human behaviour in terms of the methodologies of 'hard' science are usually required to produce evidence of order for their employers and for the advancement of their careers, so it is not surprising that this is what they find. Those who contract social scientists to report on some applied problem expect the results to be expressed in quantitative form because that is the logical form in which business and governments function.

Such quantitative results would seem to fictionalize the basic and continual diversity of human behaviour in any environment. No researcher is going to end their research by stating that they have dealt with a community of one hundred families or whatever is studied, among which there are a number of low common denominator factors such as citizenship, being the subjects of research, residence in a definable community for a definable time, that is as far as it goes. Each of those families will see themselves as indeed they are different in what they personally assess as essentials from every other one. So the social scientist gets and perhaps creates order out of this mass of individualisms.

ABSENCE OF ANTHROPOID UNIFORMITIES

While there is plentiful evidence of insect uniformities in the behaviour of bees and ants and of course earlier in that of amoeba, there is no evidence that adult chimpanzees either in captivity or in forest freedom are not individually different and indeed researchers have identified them by their differing personalities. Since chimpanzees in the wild even with prolonged observation over the years by both Goodall (Goodall, 1986) and Reynolds

(Reynolds, 2005) in Tanzanian and Ugandan forests, can only have their lives described in terms of observed incidents, patterns of behaviour, rather than in time controlled quantitative terms.

Surely there are useful parallels here for research on human behaviour. Of course, chimpanzees are in the wild and cannot be controlled or confined for research purposes. But then neither can human beings except under as artificial conditions of experiments which rather inefficiently parallel the caging of monkeys. We accept that we cannot quantify wild animals except under very artificially defined circumstances, why then do we assume that we can quantify human behaviour over which we have very little control and similarly very little overall quantifiable information. The only difference would appear to be is that humans can be asked questions and usually provide a high proportion of unverifiable replies. Most of human behaviour is outside the possibility of accurate observation and occurs under the influence of environmental and historical factors of which the researchers can find out very little.

LIMITED PARALLELS TO THE REQUIREMENTS OF SCIENTIFIC KNOWLEDGE

The 'hard' sciences start their research with required methodologies on material which are both more or less permanent in the short term or verifiable by machines which operate independently of human influences except in so far as they are activated by human choice. It seems necessary to conclude that research on human behaviour can never meet these exact conditions because the factors to be used are organized by the researchers themselves and more particularly because not only there is the constant varying of the material but because so many of the factors are either unknown or indefinable. Much human behaviour is based on indefinable emotionally based ephemeral influences.

There are certainly events which are sufficiently isolated to receive the attention of social scientists in which cause and effect in the crudest sense is obvious enough. The members of fundamentalist Christian sects in the southern United States who test their faith by the handling of poisonous snakes and the drinking of poison (Alther, 1975) have a consequential death rate just as the mass suicides of some nine hundred members of the Christian Assembly of God at Jonestown in Guyana came from the drinking of cyanide and orange juice (Kilduff and Javers, 1978). These connections are clear cut and methodologically sound connecting poison and death but such arid explanations miss out all the complex conscious and subconscious thinking which would have made those otherwise 'normal' people behave in such seemingly illogical and self-destructive ways. Approach such isolated and unusual social events and we have clear cut narrow explanations which are inadequate if they are applied to wider and more commonplace human behaviour.

Most human behaviour does not stand out as so atypical as to merit close and isolating attention and, therefore, is never likely to provide data which fits in with the requirements of scientific methodology. It is thus rarely possible to connect a behavioural event with simple lineal causations. With the nine hundred who killed themselves at Jonestown or killed their children there would have been as many reasons as individuals and to group them together as a mass suicide paralleling cattle being slaughtered, is to diminish this important individuality. Of course we can jump to the conclusions that these people were all in some way mentally disturbed and not acting according to the standards of the societies from which they came. There is the Eyam case in the seventeenth century where two priests of different Christian denominations decided and influenced the villagers not to flee from the plague as it would spread that dread disease to other nearby villages; one of their wives and 260 out of about 350 villagers died because of their altruism (Daniel, 1966). We can only guess at the complex and varied motivations behind which may have made this community altruistically isolate itself.

Violent crime and riots correlates well with high temperatures in the United States as well as to economic declines and the prevalence of drug addiction. But these are generalities covering large numbers of people who are dissimilar in a very much larger number of factors and it has never proved possible to extend any understanding and correlations to the anticipated behaviour of individuals. Indeed if it was possible to do so many issues of laws and order such as probation would have been solved long ago.

THE FINDING OF SOCIAL BEHAVIOURAL ORDER

Social scientists in researching human behaviour in either its extreme or rather average forms are faced with the alternatives between attempting to quantify what they find to be occurring or to find this too impossible to attempt. Both quantitative and qualitative research methods are suspiciously easy in their own ways. There may be factors in the choice of either of these two approaches which are personal to the researchers and do not result from any appreciation of the difficulties involved in quantifying. This may require fieldwork involving direct relationships with a large number of strangers which some introverted researchers may find difficult. There is the quieter qualitative method and letting the atmosphere of the community and their problems become known to them by a longer term and more indirect approach. Most researchers are funded for a limited period and this does not allow for any prolonged absorption into the issues confronting what are in practice strangers inevitably separated from them by wide social distancing. They are in a hurry forced on them by the conditions of their employment and the only way that they can show results is to quantify their observations or work on what statistics are already available. Statistical tables and boxes filled with completed questionnaires show that they have been busy as researchers getting such results.

This can be accurate enough in its way as Kenyan prison records showed which guards had charged prisoners with offences against the prison rules and from this data it seemed reasonable that some warders needed this way of enforcing their authority while others managed to do this by their personal abilities or were just too lazy or too ineffectual to bother. While, of course, it is possible that the absence of data is in fact a true illustration of what is going on, this is not necessarily so. The Sukuma can divorce through their local courts which are supposed to be run according to their customary law, but the records show very few divorces. This did not mean that their marriages may have been unusually stable but probably that they wanted to settle domestic differences in their own ways as they mistrusted the court procedures administered by those who were only officially unbiased.

There may be a more subtle form of bias undermining the broader approaches to research in its relationship to public opinion by which certain behaviours are predefined as unworthy of any binary considerations so that views which oppose this may not have any public voice. In this way the data on which probabilities are based is biased from the start. It was assumed quite rightly that expert witnesses used by Finish tobacco companies of whom 33 out of 45 were funded by these groups (Heikki, 2007) were producing evidence in favour of the products of those who were in fact their employers. Overall what these witnesses declare to be the results of their research is going against public opinion and not that their data was professionally false; smoking is bad and that is the end of the discussion. This is in the context in which more or less every public issue in every society develops a range of pressure groups for and against the matter under discussion.

We are perhaps forgetting in this context that bias can in fact be binary and that valid research can be done on both sides of this public opinion divide which is itself not likely to be uniform and anyway probably dominated by professionals and high status persons. There are innumerable studies of the adverse effects of alcohol but there are few which show that in social environments which are inevitably stressful, alcohol has the beneficial effect of making life a little pleasanter. The way that orthodox Jews combine moderate drinking with religious practices correlates with very low rates of alcoholism, certainly infinitesimal in comparison to the alcoholism of Irish and Scottish Roman Catholics (Hyman *et al.*, 1980).

Apart from the doubtful accuracy of all statistics which cannot be supported by collateral data, such as might be the case with hospitalization from dangerous diseases, they are predefined abstractions from much wider fields of social behaviour and in this sense they are impositions of artificial reality apart from the fact that they are now historical rather than illustrations of contemporary behaviour.

THE IMPOSITION OF ORDER ON DIALECTICAL INSTABILITY

In research just as much as in private life there is a quasi-genetic need for orderliness but there is in this an essential difference. While at the same time there is the disturbing need to change as an essential need to adapt, every individual sees the organization of their own lives as orderly wholes threatened by the disorderliness of the surrounding society and in this there are many forms of supposed rationality. The researchers on the other hand whatever their own personal forms of orderliness, are outsiders who have a personal and professional interest in finding order in what they observe and thus making their observations and conclusions manageable. There need not be any coincidence with this imposition of orderliness and how the societies and people observed experience their own lives. The manageability of data on social behaviour is imposed through the creation of categories and their imposition on unstable activities which have no such simplicities; they are different people with their own separate role expectations.

Of course, it is correct enough that there are obvious and seemingly clear cut differences in society which everyone sees and accepts such as age and sex differences and a number of other classifications in which there are implied binary attributions about which everyone there will seemingly agree. But can these be made into watertight classifications more or less for the convenience of social scientists and are the methodological children of Comte and the European Enlightenment. Some women are 65 years of age but whether they can be classified as old women is a matter of their individual personalities and the circumstances in which they live and similarly there are many eighteen-year old who are not teen agers in any social sense of the term. Apart from hermaphrodites, there are many very male women and very female men in their social behaviour and personalities.

But what are the boundaries of such classifications which make binary decisions so easy as to dominate their categorizations in commonplace statistics. Some are no doubt obvious enough when we put into our notes the observations of a very old sightless woman who cannot write at all and who has lived all her life in the same house in Saharanpur with a shrine to Krishna on the wall beside her wooden bed. The very convenience of such a person for the needs of social scientists who have come here by train from Delhi because they have heard of her redoubtable memories of Gandhi's campaign of peaceful opposition to British rule. We will have to admit that it would be difficult to put her into any of the boxes required by categorization without destroying her essential and indeed unity. It may not be even reasonable to describe her as unusual as in any sense of social understandings all the inhabitants of Saharanpur are equally unusual. Among her neighbours and relatives there may well be a senior professional soldier, a refugee tailor from what is now Pakistan and a boy with Down's Syndrome.

What are the social differences between 49 and 50 years old and between those who got 65 per cent rather than 64 per cent in their final examinations and were thus categorized as in different categories of excellence because these people go into different boxes from which different conclusions are reached. What can be the justification for making the cut-off points even rather than odd numbers since these are certainly not points of division dictated by social behaviour. What constitutes domicile when individuals are migratory or spend the majority of daylight hours several miles away from where they are unconscious in sleep or in semi-conscious intellectual neutrality watching television. What constitutes putting an individual in a box labelled marriage when its only social significance is a legal definition as the case of an English man who had left his wife after three weeks but they remained legally married until he died thirty-five years later. The whole process of categorization and putting human behaviour into boxes created by outsider scientists and bureaucrats should be accepted as methodologically suspect.

In the study of bacteria or the elements of relatively static materials there can be no common-sense objection to the imposition of categories but there will still be the problem of the dividing lines between one category and its neighbouring ones. On the other hand the dividing of human behaviour into seemingly exact categories which have no recognizable part of the understandings of those being studied goes against this same common sense. Some African traditional societies divided their men into age grades with each grade having a distinct name but the time that cuts off one grade and creates a new one is the result of social pressures; the restiveness of one group to get promoted and the numbers of younger men waiting to get into the system at the bottom. There might be a ten-year difference between the oldest and youngest members of the same age grade.

Categories in some cases have exact overall social consequences. To be categorized as a Roman Catholic in Northern Ireland or as a Muslim in India would have overall social significance dictating place of residence, marriage partners, schooling, employment, places used for socializing and political involvements which may not be closely related to the regularity or intensity of their religious beliefs and practices. Such categorizations are probably of little significance in Oxford or among middle class professionals generally.

Education by the recording of examinations passed is an ill-defined category except as a bureaucratic device to filter people in and out of possible employments. It is not only that primary school leavers have varying abilities to the extent of their literary Skills but even the quality of degrees for employment is dictated in part by the reputation of the universities and departments concerned.

There are often categories which the social science profession and its researchers have created so that they can communicate with their colleagues in other universities and research institutions. Anyone involved in marriage counselling knows that the only similarities between the couples they see on a particular day is that they are legally married and are consulting the same person on the same day and this would apply as much to couples who are Norwegians, Nicaraguans and Nagas who are in dispute over what are usually indefinable but negotiable issues.

Categorization is an essential requirement for any quantification of any aspects of human behaviour if there is going to be any hope of scientific exactness and the word 'hope' is an essential element in this approach. It rarely justifies the exactness which is usually attributed to record numbers. Bureaucracy can require the provision of a range of facts which are necessary for the fulfilment of certain procedures. We have already pointed out the inaccuracy of census enumerations but every bureaucratic procedure carries with it systematic inaccuracies over hours of work, insurance losses, tax statements and probably all career histories. Social scientists, social workers and the police recording the details of a domestic disturbance from those involved will often wonder whether they are dealing with the same event. Even the details on birth and marriage certificates are often statements of hope and intention about how they wish to be socially accepted.

Medical records are inseparable from the quantification of human behaviour. Those who try and produce reviews of the prevalence of a particular clinical condition often find that the different physicians use the same phrase to describe a particular or different condition. There is an obvious need for agreement on what constitutes a particular condition but unless this is established by laboratory procedures there is little possibility of this if only because a single patient may be suffering from multiple morbidities. A group of six internationally accepted experts participated in an e-mail administered Delphic process on what constituted lower-back pain for which the published literature provided fourteen sets of symptoms. These experts reached 97 per cent consensus resulting in three sets of pathology outcomes, two sets of functional limitations and participation outcomes and thirteen sets of symptoms and care-seeking outcomes (Griffith *et al.*, 2007).

Even accepting the care with which these professionals with long experience of this particular physical condition, have reached agreement on these varied definitions, their categorizations are likely to be no more accurate after this exercise than before. They are dealing with a single condition in different people. It may be that the diagnosis is more for the convenience of the physician, the institution for the allocation of funds and staff than for the sufferer. Each physician will be interpreting what he or she sees in their clinical evaluations. There can be no real hope in any greater accuracy in any such categorizations of physical conditions and immeasurably less so in placing someone in the category of schizophrenia.

The medical profession with its increasing use of mechanical testing and the relegation of the patient to be subordinated to these processes, has become aware of the drawbacks to this 'boxing' of sufferers into predefined categories. Sensitivity to language and emotions of the patients is seen as the making of the superior clinician and by this overdependence in 'boxing' leads to most errors in which thinking is guided by stereotypes (Groopman, 2007).

There are also problems over the veracity of data as when pregnant woman state that they have experienced violence from their partners and their replies to a Child Abuse Potential Inventory which rate them as three times more likely to abuse their children (Casanueva and Martin, 2007). This may well be so but without corroboration from medical and social welfare records that there has been violence, such conclusions are little more than speculation.

We have to conclude that whatever categorizations are used

they impose some implied accuracy about some aspect of human behaviour which is thus made both static and dated. In doing this it obscures the fact that the enormous variations which occur in any activity is a necessary part of the dialectics leading to personal survival.

THE HANDICAP OF CATEGORIZING HUMAN BEHAVIOUR

The basic problem in social science research into human behaviour is the urge to categorize what humans do and the variety of such activities and their constantly changing nature. Any categorizations must always be inaccurate from the moment that they are made and increasingly so from that moment onwards, not so much because behaviour may not be susceptible to such boxing in but because in every activity there are inevitably unknown influencing factors. If there is some degree of accuracy this is likely to have been achieved as a bell-curve of restricted range of scalable facts.

Thus all social science researches not only start with a range of variability about which its illusiveness makes it impossible to categorize with any degree of accuracy. Whatever is recorded with this presumption of accuracy is constantly subject to additional variations. The individuals themselves are changing by the processes of ageing, their inter-relationships will have varied and the social and physical environment in which they behave is changing. An individual may catch the same grossly overcrowded commuter train into Mumbai or Manchester every working day but to categorize this as a repetitive similar act is to simplify each event out of its social specifics.

It seems reasonable to suggest that categorization except in its simplest forms has not been seen by societies as a necessary and useful development in how they organized their thinking and their lives. A study of ethno-biological categories in several traditional societies (Berlin *et al.*, 1973) definable in terms of linguistic and taxonomic criteria, found no more than five; they concluded that it was unlikely that any traditional society had worked out a process of thinking in such asocial terms. No society has seen any social need to develop systems of categorization which are independent of social needs. As used in the social sciences it is a system developed from the European Enlightenment designed to record 'hard' data rather than to reflect cultural differences and processes of variation.

The supposedly clear-cut division between the sexes has most traditional societies distinguishing between male and female prior to puberty; after then the division is one of social positioning relating to menstruation and fertility. Blackwood (Blackwood, 1984) noted the appearance in traditional societies of gender definitions which were more flexible and wider in scope than those used in Western cultures. The data amassed by Lang (Lang 1998) supports that contention by detailing not only a variety of gender constructs, but a variety of ways in which each one might be played out in a culture. Ultimately, gender constructs may be more profitably seen as sets of interacting continua, rather than as sets of strongly bounded categories (Segal, 1999). From this conclusion that these traditional cultures did not divide biological sexuality into a simple binary classification so we can see that there seems little likelihood that there can ever be any cognitive process of categorization which is independent of rather narrow social interpretations. An interesting side-line to sexual categorization comes from contemporary Iran which has no religious objection to sex change surgery.

Most attempts at probability are based on statistical analyses which developed from data arranged into categories to simplify examination. At the same time there is a tacit acceptance of the impossibility of treating each individual and each social situation in the reality of their difference; accepted as a numerical fact by all social scientists who assess their information in terms of static quantifications.

What are these categories into which social scientists place their data. The placing of this data into categories follows an assumption that events relating to human behaviour are discrete enough and identifiably similar to other events to be grouped together for analytical purposes. Once social scientists have accepted as they must that individuals in their behaviour are distinct and that even with identical twins there are likely to be differences in social experience which will be reflected in some aspects of their social activities, they have in fact but not apparently in practice accepted that this process of categorization is a process of falsification. Watanabe (Watanabe, 1969:376-9) states that beyond the fact that two objects can have the same weight 'there exists no such thing as a class of similar objects in the world', while stating more obscurely that 'any two things have exactly as many properties in common as any other two'(Goodman, 1972:443).

We categorize what we see, hear, taste and smell because we are biologically enabled to do so as far as the culture in which we are socialized suggests that we should classify. There has been considerable research done into the seeing of colours. Whatever the reasons some cultures do not see colours in the same way so that the Tanzanian Sukuma do not distinguish blue and purple or orange and yellow; shown a piece of blue paper some describe it as 'Reckitti' after the blue washing powder. The Hangaza of Ngara found it difficult to distinguish red and green using the Ishihara test for non-literates while their neighbours just over the border in Ruanda had much lower rates because the children were taught colours in primary schools (Roberts and Tanner, 1967); there was no biological factor but only a cultural difference. A Greek on being asked by an Englishman seeing a disturbance among Greeks which appeared to be verging on violence, replied that it was just a very well argued disagreement; so English and Greek people would describe the same event in very different ways.

We can see from this that even when the differences are seemingly obvious, culture affects categorizations and so we can expect other cultural difficulties in what social scientists create as categories and how their respondents reply to these professionally created divisions. In discussing events which have cross-cultural component made more difficult by social distance factors, it is probably an exception rather than a common occurrence to find people having even approximately similar understandings of a single pragmatically isolatable event. When it comes to events which have an abstract and perhaps indefinable element the possibility of agreement clear enough to put them into similar categories is negligible.

It seems obvious enough that what societies and individuals may or may not do, can be based somewhat inaccurately on broad band demographic characteristics. But the initial and pervasive difficulty is that a category has the characteristics of a box which has clear cut edges and for anything to go into such a box it has to have certain characteristics or remain outside. It cannot be on the edge straddling both aspects at the same time because that is not logically acceptable but common enough in human behavioural understandings which is not over concerned with such abstractions as logical consistency.

There can scarcely be a questionnaire or data sheet that does not record at the top the age of the person responding or about whom data is being recorded. Of course there are obviously differences between the old and the young but to tie this distinction to their numerical age, ignores the fact that people may not act their age or be treated socially according to any numerical definition. This is a bureaucratic system created by Western societies to fit in with their legal needs and welfare requirements. In Sukuma society the unmarried of whatever age are not really accepted as adults.

When all behaviour is in practice both individualistic and situational categorization in any form must create serious doubts about the numerical validity of what has been cumulatively described. Legal codes lump together various types of crimes without regard for the situational factors which make each case distinctive; snatching an apple from a market stall and a bundle of currency notes from as bank are both theft but have nothing in common. Marriage is a legal state but the Sukuma have eleven types of marriage with distinctive names and contemporary Israel has had to pass laws to enable the widows of dead soldiers to remarry without being formally released from their deceased husband's brother's obligation to marry them.

CATEGORIZATION AS DOUBTFUL EVIDENCE

Researchers in the social sciences with their special interests are really engaged in fishing expeditions into unknown waters. They wish to find out from their clients whether they have ideas and practices which are part of their existing special interests or the unconscious ones which come from their personalities and from their socialization. It would seem then that these researchers are in most cases are not seeking new information but are providing whether intentionally or not fixed menus from which respondents can choose.

A schedule in a questionnaire or in the mind of a researcher are in effect a prepared list of leading questions which would be disallowed in Anglo-American legal procedure as suggesting to the respondents the area within which their replies should be provided, yet they are accepted as a form of acceptable truth. These schedules tell the respondents almost at once the range of acceptable answers; in a broad sense they find some data at least which conform to their needs. The Sukuma have no word in their own language for religion but provide what seems to be religious information when they may be describing their existential tribal behaviour. The red in the Rorschach test never got blood related responses from the Sukuma because they said quite logically that it was black almost at once. Ugandans on being given the paired word test would reply bananas or food as the pair with mother, while the more educated ones would reply father.

To put it bluntly quantification in relation to human behaviour is unnatural. Almost all of what we learn as we become members of a particular culture is passed on informally as part of some interpersonal relationship; it is not part of behavioural patterns which have and indeed could have firm edges. Then social scientists start to quantify because that is within the paradigm within which science operates, despite the fact that numbers are not an important part of social life; they are an imposition. The inhumanity of quantification is shown clearly in the differences between computer programmes and how cultures classify behaviour (D'Andrade, 1981). The steps in almost all computer programmes have to be exact and we know that this is just not possible for human behaviour which is too individual and environmentally varied but the computer requires the imposition of artificial exactness. The people being investigated have to be classified in binary exactness as either male or female and of a certain age rather than in terms of environmental variations. Counting distorts understandings of human behaviour.

3

The Presumption of Social Order

Data have to be collected and this process involves individuals with not only personal idiosyncrasies but with patterns of thought and understanding dictated by the cultures within which they operate and their conscious and unconscious socialisation up to the time of and during the research in which they are participating.

Social science research is carried out by four types of people who have similar characteristics and have been subject to the same popular and professional socialisation which affects not only what they experience but the form in which they organise and interpret their data.

Firstly, there are undergraduates undergoing required training in the social sciences and carrying out small scale research projects within or near to their university under closely regulated conditions. Then those working for a higher degree with specialised research projects similarly under professional supervision and institutional regulation. Next in higher status comes the career motivated research by established academics which is evaluated by their professional colleagues. Finally, those of equivocal status, hired researchers who do applied research for money outside the institutional control of universities or research institutes. Out of 124 meta-analyses into hypertensive drugs, 49 projects were financed by drug companies and although it was concluded that this was not associated with favourable results, they were associated with favourable conclusions (Yank *et al.*, 2007).

There is a primary factor which is common to all four types of researchers with the partial exception of those with private finance or who choose to do research within their range of interests without having to get funds or the permission of their superiors or those they are researching. They are all employees whether as salaried professionals in universities or research institutes or more directly as people being paid to do tied-to-time specific research. At the back of all their minds are the bread and butter issues of what is going to pay the rent and their food? In this they are no different to petrol pump attendants or cooks in a McDonald's franchised restaurant. Subsistence Bengali farmers have day-to-day needs which are more diffused and do not have any involvement with the carrying out of research. Researchers certainly know well enough that their employers are in a dominant position to dictate what they expect from them even if this is lightly administered within the code of academic freedom which itself is not a universal factor. They carry out their research within a system of financial constraints from economic reality and its bureaucratic administration.

It seems likely that the disinterested search for new forms of knowledge is a rarity and probably confined if it exists at all to established researchers at the top of their careers. Yet even there they are likely to be influenced both by public opinion and professional fashion (Kuhn, 1962). Break-through work is rare indeed in relation to the numbers of men and women engaged in research and their range of topics.

Lower down in the professional scale ideas and practices are going to be correlated to the market trends of public opinion. Compilations of research show the groupings of research changing from decade to decade and the Ford Foundation as much as the British Ministry of Overseas Development are going to distribute their grants within their own ideas of usefulness which may not coincide with any degree of closeness with the academic interests of researchers or their universities; they have constraining budgets which are just as limiting as personal ones. Such restrictions are universal and a report from Chinese Central Television commented that pilgrims spent as much on incense on the sacred Mount Hengshan as was available in the budget of China's Natural Science Foundation (Shi Meifen, 1989). These correlations to public opinion are not necessarily national ones as in sub-Saharan Africa much of the funding for research will be coming from overseas sources dictated by their interpretations of need.

There is also the common factor in researchers that they consider themselves to be intellectually gifted and that they have a free-ranging ability to think in original ways which provides them with the means to gain special understandings into human behaviour through their work. Why else would they be working in and supported by organisations which are publicly considered to employ some of the cleverest people known or thought to live in that society?

Their pattern of thinking is not necessarily correlated to any such self-assumed ability to think in original ways because they are just as much cognitive creatures of their own socialisation as anyone else. They have been brought up and indeed enabled to work as researchers through and within the pervasive structures of multi-level wide-ranging bureaucracies. They do not share many characteristics with subsistence farmers or daily employed workers whose lives are largely conducted outside the narrowing formalism of a structured society run by bureaucratic needs.

Unless the researcher is working with records to which the public have access or is doing research about their existing work whether as a practising doctor or lawyer or an employee of McDonald, they are automatically tied into another institutional structure. Their research proposal will have to get the approval of their university department as well as their ethics committee in addition to the permission of the social, economic and political institutions or areas in which they hope to work. Local authorities, social welfare departments and business firms have to be approached with diplomatic skill and possibly some deception. All these are confining structures rather than ones that are making the researcher think in terms of liberated and innovative thought. In crude terms they are well advised to beware the unexpected consequences of their intrusions.

At the lowest rank of researcher are the undergraduates who may flatter themselves that they are 'free spirits' able to think and behave in ways which are independent of the conservative and bureaucratic structures of their society. These men and women are maintained by government grants, bank loans or parental support, have their lives ordered quite explicitly by university regulations, teaching time-tables, course and residency requirements. Their personal lives are ordered round these institutional structures which will include bus time tables and student passes, places with the cheapest food and generally where their university has organised for them a preferential and highly structured standard of living. There is a certain latitude in how authorities treat these younger men and women but their freedom of thought and action is restricted within a paradigm of unavoidable orderliness.

The post-graduate researchers to an even greater degree have to lead professional and personal lives dictated by the orderly bureaucratic structures of their society. This is often combined with the need for the supportive patronage of those higher up in the university status structure. Formal behaviour is dictated again by university regulations and the getting of grants combined with semi-secret secondary employment as grants are rarely generous. They can only spend on research the funds which they have acquired. Library access may be free but time is not and they will prefer research which does not involve inevitably expensive and time consuming travel. They have the same standard of living restrictions as any other adult in that society.

Almost every aspect of their research activity will be costed particularly when their research work involves overseas travel requiring visas and the approval of the host country and a university there. It seems likely that in almost all the ideas the hopes of these researchers will be modified by these institutional requirements which may appear to them to be peripheral to their enthusiasm for the project that they have created as a personal dream.

Finally, those who have established positions in universities or who act as independent consultants. In many developing countries university salaries are insufficient for anything approaching an acceptable professional standard of living so that many have to give outside work a priority over what are the official requirements of their university status. Their minds will be attuned to the requirements of their part-time or potential employers and in such cases they are market oriented.

Whatever their residual ideas about the necessary freedom for innovative research, they will always be limited by what they are able to do within the macro-structures of their society. There will be restrictions imposed by tax regulations, social welfare and health provisions, schooling for children, university terms, cost of postage, secretarial help, mortgage and rent payments; there is an almost endless list of constraining factors.

All researchers from as far back in their lives as they can

remember will have existed in a regulating social system. Whatever residual ideas researchers may have had about the intellectual freedom in which they might hope to operate, it will be essentially limited to what they are able to do within the restrictive paradigms of the societies in which they are living. In some ways nature may provide the opportunity and indeed the ability for a few to think freely which may be no more than the cognitive system into which they have been socialised. For most researchers they will always be operating and thinking from start to finish within the ordered patterning of their society.

THE MIND SET OF REGULATION

While thought may or may not be individually creative, its physical expression in speech is likely to be broadly within the paradigms of the society in which each person has been socialised. When these thoughts have to be put into writing in order to convince other people of their correctness, they are likely to be even more guided by what the anticipated reactions of the recipients might be.

We have seen that would-be and existing researchers unless they are self-financing and self-supporting have to fit into a well established bureaucratic system of applications for grants for which only a small minority are successful. Donors have limited funds to give to the few who are selected out of thousands of applicants.

Research does not occur in a framework of practice which would enable genius to show itself in outstanding results as often as not these come to 'hard' science researchers by chance. Such striking results cannot occur in the 'soft' conclusions of the social sciences. Thus it seems likely that what they do and how it will be administratively and financially supported will come from broad reactions to general public opinion and more specifically by the professionals who are involved in supporting certain types of research rather than others about which little is known. While schizophrenia can be considered to affect a proportion of people in any society and could not be related to periodic mass infections, research on this distressing condition has fluctuated. Published research on schizophrenia has peaked in 1975 and 1985 doubling the amount published in 1970 and 1980 (Mueser and Berenbaum, 1990). We do not know what may account for these obvious fluctuations but editors act as gate-keepers for what may be published. The Editor of the *British*

Medical Journal commented that he pushed publications on pancreatitis because his brother suffered from this disease and that the journal published on toe-nail fungus because so many of the editorial team suffered from it (Editor, 2004).

The constraints from being in practice employees is shown even more specifically in the system of grant applications and the grant agencies peer review policies (Meyers, 2007:301-3). There is a mind-set of conformity "(Applicants for grants) will tend to submit only proposals that are likely to be approved, which is to say, those that conform to the beliefs of most members on the committee of experts. Because of the intense competition for limited money, investigators are reluctant to submit novel or maverick proposals". There is the further constraint that "the peer review system forces investigators to work on problems others think are important and certainly not to look for results that might undermine their own positions." Even the form in which applications may have to be made is often laid down and it would be hopeless for as researcher is expected to get financial support on the hope that he or she may find out something of value; this might indeed happen in 'hard' science for an applicant who has a proven record of success but not for the 'soft' social sciences. There would appear to be an enforced regularity in research work which reduces rather than enables the explication of chance and probability.

THE EXPECTATION OF SOCIAL ORDERLINESS

Researchers in the social science coming as they all do from an ordered intellectual environment and usually have as well experienced their lives as an orderly progress up the professional ladder. They are predisposed perhaps even intellectually obliged to see the same process overtly at work in societies comparable to their own and latently present in less well bureaucratically structured ones. It must surely be kept in mind that the obviously well-structured Western societies are not much more than a century old. As a balance to this people in these 'well-ordered' societies see their own behaviour differently and are often preoccupied with fitting their individualisms into these written requirements. The ways round the regulations are a preoccupation of members of such organisations rather more than the fulfilling of the required uniformities. There is rarely any exact coincidence between legal and bureaucratic requirements and what people actually do or indeed see their own behaviour. Prior to this recent bureaucratic overlay all societies worked within highly adaptable situational considerations within broadly defined non-literate paradigms.

It would seem likely that those who have researched the past and working almost inevitably from either a limited number of documents skewed to high status writers or empirically suspect oral history, have imposed the order shown in their meticulous and thoughtful reconstructions. Order is an abstraction not necessarily a social reality beyond its own definitions.

The point must surely be that all types of researchers do not approach their work with open minds expecting to find and to retain in their conclusions the disorderliness of the unexpected. Nurture got there first with a constraining understanding of order within which they have been brought up and which academic life sees as a professional necessity. In the minds of social scientists there is a social and bureaucratic paradigm within which they approach the possibilities of their research. This means that they are necessarily if unconsciously conformist to the structure and indeed bureaucratic requirements of the research industry in which they are employed. Every social scientist takes notes and then later settles down to working them into order. The Sukuma have some general understanding that ancestors and unrelated spirits can influence their lives which the anthropologist turns into a system (Tanner, 1969). The reality is that every event attributed to spirits is different in how it is interpreted and how it is ritually neutralised; it is more a do-it-yourself occasion than something that has any systematic requirements. This is not social behaviour as it is in reality but how it is required to present itself to academic supervisors, examiners and publishers.

DETERMINISM

At the back of all scientific thinking and the social sciences include themselves in this, is the fact of successful scientific determinism which has existed as far back as records exist and increasingly so since the European Enlightenment. The range of scientific determinism has been so enormous and constantly enlarging that it has led to a general feeling of confidence in the further inevitable expansion of linear understandings and causation.

This confidence in relation to human behaviour has to be balanced against the encroaching factor that the balance of what is unknown and perhaps unknowable remains as large as ever because of its instability and the inability of any linear approach to cover its pervasive occurrence.

It seems likely that scientific determinism can be as effective or ineffective as the situations in which it operates. It may be effective under particular and necessarily or accidentally restricted conditions in a defined area and time and for certain people and indeed it ought to be successful at one level of understanding but not at another. The connection in Muslim societies between the washing of face, hands and feet before prayer in contaminated water and the level of parasitical infestations is beyond argument. But to relate the level of infestation to the more devout Muslims in Egypt who are assumed to wash five times per day cannot have the same level of exactitude. We do not know the individual differences in frequency of prayer in which there is always likely to be a shortfall between what is required by Islamic law and what actually is carried out by individuals who act according to their daily social and physical situations nor the extent of the washing as it would depend on the accuracy of self-reporting (Farooq and Mallah,1966).

Linear determinism is successful because the factors under consideration are factually limited and have a primary significance. For most acts of human behaviour there are very many more factors involved than those that establish primary connections; the somewhat childish but unavoidable fact that in considering any human act everything is connected in some way with everything else. It can only be made orderly by restricting the factors being considered to those that are more amenable to observation and recording.

Social scientists who have brought themselves to assess social behaviour in deterministic and structural terms are unwilling to see the extent of behavioural variations in even the simplest of human acts. Parallel Distributive Processing which states that the human mind considers a range of factors before acting at a speed far quicker than the most modern of computers, has not been able to implement this much beyond the choices involved in typing. The behavioural complexity involved in a single act of personal worship, commitment to a particular partner in business or marriage or in hunting expeditions means in effect that reality is always both individual and timed and perhaps beyond any explicable understandings.

This is not just a question of individualism but the social fact that people do very little in personal isolation and so there is always the uncontrollable compound 'interest' of what occurs to this behaviour when it happens in the context of another or indeed of thousands of others. The last Kumbh Mela on the Ganges River is estimated by the Indian authorities to have been attended by some seventy million people. We have to start with the assumption that these people have gone to some expense and trouble to attend and that to have come there must have been the anticipation of a peak social or religious experience. It is rationally impossible to see such numbers as having similarities except in the sense that they have attended but even that is suspect since we do not know what is involved in any individual thinking and behaviour in what parts of this event which he or she has attended. Children came and so must have a number of mentally handicapped people as well as the representatives of commerce who would have hoped to benefit from coming. Christians, Muslims, Jains and Parsees were there apart from the Hindu majority. Of course, this is an extreme example because this was the largest known human gathering for a single 'purpose' far bigger than the mere two million Muslims who went on the Hajj pilgrimage that year.

Even if social scientist researchers cut down their project to the Christmas lunch of a single German or Indian family they will be faced with just as many possible factors as those working on the Kumbh Mela. The reduction in numbers does not necessarily make for any growth in simplicity except as a result of the predefinitions and preconceptions of those researchers.

It is not only that social scientists are trained along the predetermined lines of Western scholarship and rationalism and the general orderliness within which their lives are conducted that determine conclusions but the culturally tinted spectacles through which these researchers view the behaviour which they are viewing or recording. It is an enormous leap of hope to assume that Indians and Indonesians, Germans and Greeks are meaning or indeed seeing the same thing when they are looking at some common place domestic activity much less something as complex as the Jain ceremony for a family to enter total commitment to a life dictated by Jain thinking (Mehta, 2004:456-490). In Mehta's description of a family's ritual of dedication we have enough details to both understand and sympathize with the extreme 'illogicality' of what these adults have done in leaving their life of middle class wealthy contentment as diamond merchants in exchange for the homelessness of itinerant mendicant Jains. It seems doubtful that if he had worked on this ceremony in any linear sense that the results would have added anything more and very probably very much less understanding of this extreme behaviour. The orderly restrictions of linear thought should perhaps be seen as diminishing if not evading the impossibilities of hoping to understand human behaviour.

Those who have brought themselves to the hope of assessing human behaviour in deterministic ways are perhaps unwilling to see that societies are in practice organised round deviations from this problematic exactness. However exact the rules and regulations may be these are always being challenged by chance either expected at some future date or not anticipated at all. It is certain that a structural analysis of any social behaviour is an artificial creation in the extent to which it approaches narrowed categories.

THE LIMITATIONS OF CAUSAL EMPIRICISM

The 'hard' sciences are so used to immediate linear causes to explain changes in largely static inanimate matter or in animate materials which have long-term characteristics that their thinking has dominated much theoretical work of social scientists. Social science researchers have been content to assume similar patterns of immediate and linear causation can be applied to human behaviour. It is more appropriate to apply Victor Turner's approach to the meaning of a symbol in suggesting that each will have a fan of meanings (Turner, 1967:19-47) and that in any exact sense will be ephemeral.

Within this elastic determinism there may be priorities laid down by the paradigms of that society but how they are applied to particular social situations is one of particular environments. The elements may not have any fixed characteristics and any simplistic statements of causation abbreviate what has occurred and its consequences.

Of course, there may be primary and easily attainable reasons for what has occurred. The women was hit by a car and can no longer walk and the man lost his job because of persistent absenteeism but these are simplifications of complex events. But why was she inattentive when she knew the rules of the road and why was the man unable to work the more or less regular hours like the rest of the factory staff. Most people in most societies would never be satisfied with simplistic causal explanations and in this sense they have always taken a more qualitative and wide ranging approach to human behavioural events which is now been adopted by many social scientists. Most people in most societies are not satisfied with simplistic explanations and want to know 'why' events have occurred in their lives and they are more inclined to go to diviners than to social scientists and statisticians for satisfying explanations.

Any attempt to find out the causes of social behavioural events involve concentric circles of relative entanglement, relative accessibility and relative ascertainability. Some isolatable and important events such as the Japanese attack on Pearl Harbour and the assassination of President Kennedy have been extensively researched so it is clearly possible to give any event comprehensive coverage for finding out causative factors provided that the costs can be covered, the necessary researchers present and their overall persistence.

Not only is there the need to overcome the narrowness of deterministic reasoning and the cultural need to disentangle order from the constant variations in human behaviour but to accept the confining nature of resources. Most researchers accept that there are vast gaps in what they may well feel that they need to know for any adequate understanding of any human behavioural event. The shortfall is not due to any intellectual inadequacy but the absence of adequate funding and time. It would seem that this pattern of explanation has to make a virtue of necessity, the shortage of funds and time. Overall this understanding of the factors limiting as much as enabling conclusions about human behaviour has chance as a dominant factor and any assessment of probabilities is based on an inadequate range of data.

THE FICTIONS OF CAUSATION

Of course, there are many events for which the primary causes are obvious but there are these events which are really accidental could be seen as social mutations. We have to accept that no one whatever their intellectual capacity are predisposed to accept simplistic explanations. Social science reasoning is relatively easy as the event which they are analysing has already occurred. Many explanations are worked out retrospectively in the sense that they know the last chapter in the book and, therefore, it is not too difficult to fill in what may have led to this ending but what may have occurred before is now beyond investigation. It is rare for an event to be known in advance in its totality.

There are certainly predisposing and precipitating factors and they are at the ostensible head of what may have caused the event. The wider range of factors are more likely to be non-lineal. If analyses are expressed quantitatively and often to several decimal places, then the accumulation of minor factors may well be influential.

It seems likely that causation for human behavioural events can be seen in the lineal understandings of 'hard' science and that the commitment to lineal causation is an ideological one. There can be no such thing as simple lineal sequences either in the behaviour of Kung hunter gatherers in the Kalahari or in the affairs of a Mumbai business executive. There have to be conscious and unconscious primary and secondary ones on the fringes of immediacy as well as touch and go factors, but above all there are singular disruptive and unforeseen occurrences.

THE RESEARCHERS' CHOICE OF METHOD

Whatever methods are chosen by researchers it will to some extent limit what they are likely to find. A psychologist studying individual behaviour in one to one sessions is likely to find wide variety. The sociologist studying patterns of marriage is likely to find a pattern of shared conformities. This is not so much bias as just choosing the entrance way to a problem which dictates the likelihood of the finding of certain factors. An example would be social science researchers finding out the quickest and presumably the cheapest way of choosing students for university places. A project based on linear factors in which the results of tests were correlated to demographic data can produce adequate results identifying trends.

If on the other hand the aim of such research is to find out a much broader picture of motivation and the factors which might be correlated to success or failure then a linear methodology is not appropriate (Remus and Jenicke, 1978). In such a choice between methods researchers would have to assess whether they have the time and the funds to attempt this more complicated work.

In working on the abilities of bankers to evaluate the ratio of assets and liabilities of people applying for mortgages, then a linear approach showed that only 9 out of 48 succeeded (Libby, 1976), but similarly this approach tells us nothing about what might make a better evaluator of financial data. So the choice of methodology might be the division between applied research working for a defined end of who are best qualified for particular work and wider academic research in which there can be no such narrower objectives.

VARIABLES OF CHOICE IN RESEARCHERS' METHODS

In hard science most research work is controlled by the nature of what is being analysed and there are generally accepted standards in the scientific community as to how this work should be done if the results are to be accepted as accurate according to these professional standards. In comparison to social scientists, hard scientists have not much choice in matters of methodology. Any researcher attempting to initiate new procedures has to undertake a long process of convincing their colleagues that they have broken new ground long before the publication of results.

This type of situation cannot apply in social science as although there is considerable peer appraisal of any individually published research, there are no profession vide on approved lines as to how each piece of research should be done. Each piece of research faced with social and individual variability is in practice a new field. It is perhaps generally felt in the scientific world that studies with a more or less firm statistical base are just about acceptable. Anthropological field work which has no methodological basis is marginal at best (Kumar, 1988) and that some works which appear to be based on no known data (Castenada, 1968) should be classed as works of fiction. There is the simple fact that the reduplication of research which is necessary for its scientific acceptance just cannot be done for social science work. Even the most thorough piece of work such as a study of Navaho philosophy (Ladd, 1957) working from a one to one relationship between the researcher and a single tribal elder may be seen as an important basic work on Navaho, American Indian morality. It is in reality a piece of isolated scholarship which individual readers have to assess for themselves.

So in practice social science researchers are on their own to choose whatever variables they should study in whatever way they find personally possible and congenial. There is perhaps a general feeling that there can be little understanding of a general topic until some basic data has been obtained on the lines of a census of who lives where and who is related to whom without realising that this is a particularly Western way of approaching social environments. A researcher from an Eastern background might see the recording of constantly varying characteristics as a waste of time, even if such data is accurate which in itself is a big assumption.

Researchers usually approach their projects with ambitious ideas as to how much they can accomplish in the time available. They may not realise that their effective understanding of human behaviour in the desired contexts depends very much on establishing good relationships with a small number of informants in a general environment in which they are accepted as tolerable as much as tolerated outsiders. This may be a long process affected by chance.

Researchers usually start with a social environment using variables which they consider to be both reliable and readily available. However, even the sexual classification may be social as much as biological and Tanzanian census enumerators asked under what heading should they put individuals who were neither male nor female and in asking that question they certainly had some persons in mind.

Age in the statistical sense is largely a creation of bureaucracy. A baby may not exist socially until it has been through a ceremony of social recognition and been given a name or they may age a child from the date of conception. Others even if they know their age because they had their births registered may not be willing to disclose it publicly to a stranger for fear of jealousy when there is high infant mortality. We know from Western censuses that people stay at the end of a decade and avoid declaring that they are now in their 30s or 40s. Tanzanians might know that they were born in the year of Independence rather than knowing the actual date numerically.

Almost every variable which is selected has to be attached to a series of socially different people. What constitutes a marriage is a social variable unless there is a legal document in support and where an informant lives may not be exactly locatable when houses and streets are not numbered or mapped and many have migratory lives so that their address in one season will be different to that of another. Large numbers of Tanzanian Hangaza went away to work as migratory labourers in Uganda returning at the end of the year. A census in the middle of the year would give a grossly distorted sex ratio of females without men. So overall these check lists of variables, however, carefully done even with the help of local informants would not necessarily have any long-term factual reality.

When it comes to religion which in the Western understanding means commitment to a particularly defined faith, it is virtually impossible to get an answer which is not subjectively and objectively interpretable in different ways. Most people who state that they are Buddhists or Christians or whatever show different forms of commitment for different occasions and indeed for different days of the week. Most African Christians practice some form of their quasi-traditional beliefs in parallel to the requirements of Christianity particularly when they have troubles. Very few Buddhists practice the abnegations required by the philosopher Buddha and mostly they have turned him into a god or created local spirits to whom appeals for intervention can be made (Spiro, 1971).

In traditional societies ethnicity and religion are indistinguishable so questioning an old tribesman about his religious affiliation would get the reply 'I am a Sukuma'. However to be a Muslim is distinguishable at least in some ways from being a Swahili or Pakistani, even more when the culture would appear so basically contrary to what Islam requires as with the matrilineal Yao in southern Tanzania.

ACCIDENTAL VARIABLES IN METHODOLOGIES

Apart from the variables which however exact to record may be found in some form in all societies, there are important ones which erupt in the course of social research which have to be taken advantage of because such opportunities will not last for long. The researchers may be there when the Indonesian tsunami struck, the floods occurred in Bangladesh, the earthquakes in China and Kashmir and the prolonged droughts in eastern Africa and Australia. The ways in which these disasters hit communities and individuals is of importance for understanding the methods with which inevitable misfortune is coped with. In such situations the researchers have to collect data from sufferers with a minimal interference with their survival necessities and as far as possible detachment from any personal involvement beyond note taking and a camera. The researcher has an unstable involvement with his or her field of enquiry in which there is always a clash between human instincts and detachment.

Then there are ideological disruptions such as the civil wars which exist in or have occurred in the Sudan, Uganda, Columbia, Maputo, Myanmar and Somalia so that researchers cannot work there. They will have to use secondary sources but data from displaced persons may well be of doubtful accuracy. These outbreaks of disorder as in Cambodia, have been started with leaders borrowing their ideologies from Western socialists and communists or from the agnostic policies of Jawaharlal Nehru, the first Prime Minister of India, a Brahmin by birth who received a secular education in Britain. It would seem that social science understandings of human behaviour are skewed towards relatively stable social situations.

There is also the problem of the developing new political and social awareness which may make getting quantifiable data from a large sample of people in any community more difficult. Many people anyway may dislike the rota approach to the collecting of data about themselves and their neighbours. The overall growth in people seeing themselves as individuals paying taxes as a named person, getting educated as a particular person and finding themselves in employment in which their employers have no interest at all in who they are outside their work capabilities, but above all having themselves registered as an individual voter of interest periodically to politicians. There is also the primary fact that property in the form of cattle and harvests cannot be hidden but money can be hidden away from the claims of indigent relatives.

So it may be that in developing societies there is the same steady movement to individualism. Social scientists will have to learn the skills of gaining the confidence of the individuals from whom they want to collect information and with this the increasing difficulty of collecting data from some predetermined samples. Social scientists may be well trained in the use of depersonalized methodologies but much less well trained in how to gain the confidence of strangers from whom they are separated by very wide margins of social distance because of their education, sex, age and ethnicity. A theoretical commitment to equality is much easier than putting oneself into the position of wanting information from people who have no reason from their own cultural standpoint to provide anything to strangers.

Researchers may thus find themselves committed to methodologies more suited to work within Western societies more committed to individualism but who still have memories of traditional communalism, although they are themselves interested in personal advancement. Thus it may be more difficult to see in these societies the sense of social order which traditional verbal history may suggest to have been the norm and which forms of quantification tend to perpetuate.

There is also a change in the social and political atmosphere in which social science research takes place. In what might be called the colonial phase of social science fieldwork the researchers were much freer methodologically to do what they wanted. Now subjects for research particularly by expatriates are vetted by national committees and the local universities to which researchers are affiliated. Their sensitivity to this supervision may restrict more open enquiries and indeed many researchers may feel the need to demonstrate their political ideals by showing a general sense of equality. Nationals who have to live with their published results may feel the need to self-censorship or restraint in what they do in research. The theoretical need for the scientific underpinning for what methodologies should be used may have to be modified by the social and political realities of the situations in which researchers find themselves.

THE UNLIMITED RANGE OF METHODOLOGICAL VARIABLES

Whereas in hard science the variables of participation are limited by the methodology for the research laid down in advance, this is not so with social science fieldwork. The methodologies which are used depend on the social situations in which the researchers find themselves. For a start the cooperation of those in the proposed area of research cannot be assumed or indeed cannot be used because it would lead to subsequent biases in the information received. Evans-Pritchard records the non-cooperation of the Nuer in his work which would have required information passing through interpreters whom the Nuer would have despised as outsiders so that his methodology was confined watching what went on from his tent. Later a para-military raid terminated any hope of cooperation so that he packed up and left.

Much research into subjects which are too sensitive for the necessary data to be publicly pursued would have to rely on odds and ends of information picked up in undirected gossip. This is a time consuming method which relies on patience, a good memory since taking notes would be impossible and a good knowledge of the necessary linguistic code. A national may not have any particular advantages in this as the English spoken in universities would not make the dialects used elsewhere to be necessarily intelligible.

Even in communities which have only a limited number of literates predominantly with only a primary education there may be written records connected with health and religion. Hindu places of pilgrimage sometimes issue certificates for those who want evidence that they have been there on a pilgrimage circuit. Churches often keep punctilious records of baptisms providing data on names. Government offices often have out of date tax registers which can provide data on names and population movement. Almost all health facilities keep records of patients, diagnoses and the medicines they have given. Thus there is the sporadic availability of written records but there is no consistency in their contents.

Any bureaucratic organisation will be keeping records and the amount that is recorded may well show how and for what reasons the facility is being used or not used. The millions of Tanzanian Sukuma have a local government system of courts which can be used for civil suits and the records show that these courts were little used for the settling of marital disputes over bride-wealth and divorce. Since it must be very unlikely that these people have an unusual stability in such relationships this would suggest that there are local systems of arbitration. These would have been easier to use than a court system organised round judicial principles which contradict their traditional system of compensation and communal interests. The importance of bureaucratic records may be to show the purposes for which their use is avoided.

In the absence of any agreed methodologies based on pragmatic necessity, what methods are used in practice depends on a combination of the situations in which the researchers find themselves, the influences of the schools of thought which they have been under during their education and above all what their own personalities enable. It may be that out-going people with attractive personalities will use interpersonal contacts while another of a more retiring nature and an inability to learn and use the linguistic codes of other cultures will find extracting information from gossip too difficult. They will rely on observation and the use of whatever written records there are even in largely non-literate communities.

With scientific aims predominating it may be that social scientists attempt to pay too much attention to such variables as age, sex and location which are either inaccurately available or change almost as soon as they are recorded. If we take the fact of attending a ceremony in the sense that people have passed through a door for the ceremony, stayed there for its duration and then left, we have some numbers of very little significance. Coptic services in Ethiopia are long and many are asleep and indeed lying down to do so; their churches are small so that large numbers are attending in the courtyards out of sight and sound of the ceremonies. In any sense of understanding what is going on and its significant numbers mean very little except in terms of noting the alternative uses of time, and issues of transportation and sanitation. What methods can be used for the study of the last Indian Kumbh Mela which was attended by an estimated seventy million pilgrims. Researchers can pick on a few pilgrims from whom they may be able to gain the dimensions of some of the issues involved in such an enormous religious occasion. Only the government departments involved can provide numerical data from which some behavioural consequences will emerge. Hinduism itself could not bring any order out of such chaos because it has no centralising bureaucracy and on arrival on the banks of the Ganges each sect would be concerned with its own interests.

So researchers in approaching a religious ceremony have a number of restricted methodological opportunities open to them since they obviously cannot intrude on the privacies of anyone while it is going on. So this may mean talking to people afterwards in which they will be presenting to the researcher what they feel they ought to say about their participation; that they were just there would mean the accumulation of self-assessed data. Yet to record that many were dozing, reading, could not see or hear what was going on may well miss what is important for these participants. In terms of any scientific methodologies this fieldwork is probably no more than professionalised guesswork which has to be evaluated in terms of the researchers' own reputations and presentation.

So in addition to the enormous number of ill-defined or indefinable variables which are part of all evaluations of human behaviour there will be a number of possible ways of approaching such research. These cannot themselves be assessed on any scale of scientific adequacy because what is done is both personal and situational. These so-called nuisance variables (Meehl, 1970:810) will have been recorded but without more specialised studies we cannot be certain of their social and psychological importance since they are influenced by other variables both inside and outside the project (Fisher, 1966). What is certain is that in any social science research project the methodologies used ensure that more will not have been discovered as will have been found out. Even theoretically there is no possibility of any universal comprehensive coverage.

FEEDBACK LOOPS—THE INFLUENCE OF THE RESEARCHER

In hard science the range of research is to some extent predefined and feedback loops are eliminated as far as possible by reducing the involvement of the researcher and confining the range of the research as far as possible as in research into illness and the use of particular medicines and surgery. The range of change is expected and is the basis of the research in the first place; patients are expected to change. This is not usually connected to the unpredictable behaviour of the researchers and only their formal activities would be considered acceptable as data.

Social science research can only rarely operate in any such predetermined more or less fixed lines. During the course of any research which is likely to be lengthy rather than short and consist of the interrelationships of innumerable variables, there are likely to be several feedback loops.

Unless the researched people have had considerable experience of inquisitive strangers, the appearance of outsiders who appear to have no specific roles which can be accepted as that of teacher or nurse, they are going to have some effect. It has been suggested that the Yanomano (Chagnon, 1977) who were described as the fierce people were in fact made into this by the researcher giving them iron tools which they used aggressively to dominate their neighbours. Further that the researchers also brought disease to them and withheld medicine in the interests of their work (Turner, 2001). There are moral as well as methodological issues facing the individual researcher.

If correct these are extreme cases but whatever the researchers do it can be certain that they influence others in whatever interpersonal relationships they achieve.

Gulliver in his work on the Tanzanian Warusha on their closely settled mountain reported that the pitching of his tent on a patch of grass disturbed the grazing patterns of his neighbours (Gulliver, 1957). Briggs who lived with an Eskimo family throughout an Arctic winter (Briggs, 1970) and the French woman who lived with a north Indian Brahmin family for some months, must not only have altered those families pattern of living but have had some effects on their ways of thinking about foreigners.

THE RESEARCHERS' OWN PROFILE CHANGES

In the course of any research particularly when it is prolonged by return visits, they will age and take on a different demographic profile; they are likely to marry and have children, live in a new environment under the influence of different academic colleagues and friends even change their religions as was the case with Victor Turner. Margaret Mead when she first visited Manus and who last visited the same community forty years later must have been virtually a different person. In between visits the whole pattern of thinking will have been altered by their own academic contacts and reading.

THE EFFECT OF RESEARCH ON THE RESEARCHERS

Everyone including researchers live in a personal world which is subject to constant external and internal influences and the deep contact with people who do not think and behave as they do for their own reasons is bound to be a personal shock although it would have been intellectually expected. There are substantial differences between the conscious and unconscious understandings of a patrilineally socialised and highly educated social scientist researcher understanding what is involved in matrilineal societies and meeting men who are responsible for their sisters, children and the killing of animals in sacrifices. The actual seeing of different social realities is always likely to be a shock that people actually do behave in these 'peculiar' ways. The man who inducts the Sukuma chief into his new role will avoid speaking to him directly even when required to give evidence before him in a court case shouting his evidence from outside the building. The Zigua woman will not enter the same room even the verandah in which her son-in-law is sitting. This is not so much culture shock of the tourist but the shock of realising the rational realities of these differences.

Chagnon writes of his emotional even physical horror in first meeting the Yanomano with their obvious savagery and disgusting appearance shocking to even the most liberal minded Westerner. Powdermaker's shock on realising that she was alone in a totally strange environment when the boat delivering her to Lesu went off. Almost all researchers in their fieldwork in communities or environments of which they had previously no more than theoretical knowledge are exchanging an environment of some security which they know and are known for the social isolation for which they will have had no previous experience.

Certainly Turnbull came to dislike the Ugandan Ik but his dislike while other researchers record their difficulties over the domestic violence which they may witness. Knowing about malnutrition and disease and seeing it in social situations which their outsider understandings would see as unnecessary brings with it the shock of their personal impotence. The researchers are not all that detached from what they experience as they would theoretically wish to practice and indeed should do in any scientific approach to the evaluation of human behaviour. There are unpleasant people and unpleasant practices in any society but research into behaviour different to one's own makes this starkly obvious.

THE UNSCRAMBLING OF LOCAL SITUATIONS

Most published studies of social behaviour produce data providing a sense of order in what the writers have been researching with professional care. One of the illusions of social science research is that the seeming logical simplicity of the research design will be maintained once the fieldwork starts; this is of course a relic of hard scientific research.

Any event whether social or in the mind is in a constant process of change and putting what is seen or told them into writing produces an illusion of stability and order. In a Hindu ceremony which lasts several days the researcher is faced with a mass of publicly available data over and above what may be withheld from him or her. There is an imposed orderly theme on what has been recorded but at what level and in what form can this be described as orderly. It may well be that there will be as many understandings of what has been going on as there are participants. Are we entitled professionally to take the view that the priests are more important because their theology states this to be the case when they are just doing the job for which they are paid and which they may have more or less inherited. While the non-literate peasants in their thousands are there for the relief of distress and anxiety and as a break from the monotony of their subsistence agricultural work in a community which is still rigidly defined in terms of caste. Such a social situation in its difficulties for research cannot be any more difficult than studying rush-hour behaviour in and out of Mumbai or a political meeting in New York or Havana. What is the orderliness to be recorded in a Coptic religious ceremony or a Japanese No play when many of the participants are asleep. It is not surprising that a researcher viewing a public Hindu ceremony gets the impression of organised chaos for which a new methodology is needed to cover these realities.

In many cases researchers end up with more material than

they can process and which does not fit in with either the original or subsequent hypotheses. This is particularly so when the complexity of a community's social system emerges and they are forced to recognise that there are no simple straightforward systems; even a 'simple' temporary camp of hunter-gatherers is a location for ongoing change. There are numerous sub-systems in constant change for which there are temporal, causal and formal explanations (Rappaport, 1979: 152).

The researchers have the personal process of unscrambling the data they have collected to make it as orderly in their professional eyes as it is to those they have researched who may have a somewhat similar feeling of orderliness without having given it any thought. However, in their approach to this accumulation of divergent data it seems likely that they will pay more attention to critical or random events which catch their attention.

ORDERLINESS AND RANDOM EVENTS

Hard science research from the start is almost always carefully documented and each process recorded so that in a sense unusual breakthroughs do not come out of the blue but to those who have prepared themselves for alternatives by extensive preparatory work.

Social science research cannot usually have this rigidity because what is being attempted cannot have firm edges and has to accept change as part of what they are observing. This is built into social behaviour not only the linear demographic ones of birth and death but cyclical changes in agricultural work but equally present in the accountancy year of business and the institutions of government. The assumption of consistency is more a belief than a reality and as Winston Churchill commented 'a day is a long time in politics', as it certainly is in social science research which is always going to be affected by not only random events but of ones which catch their attention as being outside their expectations.

Fluctuations in the strength of electricity supplies affecting computer calculations can be identified and allowed for but there are whole ranges of random events which are usually in the Western world attributed to acts of God or good or bad luck (Gunther, 1977). Luck comes up in a number of personal stories

(Popper, 1974:36-7) as well as in scientific ones. In a detailed study of the possibilities of the voluntary control of heart beats using twins, the author wrote "we had our greatest luck with pair three" (Khokhlov, 1983). It is rare indeed whether a scientist or a social worker much less more ordinary people in western societies who do not use the word 'luck' quite regularly in referring to their own experiences. It is just as likely to occur in social science research as a helping or hindering factor as to whom and what they encounter under what circumstances. It is disorderly factors rather than orderly ones which dominate social science research.

THE SHEER NUMBER OF VARIABLES

We have already noted that there are varieties of methodologies depending on situations as well as on the researchers' own abilities and needs. The further and more extreme problem is the identification of variables on which to concentrate. Hard science does not have the same problem of innumerable variables because its experiments and observations are often self-limiting. The social sciences in their work on human behaviour cannot define the parameters of their work because of the sheer number of variables involving the people and their environments. The boundaries of interest and involvement are artificial.

It is not just this built-in factor of social variability but individual variability and the coincidental or accidental environments in which they spend their lives. There is also the fact that these variables differ in both quantity and quality from the different viewpoints with which they are observed. The researchers themselves have their specialisations with which they observe as well as the biases from their socialisation; they observe and find the variables which they have been trained to see and wish to see. The feminist and her male counterpart will each see variables from their points of view whether it is in domestic or in religious behaviour.

Those who have been influenced by Turner's binary viewpoint will see in their observations an endless series of these oppositions, up and down, left and right, black and white, wet and dry, male and female; these indeed exist but it is often not at all clear whether the Ndembu from within whose culture this way of analysing was devised are aware of this binary approach. To the Western way of thinking with its background of scientific logic it has an almost instant appeal, but do Westerners in their own day-to-day thinking divide up their experiences in such clear binary categories. We all speak a natal language of which we do not know the grammar as Wittgenstein commented, "The description of the grammar of a word is of no use in everyday life; only rarely do we pick up the use of a word by having its uses described to us; and although we are trained and encouraged to master the use of the word, we are not taught to describe it" (Budd, 1989:4-5).

Then there are the variables which precede a social event. Apart from the fact that we cannot know with any exactness how and about what people think and that what they say they think is not necessarily more than the isolation of a particular line of thinking occasioned by the circumstances in which it arose. This process has probably been as complicated as the rapid working of a computer which has been suggested by Parallel Distributive Processing; the almost instant filtering through the mind of innumerable factors (Rumelhart *et al.*, 1986).

Then there are trails of backward connections which are in fact limitless if we consider the existence of possible socially hostile genes obvious enough in the case of the inbred Amish communities with their number of very obvious genetic abnormalities. We do not know and perhaps never will be able to know the full range of useful variables as even the so-called nuisance ones must cumulatively have significant influences collectively on individuals which must be another factor reducing the possibilities of accuracy.

THE BACKGROUND OF CULTURAL FACTORS

While culture is certainly an important part of social understandings and references it cannot be considered as part of any scientific observations. It cannot be defined since it has no boundaries and contains an unlimited number of constituent parts; it is perhaps overloaded with intellectual concepts in art and literature when it should just as much contain the popular themes in Mumbai's Bollywood productions, popular comics in Japan and Barbie dolls in the United States.

Even in small socially cohesive community with a visibly distinctive way of living based on religion such as the Amish and Hutterites as well as the Hare Krishna devotees will have internal variations between communities. Those that are in transport nearness to their fellows will be socially and behaviourally different to those who have had to purchase land further away. In an Islamic community, however theoretically theocratic, there will be substantial differences in the parallel popular religiosity practised by individuals as in the use of the Koran for divination and what is required by orthodoxy.

The density of cultural influences can never be a constant feature in any community or family as between adolescents and the elderly, the largely urban and the rural and those who have been employed in distant rather than relatively nearby jobs. There will be even greater differences between subsistence communities with an annual cycle of work and those working in the oil fields of Iran and Iraq and urban super-markets.

Nevertheless whatever culture may be, it is something which is more than subliminally influential in ways that distinguish Eastern and West societies, Shia and Sunni differences in Iraq and Protestant and Roman Catholic ones in northern Ireland and no doubt between the nationally divided East and West Bengali.

There are descriptions of Hindu behaviour in the famine of Bengal 1943 replicating reports from the mid-nineteenth century in which charitable Christians and no doubt well-meaning agnostics have offered food to starving Hindus which they have refused as polluting knowing that their refusal would lead to their own deaths. So clearly in some situations culture has a dominating but diffused significance.

Of course, this is an extreme example but there are many examples of culturally conditioned behaviour such as the carrying out of appropriate behaviour in religious centres by people who are no longer committed believers. The use of the left hand being considered to be both ritually and biologically polluting as in the avoidance of menstruating women in orthodox Judaism which would not be connected in their thinking with what Westerners and educated people generally would see as out of date prejudices.

The reluctance of Hindus and Muslims to marry endogamously and exogamously respectively will surely continue in families which have migrated into totally different cultural environments as we have seen in the number of enforced arranged marriages of women in British Asian families. Whatever culture may be some aspects of it are considered to be and indeed are binding, are often ill-defined variables which social scientists find difficult to record accurately. These issues affect both chance and probability

NETWORKS IN THE FIELDS OF RESEARCH

The boundaries which have to be created for research projects can be laid down geographically as well as numerically but there is always social and psychological leakage which prevents any attributions of order. Whatever boundaries are defined for a project there are going to be substantial crossings over however isolated and underdeveloped a community and individuals may be. Villagers in Tanzania may have worked in the South African gold mines and crofters in the outer Scottish islands may have worked as seamen and have a knowledge of foreign ports which English professionals can never equal.

No modern society however geographically isolated is without numerous outside connections through mobile phones, television and transistor radios; and there is the Swahili adolescent walking along the main street of Pangani, an East African coastal township in a step which he said he had copied from cowboy films. In eighteenth century France long before railways and the modern telegraph news of important events such as the outbreak of the Revolution and the fall of the Bastille spread across the country at amazing speeds averaging 4 miles per hour (Robb, 2007:140-1). We also have the Chinese monks travelling to India and back just as a Chinese fleet did to eastern Africa, and the movement of traded objects shows substantial movement over long distances. Isolation from over the social border influences must be considered as no more than a wished for ingredient in social science research.

The topic of research may be treated as the centre of a network but this is as likely as not the result of the researcher's personal attention and it may not be the way the community or individuals see their social and psychological environments. It is reasonable to have one's interests as the focus of research as long as it is recognised to be what it is, a personal abstraction. But there are always difficulties over even this as there are overlapping networks not only in the individual sense but there will be different ones for different activities even within a single religion or community. There will be different ones for communal and personal devotions and those related to rites of passage, annual festivities and the specialised groupings which have different social focuses.

THE ABSENCE OF POSSIBLE DEFINITIONS

In the social sciences it is not possible to provide watertight definitions for theoretical concepts which have the same validity as chemical formulae and the anticipated workings of mathematics. There can surely be no social scientists with any sense of reality that they can create hard definitions rather than accepting them as personal definitional ideas.

"The important point for methodology and psychology is that just as in statistics one can have a reasonably precise theory of probable inference being quasi-exact about the inherently inexact, so psychologists should learn to be sophisticated and rigorous in their meta-thinking about open concepts at the substantive level" (Meehl, 1978:815).

However, by leaving the attempt to be exact about observations of human behaviour, the absence of definitions or open endedness can be considered in three ways (Meehl, 1977). Firstly, the indefinite extensibility of what the objects of research are involved in. Secondly, the inability to define the qualities of each identified indicator and lastly the important fact that the theories which we use explicitly or implicitly from our cultural understandings are inevitably short-term. There will always be a conceptual drift in the thinking of researchers as more and more information edges into their understandings (Campbell and Fiske, 1959). Our methodological demand for order should not override our almost total inability to be scientifically exact about the complexities of any behaviour.

INTENTION BEHIND INVOLVEMENTS IN RESEARCH

The social scientists who undertake research have some things in their minds before they start; it is their intention to prove or disprove hypotheses which are already available in some form in their academic culture or to follow up some new aspects which they have come across in their work. There can scarcely be any situations in which they have no preconceived ideas at all about what they are going to do.

Even if they are urbanised graduates who have read widely and have never had any experience of the social environment in which they are about to do research, they will still start with some preconceived ideas. They are not likely to find exactly what they expect. There will be similar preconceptions in the minds of those who are being researched.

It is a dialectical situation in which both parties will be in a state of constant change from what they originally thought. The understandings of one moment will never be isolated from what comes next and this in its turn will change with the similarly changing social environment.

THE NORMS GOVERNING RESEARCHERS

Human behaviour is governed by normative rules of which individuals may not be fully aware of the extent which these govern their behaviour and moreover that the so-called freedom of choice is severely circumscribed and may not exist at all. So social scientists start their research being governed by the appropriate rules of the roles which they occupied in their outside lives. It is probably impossible to get rid of these norms even if the researcher is aware of their extent. The forms of politeness in their own culture are usually applied to relationships in the new social environments in which they are working. Much the same applies to the behaviour of informants so this means that currently in the course of research attitudes of mind and behaviour of both the researchers and the researched will be consistently and constantly modified by norms of which they may be unconscious.

It is necessary to conclude that while there may be some orderliness in social behaviour it has little consistency and is subject to constant change and variation. If this order is presented as having some hard form this is probably the result of the researchers needing order rather more than orderliness as the form in which they are led to present their results.

4

The Statistical Dead-End

The production of statistics relating to human behaviour is often regarded as a necessary adjunct to establishing the correctness of any social science statements. In practice all such quantitative productions are increasingly part of history since there is usually a delay of 3 to 5 years between the completion of the research and the publication of the results. Thus the first handicap to the tabulation of any results is that they are more or less produced with the suggestion that they are contemporary but they are already out of date.

If the purpose of research about human behaviour is to provide authoritative statements we shall see that there is little likelihood of this coming from quantification. If on the other hand they are illustrative of trends around which individuals and social groups change, they suggest an accuracy about the trend which inevitably cannot exist outside an interpretable range of probabilities. It might indeed make the trend more difficult to accept since statistics in the rigidity of their tabulated form tend to encourage positive acceptance or rejection. Statistics tend to be binary reactions while trends can be discussed in the light of more contemporary data as it becomes available.

Even allowing for the fact that this may be an extreme example let us look at what particular points are made available from a survey of Americans being exposed to Buddhists (Wuthnow and Cadge, 2004). This was a random sample of 2910 adults who were asked a series of questions about their contacts with Buddhists. The answers were not presented as simple percentages to one decimal point but were shown as adjusted odd ratios from the logistic regression of contact with Buddhists together with a number of highly sophisticated statistical procedures such as 2 log likelihood, Nageckerke *R*2 and *p* value Wald statistic. This surely is adding mathematical theoretical logic to indeterminate data which may but more likely are not similarly accurate; a process of mathematical creativity.

There is here the perennial problem of the fact that these figures are not based on any defined factors as to what constitutes contact and what is Buddhism. There is no independent verification of the correctness of any replies which relate to religion, age, education and religious attendance and it may be that we should accept that there can be no possible accuracy of such replies except that they were made at a certain date and place. We do not have any evidence that those people answering these questions are who they say they are or that the answers are not imaginative replies made up on the spur of the moment.

This careful analysis of the results from a questionnaire leaves out the factors of chance in who replies and who is left out by the process of random sampling. There are also the factors of probability between those who may have met a New Age Buddhist or a Tibetan refugee prior to completing this questionnaire and those who see in Buddhism a way for coping with their own problems or in fact live next door to a Buddhist or a Buddhist institution.

There is also the question of to whom are these results directed as such sophisticated calculations would only have relevance to people who have graduated in statistics. So this published research raises many of the issues which need to be considered in the quantification of any aspect of human behaviour.

THE EXISTENCE OF QUANTIFIED DATA

Quantification of data has existed for as long as written and inscribed information has existed but it has usually been related to the counting of heads for taxation purposes. So potentially there is accuracy but humans have always disliked being counted particularly by strangers. A woman might think that it is dangerous to boast about the number of children she has had. The Lebanon has avoided holding censuses as political power rests on population size and any announced changes in population levels would be destabilizing for all concerned. The compulsory destocking of cattle in Usukuma in what was once Tanganyika, led to movement of cattle at night to avoid counting in some areas. We cannot assume that any such totals are as accurate as the figures suggest.

When it comes to the recording of data about human behaviour in which there is built-in instability of who said or did what when and where, much less why the likelihood of any accuracy which approaches the requirements of 'hard' science virtually disappears. Even allowing for the fact that the researchers have been using all their personal expertise and professionalism to make their numerical data as accurate as possible leaving aside the rare cases of deliberate falsification.

Tables of figures referring to some aspect of human behaviour exist in a social vacuum and they are in fact meaningless until the numbers have been slotted into the particular social and indeed individual environments from which they came and the methods by which this behaviour has been turned into statistics.

In what sense can these tabulations be said to exist. They certainly have a symbolic value in the rituals of social science research; they add a sense of probity to the many pages of research explanations. Figures in print are assumed to have a value greater than words in print, just as print is thought to have a greater inherent truthfulness than the transient words of even the most prominent of researchers. These figures are put into statistical form to do more than illustrate other points as they are usually printed to support a conclusion; after all they are expensive to collate and print.

QUANTIFICATION AS A PROFESSIONAL REQUIREMENT

Any social behaviour can be researched without necessarily relating it to the standards of 'hard' science; literature and art are constantly investigated and the results are classified as opinions according to the degree of expertise involved. So social science research results are often quantified in order to qualify for scientific acceptance. In applied research public bodies often seem to feel that the results given to them should be quantified as they are nervous of the opinions of social scientists. They may have reputations for having political and social views antagonistic to their own and they may feel that tables of figures neutralises this bias.

Statistics are rarely if ever primary data even if they are official records of events such as the requirement in the United Kingdom that all babies should be registered within one month of birth. Even such primary documents related to birth, marriages and deaths may not necessarily be recording correct information since in general there are no checks carried out as to their truthfulness. The cause of death may be one doctor's opinion but not confirmed by any post-mortem carried out by a third party. Post-mortems of 400 people dying in American hospitals had the clinical diagnosis confirmed in only 46-76 per cent of cases (Mercer and Talbot, 1985). In post-mortems carried out in Britain there was a missed diagnosis in 15 out of 49 cases (Perkins *et al.*, 2003).

They may be the record of someone's untruthfulness such as trying to establish citizenship as in British women marrying a series of foreigners, the status of occupations may be inflated such as professional criminals defining themselves as directors, and age and place of residence may be personally interpreted.

Secondly, there can be a record of inaccuracy and it has been found that a large number of medical prescriptions even in hospitals have been misinterpreted and this is related to safety. We can presuppose that there will be higher rates of inaccuracy in matters which are not related to safety. In Britain up to 1.5 per cent of hospital prescriptions were wrong of which a quarter could result in potentially serious effects. It was estimated that annually in the United States around 7,000 deaths are caused by such prescription errors (McLay and Ross, 2008).

Statistics in the social sciences more than in the 'hard' sciences are the end of a long productive process dominated by social factors of which only some can be partially controlled and subject to the restrictions imposed by pre-definitions. Data is individually recorded and is thus inevitably subject to such deliberate or personal perspectives. We rarely know the social conditions under which they were recorded. The data may be the outcome of a legal process as in the production of tax returns for which there may be a coordination of inaccuracies between the taxed individual, the accountant who is an employee and the inspector who will all have their own agendas covering the completion of their work-load at any particular time. Overall there are few reasons for assuming that statistics have the accuracy suggested by their configurations so perhaps there is an implicit grading of accuracy.

There are facts coming from turn-style data. A required accuracy which has no relationship to motivation such as tickets for seats on air-flights but even in this there is over-booking and fraud. Then there are statistics from the undefined wordings of opinions in which there are no identifiable binary cut-offs. We know nothing about the social environment in which these statements have been made and even less about the people who make them beyond age, name and locality but even of this we have no more than unverifiable social certainty. Demographic data from developing countries have the built-in inaccuracies which come from societies which have had no long acculturation into orderly and controlled bureaucracies.

All statistics which relate to human behaviour should be treated with suspicion as regards their numerical accuracy once they are taken to be more than indications of trends, unless they are supported by an unconnected alternative source such as hospital and police records. Even surveillance cameras tell us very little beyond what they record looking in a certain direction at a known time and place. Instead of such figures being accepted as evidence, should they not be looked at as evidence of the reverse of our lack of certainty over any aspect of human behaviour. Why then are statistics such a common feature in social science reports and publications as they are certainly a dead-end as regards their possible foundation accuracy.

They are principally evidence of personal achievement by the researchers who aspire to accuracy based on the traditions of the Western Enlightenment so that they could be categorized as a career necessity rather than a necessary part of most social science research.

QUESTIONABLE ATTAINMENT OF ACCURACY

Quantification is certainly a dead end if we concentrate on the accuracy of whatever figures have been produced and indeed to think in terms of exposing their inaccuracy on matters which are now no more than of historical interest. It is not this factor which should be of concern but the fact simpler fact that numeracy abbreviates the complexities of any human activity.

If we take a simple numerical total of the number of people who have gone through a turn-style for a performance of an opera or through an ideological one by entering a church, temple, mosque or synagogue for a ceremony, we have a number which is in fact quite meaningless for any level of social science understanding because what is involved for those people is a very personal interactive process.

There are four dimensions to any interpretive process (Duranti *et al.*, 1993 : 218). There is the medium or code within which symbolic acts are performed, the audience for the act which must include the observer, the social context in which the behaviour occurs and the action constituted through the symbolic process. Whatever the answers to these aspects it is certain that they cannot be adequately represented by a single number. They either represent a level of generality which may not be helpful in understanding the specifics of human behaviour or such totalling may be too specific and thus miss much of what is almost certainly important to any overall comprehension of the complexities of an event. Thus, it would seem that quantitative representations are a dead-end and that an alternative approach is necessary.

PARALLEL DISTRIBUTIVE PROCESSING

It has to be accepted that the number of factors that can influence even the simplest of behavioural acts of a single individual is innumerable. But such relative simplicities are rare indeed if in fact they exist at all since the individual whether Bengali farmer or Mumbai business executive are never alone. They are always in overt or covert relationships with other people whether in occasionally consistent primary contacts or in the 'touch and go' relationships of markets, walking in streets and travelling in commuter trains.

The social scientists have to be encouraged to accept that linear explanations are probably seen as acceptably valid according to the requirements of 'hard' science by the exclusion of many factors which they cannot find access to or do not consider to be important enough to be included in such calculations or do not know exist in the first place. No doubt this is a rational explanation of this particular methodology but it detaches behaviour from the people who are actually behaving. Such an approach dehumanizes what people actually do and how they may see their own behaviour. In crude terms this seems to turn research into human behaviour to be little different to the study of primates and their thinking in which habituation is assumed to be dominant.

Of course, humans do think lineally in the calculations of their bank balances in which only primary factors have to be considered without any direct considerations of the secondary and tertiary ones which are lurking in the background. Deliberate decision making in which there may be an accessible pattern of thought and social relationships does occur on a regular basis. However, as an overt cognitive process it is not all that common in comparison to the innumerable decisions which everyone makes everyday in the course of everyday living; even the taking of the next mouthful of food and the avoidance of other people in the street involve decisions. It might be that this same Bengali farmer and Mumbai businesswoman make possibly as many as a hundred thousand decisions per day; they are not aware of the majority because the decisions are not made consciously.

An individual whether they are researchers or primary school children see the situations in which they are involved as an endless series of 'wholenesses' and it is for attempting to cope with this situation that the methods of Parallel Distributive Processing have been developed. This approach accepts that the mind always works through some system of linear processing but that it works at a speed faster than any computer in considering the innumerable factors which go into the decision to eat that particular piece of mango, when to go to bed and where to put one's clothes just as much as in decision to purchase shares or marry a particular person.

So most decisions are virtually instantaneous. The social sciences just as much as the 'hard' sciences find it difficult to process a few factors at a time but become increasingly less able to cope with possible one thousand factors which are involved in the meeting of two people. Also with the growth in the number of factors which may or may not be involved, chance become increasingly a probability which becomes much more a matter of chance.

The basic hypothesis in psychology (Meadows, 1994, 2:703) for Parallel Distributive Processing is that information processing involves a large number of units working contemporaneously in parallel exciting or inhibiting one another. The important part of any such framework (Rumelhart *et al.*, 1986) is that all the units involved are in a state of activating each other.

If we extend this approach to the complexities of actual human behaviour we find that it has not got very far (McClelland *et al.*, 1986) because even the simplest of human activities such as the finger movements in typing or reaching for an object without involving a massive number of known and unknown alternative factors which make it unlikely that this approach can be used effectively for any more complex units of individual human behaviour much less group activities (Tanner, 2007).

It is also the point that attempts at this approach have ended up in the same compulsion to achieve 'hard' science accuracy with an array of complex mathematics. We are thus left with the basic premise that there is this parallel processing of information which occurs in every human act but what is involved includes many chance factors. As always numerical accuracy cannot be achieved and researchers are left with qualitative conclusions.

5

Nurture *versus* Nature

Nature and nurture is an old disputed dyad and is possibly overdone in the presumptions of geneticists that the DNA code dictates a very much larger proportion of human behaviour than it can in reality. The genetic components of any human being cannot for all practical purposes be modified except chemically in some cases and by disease and premature death. What in effect happens is that a genetic effect held by an individual bounces off the social environment in which they live. There are innumerable factors which will result in the genetic element dominating the situation as with the Ellis-van Crefeld dwarfism among the Amish and high red-green vision defects among Muslim Israelis (Adam *et al.*, 1967) which probably have limited social consequences.

This would appear to be zero-sum situations in which the genetic effect can modify a social situation in which it surfaces but the social situation cannot modify this genetic factor except by extinguishing it by preventing its continuance by reason of its social unacceptability; an Ellis-van Crefeld dwarf is not an attractive marriage partner.

It seems doubtful whether this can be an argument between two hypotheses of equal weight. Had genetics provided human beings with specific and narrow endowments and in this the inability to adapt to changing situations then human beings would have died out long ago. They would have been unable to survive in such varied and varying environments as exist in Greenland, Mongolia and the cities of Asia, North Africa and America. What we have surely is the possible genetic ability to adapt and thus to survive which is not available to such an extent in other animals.

Certainly humans have the persistent ability to be interpersonally violent beyond the necessity to protect themselves, their families and their property and indeed to kill for ideological reasons. It would be difficult to tie this into a specific genetic endowment as quite acceptable violence is socially acceptable in butchering animals for food, demolishing buildings and many competitive sports. In addition personal abuse is seen by many as just as dangerous to human well-being so there are laws to control this in many Western democracies.

It is only in small exclusive endogamous religiously motivated communities that mutations stand a chance of survival but not to spread to surrounding communities. It is such communities as the Amish which have become the object of substantial research into genetics and this has disclosed that within these communities twelve new genetic abnormalities have been discovered. Additionally a further eighteen which occur there in unusually high proportions. In the case of the Ellis-van-Crefeld dwarfism the numbers among the Amish equal all known cases in the rest of the world (McKusick, 1973).

The Ashkenazi Jewish sect similarly have unusually high frequencies of some autosomal recessive genes such as the Tay-Sachs infantile idiocy (Adam, 1973). In all such communities the very different social behaviour of such groups ensures that they will always tend to marry endogamously and the visibly specific nature of these genetic abnormalities means that there will always be a limited recessive chance of these spreading more widely into the surrounding populations.

There is another side to this pattern of endogamous communities maintaining hostile and that genes is their retention of benign ones. If there is a combination of genes involved in intelligence and adaptability, then the Jewish reverence for the Talmudic scholar, their ghetto like social groupings and the preference for such men as husbands may well have given Jews a competitive advantage.

There are also cases in which it is hard to determine whether the perpetuation of a gene or genes is hostile to the host society or not. It has been suggested that there is an hereditary element in schizophrenia and that some African diviners are schizophrenic in their ability to live in a world divided between communion with the spirits and helping those who come to them for consultations. They provide a useful social service and those who are successful and acquire a reputation would have no difficulty in marrying well.

On the other hand Muslims tend to marry their cousins and in some cases double ones through both mother and father (Tanner, 1964b) as a means to retain property within the family which has been inherited by women under Muslim law. This would retain hostile genes within families as well as reducing fertility (Roberts and Tanner, 1959).

Other religions actively discourage marriage with close relatives and both Christianity and Hinduism prohibit the marriage of cousins which discourages the perpetuation of genetic abnormalities. In most contemporary modern societies there is the free choice of partners despite a tendency to marry within localities and occupations combined with a migratory pattern of living and working in which few people have settled habitats.

We are always dealing with small populations which have made themselves so distinct as to invite research into genetics. In most cases these communities have not so much adapted to these abnormalities as absorbed them into their patterns of living. The Amish look after these defectives without question since to reject them would be against the biblical basis for their distinctive way of living. They will only remove members whose violence is a danger to the pacific nature of their lives. Nature has provided them with these difficulties which they cope with by adaptive patterns of nurture. Genetic endowments certainly lurk in the background to all human behaviours but it would not appear to have provided any behaviour which is too narrowly specific. Mutations tend to die out unless they are maintained in in-bred small populations as their inability to adapt makes them behaviourally and socially handicapped. In many subsistence societies such as the Tanzanian Sukuma the visibly abnormal baby would be killed at birth as the only sensible thing to do and it seems doubtful whether such a death would be even regretted much less reported.

Chance may allow a mutation to survive but such mass events as genocide in Ruanda and in the Pol Pot regime in Cambodia, the huge losses in Russia in Second World War, famine deaths in China during the Maoist excesses will certainly have reduced the number of recessive gene carriers with genetic abnormalities. Some of these wholesale killings would have extinguished both useful and harmful mutations but these were still chance events.

DETERMINISM IN SOCIAL BEHAVIOUR

Genetics provide an illusion of determinism into our understanding of human behaviour but this is likely to be offset by chance events. Individuals may not live long enough for their hostile genes to be passed on as they can die of another disease or be hit by a passing car. People carrying the gene for Korsakoff's Syndrome might die before they have the opportunity to breed. Recently in Uganda the medical school did not have much teaching about cancer because the anticipated length of life did not provide for many types of cancer to develop.

Nurture would seem to have deterministic elements in the major cultures such as caste influences in Hinduism. In practice culture at the level of individual behaviour is rarely controlled so closely as to be determinable in advance. In a British government requested study (Bird *et al.*, 2003:13) of the ways in which the performance of civil servants and other employees of nationalised institutions might be monitored, the writers concluded that the uncertainty associated with any method of risk assessment had to be formally included in any monitoring procedures. The main reason for not publishing the mortality rates associated with particular surgeons or surgical procedures was that those patients were never so uniform as to make such comparisons or conclusions possible.

In any attempt at understanding human behaviour we have to deal with not only the factor that we know very little about. What we are researching is human complexity and the distinct individualism of all humans in their combinations of genetic endowments and social experience which will be different even for identical twins. It is also not only the factor of this limited knowledge but that any such studies are subject to chance in the ways that research is initiated but also alongside the varying processes of investigation. Any such project is being altered from start to finish by factors over which the participants, researchers and the researched have very limited control and indeed have very little anticipation as to what might occur, where and when. However, experienced researchers may be in particular fields by chance and probability come into their areas of expertise from other areas of study and at best what results is authoritative guesswork.

There are two forms of determinism which can be considered

but they are both enabled by literacy and cannot be considered to exist as actual evidence of any consistency. There are actions which are to some extent predetermined by what has gone before and actions which individuals are required to do and in both of these situations there are as always the factors of individual differences, varied social environments and chance.

Both orthodox Islamic and Jewish law have unitary approaches to almost very aspect of human behaviour. Although Rabbinic rulings attempt to give statutory form to what orthodox Jews should do in every conceivable situations, their implications are not much different to similar rulings of Islamic jurists and the canon law of the Roman Catholic Church. Islam like Judaism has no centralising authority and jurists base their opinions on the Koran and the Sunna, the customs of nations. Its predominant meaning is taken to be conformity to the opinions and cited sayings of the Prophet as recorded in Hadith of which there are over seven thousand in Bukhari's collection (Brown, 2007; Musa, 2008). Thus as in Judaism there are not always uniform statements from a variety of specialist interpreters and those who aspire to that status. Even in psychotherapy Halakhic thinking is towards consensus over values and practice (Spero, 1980) and of course, in Islam there are the constant somewhat begrudging concessions to modernity over such matters as the rights of women and the use of the internet and Jewish ones over the use of electricity and the Israeli airline El Al flying on the Sabbath.

Thus all systems of belief have combined institutionalism with literacy almost without regard for size as we see in African new Churches such as the small Kenyan African Israeli Church Ninevah producing a written constitution, in order to create uniformities of belief and practice. With the extent of individual commitment to an institution and its controlling ideas and practices nurture takes on a greater importance and the probability but not any certainty of particular behaviour becoming more likely.

THE ARGUMENT FROM EXTREMES OF NURTURE AND NATURE

The nurture *versus* nature argument is an interminable one in which we are confronted with the easy option provided by extremes. The child with seemingly hereditary lack of intelligence and very limited social aptitudes or is an Ellis-van Crefeld dwarf despite persistent socialisation efforts as among the Amish or specialist training schools is an example. These are virtually unalterable human situations in which nature has the controlling hand but such distressing situations in human terms because of their small numbers have no overall influence on human society. They come to the attention of well developed societies which have the resources and the morality for them to survive. Subsistence societies do not create social situations with which they do not have the resources to cope.

At the other extreme we have examples of nurture in which small groups create all inclusive ways of living which often last for centuries because of their overall efficiency. The successful farming methods and humane communalism of the Amish make desertions to the outside world uncommon. Monasticism and militarism have similarly created forms of community living which have been functionally successful for which nurturing clearly predominates.

It would seem that the determining hinge between these extremes is the extent not so much that there are extensive codes of obligatory behaviour, but of socialisation of children over generations into these patterns. A scale perhaps by which this socialisation might be assessed in which small tribal groupings of subsistence farmers would have much the same overall control over their members and the advantages of maintaining social inclusion as might be the case with the modern Amish or Hutterite communities.

In well developed contemporary societies there are numerous religious and secular institutions which provide just as many instructions as to how their adherents should live. However, all such groupings operate in a competitive market place and because their members are well dispersed and have multiple memberships, both control over and benefits to individuals are less observable if they exist at all. The penalties for failure to comply are easily avoidable as often their shortcomings are not public knowledge. Nurture clearly occurs but it is too diffused to have its elements specifically identifiable

We must conclude that nature only controls human behaviour in any directly identified manner in extreme cases and even then in only small numbers of cases in small circumscribed populations.

Elsewhere there will be a largely unknown genetic component but nurture predominates in the ways that human behaviour varies with the environments in which it expresses itself. In this any predetermined probabilities will always be governed by both constant variations and individual variability as well as by the irregular appearance of chance.

6

The Assumption of Chaotic Change

It must be obvious enough that the vast majority of changes affecting human behaviour cannot be anticipated in any direct causative sense. When there is any such understanding it is retrospective and relates to narrowly defined events and in the short term. We have to accept that most changes cannot be anticipated because there are too many unexpected as well as varied factors which individualise situations.

So it seems certain that the effective use of lineal thinking in the form required by the 'hard' sciences for human behaviour can only be possible in narrowly circumscribed fields in such matters as the consequences of isolatable accidents assessed retrospectively or in the primary consequences taking of chemical substances. This is a very narrow field of accuracy in comparison to the range of behavioural decision making which occurs everyday for everyone when they walk about, eat each mouthful of food or decide when and what to do next. Even in such simple matters each individual is constantly being pushed into unexpected directions; a knock on the door or a bolt of lightning. Any such calculations would leave out of consideration such horrifying events as major Chinese earthquakes and landslides making for dangerously unstable dams of accumulating water menacing all those living in the same valley. As a result the Beichurn town was flooded and a further 250,000 had to be unexpectedly evacuated in June 2008.

In all other matters the everyday inter-relationships of people between themselves and their social and ecological environments involve innumerable unknown factors despite an overall assumption of regularity by all those involved. Conclusions based on lineal concepts of causality cannot have much practical significance except possibly as acts of professional faith in their own methodologies.

The move from this spread of real and recognisable human complexities into connecting probabilities into a theory of chaos is almost certainly a leap too far in describing the recognisably unknown nature of human complexity as chaotic. Chaos theory developed from the scientific recognition of the limitations of lineal causation and that there must be accessible relationships between variables and instability in the short-term (Elliott and Kiel, 1996).

This appears to be no more than the acceptance by 'hard' science when their work goes beyond calculating the variables in stable materials or definably limited situations that they are having to cope with more instabilities than allowed for in their existing methodologies. Cause and effect in the scientific sense of exactness may be rare indeed but there are nevertheless always non-lineal sequences which are the result of constantly reoccurring processes of adjustment to the necessities for survival.

The bringing in of complex mathematics into such assessments as the thousands of factors that might be hypothetically involved in the breakdown or creation of a single human dyadic relationship which is so analytically complex but not necessarily chaotic. This recognition of what might be called insoluble complexity which is also approached by Parallel Distributive Processing, is unlikely to be effectively coped with by the application of mathematics when the symbols used have themselves no analytical stability.

The assessment of the probability of any future event occurring when it involves immensely varied individuality is always going to be difficult but not because human behaviour is or was chaotic except possibly in a limited range of short-term situations. The immediate consequences of any earthquake for a society as for an individual experiencing an accident are certainly visibly chaotic. Reorganisation starts individually and collectively within hours and with even a short space of time complex reorganisation takes place. It seems likely that human behaviour at whatever level it is examined is pre-programmed to widely variable forms of reorganisation following every conceivable eventuality.

The definition of chaos is of a gaping void, utter confusion and disorder in an amorphous mass that cannot be analysed but it would seem that any such definition of chaos can rarely if ever be applied to the human situation. In fact from its ethological beginnings in primate life, social life appears to be invariably well ordered, with varied roles, behavioural patterns and a predictable range of activities and change. Situations which are obviously chaotic or carry the possibility of chaos such as the immediate aftermath of a tidal wave or earthquake bring into play immediate organised activities to reassert the social balances necessary for survival. Traditional societies wherever possible deal with deviance by processes of compromise rather than by binary decisions which might destroy any continuing unity. These are not processes which go beyond a range of acceptable probabilities.

In all known human social behaviour either individual or collective order appears to dominate over chaos. This applies as much to the complexities of urban living (Whyte, 1951), the social and working lives of artisans in Banaras (Kumar, 1988), the organisation of adolescent sexuality among the Muria of central India (Elwin, 1947), the family lives of poor Mexicans (Lewis, 1979), the organisation of transport for the two million pilgrims arriving for the Hajj to Mecca (Bushnak, 1978) and how homosexuals cope with their marginally acceptable social deviance (Humphreys, 1970). The dominant impression of social behaviour sustained by social science research must be of order rather than anything that could be defined as chaotic.

This obvious orderliness can mean that in the short-term participants as well as observers can state with some reliability what they are likely to be doing in the immediate future. There is a high probability that some behaviour will appear to be repetitive but when the time span of observation goes beyond this immediacy then chance starts to affect probability with the factors related to individualism and accidental coincidences but it is never a situation which involves the disentangling of chaotic factors.

Of course, there is a built-in instability in all social systems because biological and demographic changes are occurring all the time independently of any human agency. While this is going on it is at the same time being absorbed into the largely unconscious human dialectic of behavioural change. Of course, when a disaster occurs such as the Indonesian tsunami or the terrorist destruction of the World Trade Centre there is an immediate period of chaos. In the former case when unaffected fishermen returned to shore to face the almost universal deaths of their wives, they would have had to cook their own food for the first time and to do so immediately breaking the traditional customs. Similarly, the machinery for clearing away the mountains of broken buildings in New York would have started within the hour. In fact it would seem that humans dislike social and behavioural disorder and instability and that chaos is avoided almost instinctively.

ORDER INDEPENDENT OF LITERATE ENABLED COHESION

It is an aspect of Western culture that they have often understated if not ignored the fact that there have been seemingly non-literate cultures in the past such as the Incas of pre-Columbian Peru with the 'quipus' knotted strings and the totally non-literate ones such as the Xhosa and Zulus have all had complex wide-ranging social systems. There are also enormously complex societies such as Pharoanic Egypt, Muslim India and China administered by sophisticated literate elites with long periods of effective government.

So we have long periods of wide-ranging stability which do not catch the attention of historians as much as the short appearances of chaotic events which are as much a feature of developed as of developing societies. The differences may be that the former have the resources and bureaucratic ability to deal with some aspects of anticipated disasters such as the laws governing buildings in earthquake prone Japan and in California where movement along the San Andreas fault means that a major earthquake is inevitable. Other countries do not have the resources to cope even if they were willing to do so as with the dilatory reactions of the military junta in Myanmar over hurricane Nargis. Natural disasters will always be a persistent feature of individual and collective life in which survival will be a matter of chance as with well-to-do Westerners holidaying in South-East Asia when the tsunami occurred or those who happened to be away from work when the terrorists destroyed the World Trade Centre.

Then there are disasters which are the result of human activities deliberately planned and carried out. Of these the Holocaust killing of almost all European Jews must surely be the most horrific carried out as if was as an industrial project and such lesser known horrors as the Japanese occupation of Nanking (Chang, 1997). World War Two with its introduction of area bombing by the Germans and then taken up much more extensively by the Allies over Germany and the Americans in Japan killed off large numbers of civilians and virtually destroyed whole cities such as Dresden and Hiroshima. There are few people in East or West who have not lost family members in recent international or civil wars if we include the recent genocidal killing of Tutsi by Hutu in Ruanda.

There are also man-made disasters caused by political planning or mismanagement such as the post-Revolutionary famine in Russia with its collectivisation of agriculture, the PolPot programme of forced deurbanisation and rural collectivisation of social life in Cambodia killed at least a million. The Mao programme of the Great Leap Forward even allowing for unexpected bad weather is estimated to have killed some fifty million (Becker, 1996).

In Tanzania the one party government instituted nationally the more or less compulsory movement of dispersed populations into villages that would then be the basis for social advancement with schools, dispensaries and shops. This resulted in the destruction of local subsistence patterns of agriculture adapted to local ecology and major reductions in agricultural production. Such a major national policy was carried out without any adequate trials and perhaps was the result of socialist political planning by leaders who were town's people by personal living styles and education. It took some years to recognise the adverse effects and to permit people to disperse again into their time-tested systems of farming more suited by experience to their environments which the people perhaps knew all along. In Zimbabwe the Mugabe dictatorship has effectively turned an efficiently run agricultural society exporting surpluses of food into a bankrupt state with rampant inflation and dependent on international charity for the prevention of widespread starvation. Historically only Easter Island society and the Mongol invasion of Central Asia society have managed destruction so effectively (Diamond, 2005).

In all societies there are both folk memories and recent familial knowledge of natural and man-made disasters and they have always seemingly been able to reorganise themselves out of chaos. In some cases there has been preparatory organisation which has not been based on literacy or decisions reached out of the overt thinking of those in authority. It is more appropriate to see such patterns for survival to have been reached by collective almost covert thinking. The non-literate subsistence farmers and livestock keepers of north-western Tanzania who place a high social and economic value on their cattle often having specific animals dedicated to family ancestors. They keep only a few at their homesteads and 'rent' out the remainder without payment to create networks of reciprocity which ensure a better chance of survival for animals in case of drought and disease but creating obligations between primary groups which have no blood or marital connections.

East African tribal communities have a well-organised pattern of coping with encroaching disaster; the dispersal of assets by the loaning out of cattle to unrelated people so that new networks of reciprocities are created to be called upon when the owner is in difficulty and which by the dispersal of livestock increases their possibilities of survival from drought and disease, then the using up of their own familial resources, the recourse to natural resources in the surrounding unoccupied land and finally flight; a sequential process which they would implement whether they have been affected by natural or man-made disasters.

Of course, there is evidence enough of irrational behaviour such as the wholesale killing of Xhosa cattle and the destruction of grain in response to the predictions of the prophetess Nongqawuse that the idyllic past would return to them restoring their past glory (Peires, 1989) which resulted in the reduction of the population to a quarter of its previous levels from famine and the mass suicide of the Jonestown community in Guyana (Lasaga, 1980). Unusual events attract media and research attention but less attention seems to be paid to the reorganization of societies after such short periods of chaos. Disasters survive in folk memories much more readily than periods of stability as we see in contemporary Arab thinking about the barbaric behaviour of the mediaeval Crusaders which have no part at all in Western thinking about the background to what they might assess as Palestinian intransigence.

We see repeatedly that all societies even ones which are deviant to what their surrounding cultures expect and try to enforce, have the ability to organise in complicated ways even in the non-literate complexities of the ritual 'kula' ring system of the South Pacific Islanders over large areas of empty ocean (Malinowski, 1961) and the literate complexities of contemporary urban Kolkata. However, this stability is more an ideological construction of what these societies want to happen. There can be a limited certainty that what might happen next day will happen and beyond that there can be no certainties.

This ability to manage crises involves flexibility, adaptability and innovation as well as decision making leadership at a primary group level (Baker, 2007) applies as much to the highly organised professional coping with international disasters industry as it would do to an intellectually isolated group of subsistence farmers.

We can do no more than accept that human societies have always shown an ability to stabilize their behaviour and social systems within what they know to be the inevitable instability of demographic change and chance events. None of this behaviour can be classified as chaotic except in the short-term immediacies of personal or collective disaster. Probability remains very much no more than a very short-term assessable factor.

7

Levels of Inter-related Instability

Any society has different levels of cohesion from primary groups which have a combination of economic, social and religious reasons for stability on which their subsistence survival depends to touch-and-go street and market meetings. These involve no more than culturally accepted behavioural patterns of mutual avoidance in which those approaching each other make early assessments based on age, costume and overall signs of deviance or social acceptability. Chance dominates all behaviour in high density urban populations whether in Kolkata or Copenhagen.

In all societies there are always ranges of behaviour which are based on the anticipation of chance as in the markets of highland Myanmar and inner London where people go in the hope of favourable encounters between buyers and sellers with no certainty that either will meet at that particular time and place.

In small largely self-contained communities whether in the villages of the Yao of southern Tanzania or in the small areas dominated by Chinese in London or Liverpool, there are anticipatable stabilities which come from their self chosen form of social isolation, the social and economic profits which come from such self-containedness and the less profitable consequences of living elsewhere in the mixed multidimensional society surrounding them.

In the past subsistence communities have had a high ratio of anticipatable stability because of the need for defence, the social insurance which came from calculated reciprocities and the complex relationships involved in marriage and their matrilineal and patrilineal connections. There is the illusion of stability because these communities see themselves as limiting alternatives by avoiding as much as possible social relationships with people over whom they do not have complex multi-dimensional holds. In a crude sense such communities look stable and this illusion is supported by their use of plural personal terms rather than the individualism of 'I' and the behaviour of individuals seeking advantages at the expense of others with whom they are less closely integrated by social necessity.

However, in such communities there is always a substrata of instability held in their oral history and the hard won experience and memories of their older men and women. Elephants, pigs and baboons can raid their maize fields and banana groves, thunderstorms can strike fields of ripening grain, heavy rain can wash away a complicated layer of hill side rice fields in northern Luzon in the Philippines and in many Chinese valley sides. It is almost as if the outsider sees an existing community as frozen in time as stable without recognising their reactions to seemingly regular instabilities which have gone into making up this current appearance of stability.

If we can assume that among the Sukuma or Yao of Tanzania an average family in reasonable health can annually cultivate about 2 ½ acres of cereal crops sufficient to keep them more or less well-fed over the agricultural cycle. Any adult ill-health at the critical times of planting, weeding and harvesting will have long-term consequences; they would then have to rely to some extent on their social connections and their finely tuned networks of reciprocity. It seems likely that few if any are going to provide help unless they can see that it is to their advantage to do so. There is probably no such thing as a free dinner in a subsistence community in Zimbabwe or in a slum community in Rio de Janeiro.

A village near Kipumbwi in the coastal district of Pangani in Tanzania had twenty-four households of which twenty-three were connected within one extended single family so it would seem likely that unless there should be some overall disaster, a roughly equal standard of living would have been maintained by this closely knit community. The one unconnected household would probably survive because of client relationships with several of these related households. Even in this seemingly stable community there are always dangers from the road running through this village.

In such communities almost everyone whom they are likely to meet is known by name and whatever the social realities of life there must surely be a certain psychological stability in having almost all relationships in time and motion terms primary and within sight. Life is based on a virtual totality of primary relationships.

THE INSTABILITIES OF URBAN LIVING

In the urban industrial environment the primary group still remains the centre of individual life whether it is that of a drug centred community of individuals living in an abandoned house, the family living in a tower block of flats in a city centre or a suburban family living within commuter distance of the city. Its influence is circumscribed by the division of labour; the family breaks up when members go to work or school.

Even allowing for the growth of electronics there are few families whose adults work together from home in ways that parallel the togetherness of a farming family. Electronic working from home is a middle class professional activity. For most of those who are employed the site of earning is almost always away from home. Even allowing for the few who are lucky enough to be within walking distance of their work, this has meant that social life is radically segmented into weekend full-time home and weekday home in which sleeping takes up the majority of time as commuting to work takes up ten hours per week.

This means that in comparison to subsistence social environments the lives of these people are less tied to regularities and the possibility of chance events impacting on individuals and their primary groups must increase proportionately. This is particularly likely to happen in the commuting period when the individual whether men or women is consistently exposed to events over which they have no control and in environments populated by touch-and-go strangers.

Women spend more time in isolation in their homes in comparison to subsistence communities unless they are re-employed after having children or have child-related encounters. Even their touch-and-go encounters are likely to be less than most men who travel to work and encounter several thousand others whether on foot, train, bus or in their own cars.

Thus in this urban setting these innumerable chance encounters may account for infection as in the passage of germs in ritualistic gestures in religious ceremonies or in the closed environments of buses and trains, the accidents which occur everyday in any mass setting and the spin-offs from economic fluctuations over which they have no control leading to bankruptcies and drops in the prices of cash crops in subsistence communities.

A dependency on government to prevent distress from the cradle to the grave as was put forward by the Beveridge Plan for post-war Britain, may make individuals seemingly independent of having to create their own circles of supportive reciprocities making it more likely that they avoid their neighbours more than relying on them. Few nations and then only in the West have any such reliable and expensive welfare schemes. Even there and globally generally those who are socially marginal will be more likely affected by chance events than those who are more socially and economically centrally important to their societies (Ecks and Sax, 2005).

So we can see that chance and change can affect relatively static social groups since they are predetermined as likely to happen. As societies become more complex with multi-functional differences involving several roles change everyday there are likely to be more chance events affecting individuals and indirectly those with whom they are linked.

THE NORMATIVE FALLACY

Social scientists are not alone in preferring research topics that are easier to observe and whose boundaries are definable with some accuracies. A slum community in Mumbai will always be difficult to research by even the most energetic of researchers as there can never be any population sufficiently static to have their observed behaviour categorised with enough accuracy to reach conclusions. They will certainly try but almost inevitably they end up with qualitative rather than quantitative data which will fall short of their hoped for scientific professionalism.

Thus there will be a preference for the study of communities which appear to operate within definable boundaries. The Amish are just the type of social environment which is ostensibly simple and is easily identified by their style of living and their intention to be different on religious grounds. Similarly, a village which is surrounded by fields separating them from the next one is a seemingly easier object of research than an urban community in which opposite sides of the street may belong to different local governments and indeed to different parts of any national system. These social and geographical limitations are always illusory as there are constant comings and goings over these boundaries.

Whether social scientists are researching slums or definable isolated communities there is the conclusion that the latter are likely to have not only stable normative systems on which they base their behaviour but simpler ones. This seems to be a dyadic assumption as the result of averaging out of what is assumed to be behaviour common to such communities. Social science assumes as do the people themselves that there are norms for conduct as indeed there are when both observers and participants look at behaviour with detachment. Moreover this appears almost always to be a process of simplification of complicated situational behavioural patterns.

Then these norms which social scientists record in some detail always seem to be largely their own creation. There are norms, ideals which everyone in every culture holds to be correct behaviour but this is usually the product of questioning by outsiders. They are not likely to have any prior existence because codification of such matters even in societies with long standing elite based literacy and legal codes is an abstraction which would seem to have little day-to-day social functions. There is a vagueness in their practicality since they are likely to vary in their implementation according to the circumstances in which they occur.

Thus, there seems to be a process of simplification in the recording of human behavioural data or by limiting the number of possible factors which may have little to do with social realities. Firstly, the preference for the study of society or social situations which might appear to have simpler attributes because they occur in confined or at least definable situations.

Then there is the methodological factor that human behaviour is immensely diverse in its variations so that the social scientists in practice reduce the number of factors in their analyses in order that the data or the factors become manageable and indeed definable. This results in a number of similar factors coming up in analyses as if they were a vital necessity such as age, location, religion, education and marital status as if such facts had any definable hardness or indeed any connection with the topics being investigated outside very inexact particular social environments.

Any study of human behaviour shows soon enough that when norms are put into the social environments of actual observable events, they become less dominant and just ideological guidelines of some vagueness. Social scientists find it easier to record what they see as primary data without the complicated variations which go with the elaborations of the answers to 'why', for which interpretations involve many factors including the attitudes of the researchers themselves. There are very few reasons for assuming that seemingly similar behaviour would necessarily have the same reasons behind them. Islamic public prayer rituals are very obviously identical but there is no reason to suppose that a hundred Muslims going through the same physical movements would have similar thinking behind them whatever may be their degree of religious obligation.

What is similar to the intellectualised eye may be a form of bias based on social distance creeping in which enables its quantification. An urbanised researcher may see the rush home of commuters as insect-like behaviour since the same people have caught the same train at the same time for months on end. But within this crudely normative requirements there will be complicated social behaviour varying from sleeping, meditating, listening to music tapes, staring at other passengers, working a personal computer, meditating to taking adult education classes in reserved coaches on particular trains. Perhaps it is necessary to have these shadowy guidelines for behaviour not so much as identifiable norms but as ambiguous necessities which prosper in the same way that religious ideas do.

There is the methodological reality that if social scientists accept the constant variations in human behaviour then the resulting data becomes far too complicated for numerical analyses. We end up with innumerable differences experienced by demographically similar people in seemingly similar situations. There are going to be few interpersonal and inter-institutional similarities even in similar events which might aid attempts to find out anything more than generalised probabilities.

The social sciences appear to find the quantitative assessment of socially and psychologically based human behaviour with its individuality and bases in itemisation to be beyond their methodological abilities. In endeavouring to cope with this inevitable variability their approach seems to have been the reification of norms, the simplification of wording with binary answers and their research based susceptibility to scaling.

Perhaps we have to ask ourselves whether the forms in which quantitative methodology approaches human behaviour and its built-in rigidities is the best that can be devised for enlarging social science understandings and the assessment of probabilities. They might appear to be producing data in forms for the assumed convenience of their academic assessors.

8
The Dominance of Individualism

Regardless of how we approach social science research into human behaviour it has to be based on three aspects of individuality. The researchers themselves, those researched and the shared dyadic ground in which these two individuals or groups of individuals meet and overtly and covertly influence each other. Little in these three areas of individuality can be firmly defined and thus they are all important for the chance effects they may have on issues of probability.

THE INDIVIDUALITY OF THE RESEARCH EXPERIENCE

It is not a question as to whether the social scientists are adequately trained professionally or whether the perspective within which they are trained is restricting as might be argued about some medical training programmes. The issue is that fieldwork is the professionalised but in fact personal contact between researchers and subjects who are usually unknown to them in any previous social relationship.

This is an individualising experience. Each researcher is alone faced with situations which are alien to them except in the sense that they may have some book knowledge of the current theories and reports related to what they want to investigate. This previously collected data which however much it may be related to that topic is certainly more historical than contemporary. This confrontation with social and psychological differences will force them to reconsider the framework in which they themselves have been socialised and indeed educated to think.

This individualising process is superimposed on their unavoidable demographic characteristics which differentiate them in the eyes of those who are being researched. In this they are not just strangers, social outsiders but people whose basic individualism is filtered through what these people see and interpret as the social realities of age, sex and more importantly the body language of their appearance. This does not alter the fact that they are what they are probably ethnically and demographically different about which they can do very little to make themselves more acceptable.

No social scientist can sustain for very long if at all that they are having experiences that are similar to that of other researchers and more importantly that they are scientifically detached from the usual emotions associated with social relationships. Colin Turnbull with his reputation for sensitive understandings of the African societies which he had researched wrote about the Mbuti pygmies with great affectionate understanding tied to particular men and women (Turnbull, 1961). He wrote later about the Ugandan Ik (Turnbull, 1973) with a similar sensitive understanding o' the ecologically brutal conditions under which they lived but with ill-disguised dislike. Whatever the correctness of his assessments he was certainly not emotionally detached in any scientific sense in these two long periods of fieldwork under conditions of some discomfort.

Turnbull made no attempt to disguise the fact that he saw his fieldwork in terms of human relationships rather than in attempted and probably impossible one of scientific detachment. Most social science researchers find it difficult to detail their involvements with the people they are researching often commenting on what they find as exciting in ceremonial behaviour and interesting if only because it is so different from what they experience in their own societies while the long periods of boredom and discomfort are not commented on.

What separates them from their own past and their professional colleagues is the newness of these individual experiences, the culture shock of moving out of their own circle of socialisation and into a society several thousand miles away from their natal society but this may also happen even when they move into a research situation across the street. No social science researcher comes away from fieldwork unaffected by what they have experienced rather than just seeing themselves as long-term tourists on the edge of local society.

So social scientists are not in a position to assert that they have taken a detached approach to their work. More importantly by quantifying rather than qualifying, they would be imposing on the people they are working on rather than with a system of classifications which they do not themselves have as a part of their socialisation. The individual researcher is making decisions about their behaviour in terms of their own understandings; a binary process which would seem to be part of Western scientific thinking. Thus any such processing is detaching individual observations from most of the situational background in which it may have been created rather more than presented to the observer.

What social scientists record is always qualitative and individual from the inability of any researcher to detach themselves enough for the classification of scientific to be applied to their work. Every social scientist consciously or unconsciously individualises their research experiences which affects both their qualitative and quantitative evaluations which come from the inevitable individuality of all that they do.

RESEARCH AND THE STATUS OF THE RESEARCHERS

In terms of human inter-relationships whether research work is seen in terms of projects or in more personal terms, it is only possible to know half a dozen people really well within their own cultures and probably not as many as that however long the researchers may remain in communities other than their own. Margaret Mead made repeated visits to the Manus community which she first researched in the early 1920s and they benefited from this association (Mead, 1956). She was widely known as a benefactor and knew them well in the sense of a fieldworker who had concentrated on a single village. She cannot have known any of them with the depth of understanding which we can assume she had of her husbands. All we can assume is that a fieldworker is likely to know quite a lot about the people who assist them the most but that it is never likely to be comprehensive because of the inevitable social and linguistic distance between them and the time it takes to get to know anyone well. These are individualised relationships to which the researchers are likely to attribute greater social understanding than is likely to be their social reality. These are segmented relationships held together by the fact that each uses the other for their individual profit.

Beyond this circle of a few tied together by needs which on the part of the researched probably have little to do with any research objectives. Researchers have a specialised way of looking at society which comes as often as not from the bureaucratic aspects of their socialization and intellectual needs which certainly does not exist in subsistence economies. Those researched lose their individualities and become collectivised into categories.

So any researcher who hopes to have a personal understanding of the people with whom or should we say on whom they work, is likely to be confined to as few as are in any primary group and not as socially comprehensive as the ones from which the social scientists themselves came and maintain in their own lives.

Overall this situation is filled with chance as to who encounters, who under what circumstances. There is not so much any question of choice but for the researchers to take advantage of personal opportunities which are provided by chance. Suitability may be accidental and indeed this can only be established retrospectively when researchers see their fieldwork in a stage approaching completion. We cannot know with any certainty even now the truth or falsity of what those young female informants told the young Margaret Mead in Samoa (Mead, 1928). There are similar doubts about whether the very unusual and unexpected information she got from the New Guinea, Arapesh, Mundugumor and Tchambuli informants was correct (Mead, 1962). The data supplied by her informants was almost certainly filtered through a second stage of informant interpreters who may not have had the linguistic competence sufficiently varied to translate attitudes and behavioural patterns so contrary to what might have been found in even the most isolated of small societies.

There is also the factor of chance in the ability of researchers to attract the giving of information. They cannot know until they are in the fieldwork situation whether they will have the ability to attract social strangers into giving them information. Getting people in their own social circle to tell them about their private affairs in a spider's web of gossip is one thing but to get the same range of information from people with whom they have nothing in common is much more difficult. What they may have in common with prospective informants is some partially expected mutual advantage from creating and maintaining a new form of association not altogether different from the on-going semi-permanent relationships which some people have as police informants.

The number of people with whom these researchers have close contact is always going to be low because they want information from their informants and that means finding not so much talkative people as those that are prepared to talk to outsiders in social environments that will not encourage anyone to talk to very obvious strangers. Informants are commonly extroverts in societies which may not have any such role.

It may be that such people are encouraged to be talkative by their association with people who are seen to be superior to themselves at least in material possessions as well as in education. A person with some established status in his community might have fewer reasons to even consider being an informant than someone whose self-assessed status is ambiguous and find this an opportunity for enhancing their position apart from any other reasons for becoming allied to an outsider.

This is all apart from the social fact that social science researchers will tend to feel themselves superior to those they are researching not only by reason of their education but also because of their assumed trained capacity to detach themselves from what they are observing. This is the nature of their self-assumed status however inaccurate it may be according to how their professional peers assess their work and indeed how the researched themselves see their work as biased by their outsider socialisation.

So self-importance which may go along with their role as outsiders in which they are seen to be doing nothing much except scribbling away in their notebooks in societies in which such a form of literacy is not common. Overall these relationships cannot be seen as founded on any assumption of ensuring impersonal accuracy. In every aspect of such relationships there are factors of chance.

THE INVASIVE COINCIDENCE OF INDIVIDUAL IDEAS AND CULTURE

Let us assume that the understandings of how social scientists analyze and explain human behaviour is some part of the normal pattern of behaviour in any society; their idiomatic way of explaining is adequate enough for others to understand all that these social scientists want to explain.

In 'hard' science those involved have created a subsystem of communication which is not part of the more general way of communicating in the outside surrounding society, indeed it is both specialised and individualised. It is communication to and within a circle of like-minded elite with their own linguistic code.

It has to be accepted that in any population regardless of literacy and education levels, there will always be some people with above average levels of intelligence whether we are considering a community of Kung Bushmen from the Kalahari, Bengali Brahmins or Han subsistence farmers in the Yangtse valley, much less those who pass out of the universities of Delhi, the Sorbonne and Harvard as exceptionally talented. All languages are complex constructions in which a small minority use their own languages as tools for the broadening of ideas and imagination. It is unlikely or at least extremely rare for anyone to have such competences outside their own natal languages.

It is well enough known that English, Mandarin and Hindi are immensely complicated languages well able to cope with new ideas provided by their intellectual elites. Other languages which have not been committed to literacy until quite recently such as the kiSukuma spoken by five million has a verb system more complex than English as well as tonal pronunciation (Batibo, 1985) but that is not to suggest that this complexity is part of the language used by most of these subsistence farmers as this language as with others is an individualised and individualising tool. What tense the intellectual Sukuma may use in discussing some factors in their culture would be a matter of socialisation and chance.

A group of Sukuma intellectuals had no difficulty in accepting as reasonable the logic of the Azande about the causation of their misfortunes as translated to them from the conclusions of Professor Evans-Pritchard (Evans-Pritchard, 1937) while explaining that in their part of Sukumaland, they coped with the same problems in different ways.

Languages have seemingly always been able to construct meanings for new ideas which have appeared by chance in the understandings of intellectuals and once this has occurred such understandings spread along the lines of influence which are dominated by these clever and influential people. The chances of new ideas surviving may well be just the same as the chances of a recessive biological mutations surviving outside an endogamous community.

Surely it is a failure of the social sciences to propose hypotheses which are outside not so much the understandings of this minority of intelligentsia in any community but their ability to see such proposals as possible expansions of their own intellectualism if presented to them in their own languages. Hypotheses have to link in with some factors which a culture's intelligentsia recognise as useful extensions of their existing individual understandings. The Tanzanian Sukuma already have a categorisation of incest covering paternal, maternal and sibling events and they did not see that Freud's ideas of the Oedipus complex added anything to their existing understandings which seemed to them to be adequately comprehensive. Freud's ideas seemed to them to be either a rather complex joke which only Westerners might be able to understand or just ridiculous.

The whole paraphernalia of the subconscious in their opinion was quite adequately covered by their comprehensive understandings of spirit possession. As individuals it even seemed to them that their existing specific ideas on otherwise inexplicable behaviour attributable to ancestors, spirits and witchcraft malevolence was adequate enough and that to put it altogether within the idea of the subconscious was turning the potentially explicable into something that was inexplicable in their individual understandings. The Swahili dictionary describing the subconscious as something within the intelligence of the individual does not seemingly fit into any individual understandings.

It seems inevitable that chance dominates the eruption of new ideas in the minds of individuals or in the ways that outside events impose themselves on whole populations leading to original behaviour. The appearance of HIV in many societies has resulted in much innovative behaviour just as must have happened with the appearance in societies of wandering Buddhist monks moving between India and China, Muslim traders moving into Indonesia, Roman trading stations in southern India and the invasion of Alexander's Greeks on the Gandaran culture in Afghanistan. Such a list is endless and they tend to be seen as broad cultural innovations rather than as initially affecting individuals. This is just the same process as natural changes have persistently altered human behaviour and its subtended thinking (Reynolds and Tanner, 1995).

THE HOLIER THAN THOU ATTITUDE OF SOCIAL SCIENTISTS

However much social scientists may wish to assume and do their best to carry a role presentation of normality, this does not allow them to take on any role in the researched society as if they were natal members there unless they are able to assume a role by deceit which is accepted by that community as valid. The researcher to be a nurse or a teacher would be acceptable and understandable but that of an enquirer into behaviour would always be alienating. This ability to get information under such circumstances must be a matter of chance unless it comes with their overt behaviour for which they have had some training.

These men and women come to do fieldwork after a long period of higher education which separates them not only from the commonality of people in their own societies but makes them totally different to almost all if not all of the people in the society which is being researched. It is also a specialised form of education which trains these people to see social behaviour from a somewhat inhuman particular perspective which they are unlikely to apply to themselves.

This separation from more general patterns of behaviour as a result of their education and socialisation into a specialised professional sub-culture means that these researchers will always be filtered out of more ordinary forms of behaviour and come to see the objects of their research in special ways. This is not an impersonal process but a specialising and elitist one.

THE HANDICAP OF RESEARCH BY AUTHORITATIVE AND LEARNED PEOPLE

It is not only that the social sciences need to stress the individuality of human behaviour but that their research is to some extent compromised by the individualism not only of the researchers themselves but that they are usually working in a form of isolated professionalism which stresses their own individual distinctiveness.

How can we be sure that the analyses of human behaviour particularly in the context of probability are providing a form of reality which those researchers involved have found intellectually and professionally acceptable. It is indeed correct that they have produced competent results from their own data but that their conclusions may not parallel the realities with which the researched people have run their lives.

Sometimes assessments of a human situation are deliberately and perhaps sensibly restricted. If a person is being assessed by a physician from medical perspectives, it does not make sense in that context to go beyond a clinical approach. However, the ill persons are experiencing their misfortunes in a far wider total sense (Landewe and Heljde, 2003). The individualism of one person's professionalism has in effect separated his or her understandings from that of the other's individualism; a widening gap created by professionalism.

The people who are being researched may not have the linguistic abilities to express their deeply felt feelings. Whatever their intellectual standards there is a huge divide between these limited capacities and the highly developed ones of the social scientists who have approached them. These men and women have learned to express themselves well in the talkative university environments in which they have spent some years. For most social environments outside this rather specialised one, there may be similarly specialised vocabularies and grammars of some complexity. For more general use there are simpler limited vocabularies to which we must accept that complex emotions are contracted rather than detailed.

For the limited number of people who become part of the samples used by social scientists they are often being asked to reply to complex questions which are not part of their general way of thinking. While there may be philosophers in all societies their complexities of thought do not enter into the thinking of their neighbours. In fact those who are questioned are encouraged to produce opinions on matters about which they have never had to give any thought; Wittgenstein and the Buddhist Patimokkha rule book for monks are not part of the thinking of most European urban population or of subsistence farmers in Thailand.

Sometimes conclusions from this elitist thinking go far beyond the range of any data from their researched populations as the conclusion that all fathers are in an oedipal situation over their daughters' emerging sexuality (Katz, 2002). Perhaps elitist thinking from its existence in pronounced social distance is always going to be biased. Doctors in providing treatment are influenced in the selection of treatment options by their estimate of how many good years could be expected for the patient if it was successful, the influence over their thinking of entirely personal estimates of probability (Rakow and Bull, 2003).

THE LOSS OF INDIVIDUALISM IN SAMPLING

If we accept as we must that almost all behaviour is based on individuality whatever the intellectual and social status of those being researched, then any accumulation of data from large number of individuals is going to obscure any variations which must be there. If we take a study of income dynamics and the dissolution of marriage or cohabitation in the Netherlands (Kalmijn *et al.*, 2007) which involved 3,417 marriages and 9,725 cohabiting relationships, it was found that the higher the females share of the household income, the higher the risk of separation in both marriages and cohabitations. On the other hand for income shares below equality the higher the share of the husband reduced the divorce risks for married couples but increased the dissolution risks for cohabiting couples.

Leaving aside the interesting point that their sexes were referred to as males and females which suggests that the researchers saw these couples in detached dehumanising terms almost as if they were making a natural history study of primate behaviour for which there would be limited data for assuming any great individual differences, the conclusions are linear ones related to income differences in the maintenance and dissolution of shared relationships between a man and a woman not just men and women in such simple collective categories. Each of the 26,284 people in this survey had their personal relationships assessed in terms of their admitted incomes which were a part but not necessarily a dominant one in the complex relationships of these couples. By any standards this may well be seen as a crudely simple way of assessing these relationships. This quantification must not only have simplified these issues but obscured a wide range of other undoubtedly important factors.

It is open to speculation whether the results would be much different had this study been more detailed and confined to no more than ten couples in each category. Such an approach would have shown the underlying individualism in all such relationships and provided important points which would have been missed in any mass sampling.

On the other hand the detailed information from a small sample of five sisters over the death of a sibling (Van Riper, 1997) served a dual purpose of allowing these children to describe their loss in their own ways and for the conclusions to be put in an understandable perspective as each child lived in an unique reality and their understandings varied greatly even within this one family. There seems little doubt that if the social sciences are to serve both a human and humane functions then small group research are a fundamental necessity.

THE DOMINANCE OF INDIVIDUALITY

Whether we are considering human behaviour in relation to their social or transcendent relationships, self-interest must surely predominate however modified by social distance, physical factors and external power controls. Researchers have always found it easier to exclude as much as possible the individuality of human behaviour whether it is their own roles in their work or in their approach to the large number of individuals which confront them in their fieldwork.

Despite their acceptance that individuals are inevitably different one to the other however closely related socially or biologically, social science research has always paid most attention to elements in social and religious life which are not individually distinctive but in categories which are easier to define and obtain data about without too much expense in time and effort. There may also be an element of conceit in this approach that while they are prepared to accept the importance of their own individuality, when looking at the generality of people in their field of research they do not appear to accept the need to apply this individualism to others.

By reason of this approach individuals may appear to be conforming or deviating from some group norm or necessity which have been assessed and solidified by a parallel or even a predated approach. There is no reason to assume that there is covert conformity to a particular norm in the masses of pilgrims at the Kumbh Mela, Lourdes or Mecca. This cannot mean that each of those individuals are in total conformity to the required religious norms just because of their presence there. What they are thinking at any particular moment may well vary from what they think at subsequent times and there is little reason to suppose that their individuality has been submerged in these mass activities as if they could be separated from their social behaviour and thinking both before and after. The degree of individuality in any society is going to be a very personal mixture of what is available culturally in terms of each person's intellectual and physical capacities.

In an economically developed society in which much of the small group social cohesion of subsistence societies may be absent, the individual may have a wider range of alternatives available to them both in terms of people and property. However, in all types of societies there are likely to be wide ranges of psychological and social needs so that in terms of alternative quantities, there are unlikely to be much difference between the ranges of individualism among the Mishmi tribal and Mumbai urban people. At both ends of this spectrum there are going to be individual needs met in individual ways. An intelligent Naga or Netherlander are probably going to have the same potential for extensive individualisms just as the less intellectually endowed Lahu or Londoner may well have a more limited range of individuality.

QUANTITATIVE STUDIES MISSING INDIVIDUAL EXPERIENCE

There are various difficulties over accepting this methodological approach as likely to produce answers and results which will coincide with any large scale planned application to individuals even those included in these large numerical samples.

A survey was carried out in the early 1980s into the quality of life in three Arizona cities in the United States (Zautra *et al.*, 1983) using 537 residents who were selected by using probability sampling techniques to represent the approximately 250,000 residents there. Some 85 per cent completed the required involvement. The survey group paralleled a highly diverse population which contained college-aged university students, suburban white collar residents, a Mexican-American sub-community and a large retired component. The sample were originally contacted by letter and then visited in their homes for the interviews. These interviews were conducted by 25 graduate and undergraduate students from the Arizona State University and averaged an hour and a quarter using the Social Readjustment Rating Scale extended to 65 life events (Holmes & Rahe, 1967).

For each item these respondents were asked to indicate if such an event had happened to them in the past year and whether the outcome was positive or negative. In addition a Social Participation Scale (Phillips, 1967) was used to assess the extent of their formal and informal social contacts in which they were asked to indicate the degree to which each of a variety of resources such as religious beliefs, family, friends and professional providers of help were of help to them in times of trouble. Finally, they were asked to identify their responsibilities for themselves, their families, their work setting and other areas of concern (Zuatra *et al.*, 1977); all this is supposed to have been done in a single interview.

In looking at such a comprehensively bureaucratic approach to any type of human behaviour and applying it to individuals whose life at any age will almost certainly have included variations from any hopefully comprehensive list including what may have happened to them in school, factory, family and bowling alley.

The replies to what would have been the recitation of lists without much of a lead-in would surely have suggested to these respondents the general line of this enquiry apart from semantic problems as between the understandings of Mexican Americans and elderly retirees. For the latter such a visit might be relief from the boredom of retirement and for the former suspicion over an intrusion by young students.

These are standard criticisms of quantitative assessments of anything as personally complicated as the 'quality of life' which indeed would be a little-used phrase in most households. Such approaches neglect to find out the extent to which these people were influenced as individuals by such key events and indeed whether they were prepared to give opinions at all on such personal matters.

Such quantitative data provide overall figures which indicate significances but this will not show the reasons why individuals think or behave in the ways that they have disclosed to strangers rapidly under the unusual circumstances of an interview. In Israel the number of deaths from cancer of middle aged married men has gone up by a quarter but not for women (Jaffe *et al.*, 2007) so we are left with no clues as to why marriage has had this differential effect if in fact this was the distinguishing factor.

Since we know that every individual will be experiencing their social environments in different ways there are several difficulties over accepting this methodological approach as likely to produce understandings of personal behaviour. A principal difficulty would be that we know nothing about what influences these student administrators of these questionnaires may have had on those replying. Some older respondents may dislike being questioned by such much younger researchers. Even if they came from the same discipline there can be no assumption of uniformity in how each questioner would have approached their clients, personality issues and the differences that might have come from working in the morning or evening. It would seem unlikely that any of them would have been able to treat respondents in the three major groupings in similar ways apart from the social distance factor of being in the process of prolonged higher education; there would always be linguistic misunderstandings over abstract matters.

These sampled cities or rather towns contained enormously varied populations and the quality of life for an individual might depend on factors that have nothing to do with where they were living as they might be newly married or divorced or indeed have won a prize in some local lottery or just been diagnosed as having a serious illness.

These people had responded to matters of basic importance to their lives in an average of ninety minutes and it would seem that this whole process eliminates the basic individuality of every respondent, a dehumanizing process in which chance will be the predominating factor.

ACCEPTING THE LIMITATIONS IMPOSED BY INDIVIDUALISM

On both sides of the research project individualism inevitably not only dominates in the personalities of the social scientists but in those who are being researched, but this is an unequal equation. We certainly have the quite distinctive nature of the researchers themselves about which we know little except when they are of sufficient eminence to be the subject of research themselves as has been the case with both Malinowski (Young, 2004), Colin Turnbull (Grinker, 2000) and Margaret Mead (Howard, 1989). For those who, are researched we sometimes know something about a few individuals such as Baba of Kano (Smith, M., 1954) but of the multitudes of those who have made up the communities studied we know nothing more than the collective data and the few individuals who are thanked personally for their general help to the researcher in the prefaces to their publications. More or less all we know about the individuals who have provided the data is that they came from a specific locality or from a sample of a certain number. A recent Chinese study (Hong *et al.*, 2007) listed the inadequacies of their analyses; all the data came from the self-administered questionnaires of 1845 students and that there might have been socially acceptable reporting in their replies to sensitive questions regarding their sexual and on-line risk behaviours. So we have to conclude that although we may know something in detail about researchers, those they research are only known in statistical enumerations and a few biographical facts about some prominent ones which are usually no more than a paragraph.

THE SHORTAGE OF DATA THAT INDIVIDUALISES

When someone applies to a bank for a loan that institution collects as much data as possible as to that person's credit worthiness as well as information about the market value of the proposed purchase. The bank will also consider the state of the economy and their profit margin from having their money tied up for so long in a particular piece of property. This is an exercise in probability over which every bank has considerable expertise and yet they often get it wrong both in individual cases and in the bank's overall policies. The individual loses his or her job, there is a messy divorce and the property itself may lose its value because of a downturn in the housing market as has recently occurred in the United Kingdom or the property itself may have been ruined by flooding.

Social science fieldwork is usually based on either mass sampling about whose individuals little is known except the data which those people themselves supply for which there can be little corroboration. This is a social science situation of wide ranging myopic trust which no commercial organisation would accept. The alternative is getting information from a small number of informants whom the researchers trust without any real reason for doing so since they know little of their background and base their trust on the convenience of the information which they supply so readily.

Only in qualitative work can the social scientists be said to base their information on individual viewpoints and this is inevitably less detailed than the information which is available about the researchers themselves. They accept the basic individuality of human behaviour but do not have the means to base their work on these variations. In asking medical advice a well-read doctor would say that the chances of success for this operation or its failure for a particular reason based on a known number of cases is a certain percentage. Then they will qualify these conclusions by stating that each case has to be seen as separate and thus have little to do with statistical averages.

It would seem that social science tends to stay rather with the weak averages which are provided by quantification and the provision of a limited number of individualised case studies without seemingly linking the two aspects together in illustrating the ranges of individualistic behaviour which might be expected.

In the quantification of behaviour by social scientists it may be possible to anticipate average but not inevitable trends in the length of life in Zimbabwe, the frequency of certain types of internet crime and the reduction in size of small family farming units in Bengal but not what might happen in individual situations. Social science does not have sufficient data to support much accurate understandings of the individuality of human behaviour.

9

The Biases in Research and its Objectives

If we accept as we must that there is bias in 'hard' science in how researchers choose their topics and the ways that their methodologies come under personal influences, then the range of such influences in the social sciences are likely to be much more prevalent and influential. Some form of bias should be accepted as a basic feature of both human understandings and human relationships; it is perhaps part of the necessary dialectic of adaptive change.

Bias in either the researcher or the researched is a constant and basic feature of social science research. In some cases individuals may not even be aware that they have understandings which prevent any possibility of their detachment reaching the standards required by science. Participants who were asked to state the nationality of Japanese or Japanese Americans from their pictures were correct in levels above chance (Marsh *et al.*, 2003). Even in clinical trials in which the participants had been selected by blind processes, assessors may well have guessed to which group they belonged since there would always be clues in the medical record. This would not necessarily invalidate the procedures unless we can differentiate between personal influences affecting well-being and of course, the placebo effect (Sharpe *et al.*, 2003).

It would seem necessary for us to accept that there will always be conscious and unconscious factors of bias in all research. It is a necessary part of any research to unearth as many of these factors as possible and to accept that their extent handicaps the possibilities of social science research being accepted as paralleling the results from 'hard' science. Bias affects both chance and probability.

STRESS AND ITS BIASING EFFECTS

Within a society everyone will always experience a long series of traumatic events from death, disease as well as economic and social disorder. We cannot know the extent of such misfortunes nor their effects on individuals or communities. We suspect that subsistence societies may have just as appropriate and effective methods of coping as the apparently more sophisticated social welfare professional systems of more economically developed and politically stable ones. We know that quasi-traditional healers are extremely common in all contemporary African and Asian towns and cities and we can presuppose that their numbers and efficiency in coping may parallel that of more professionally organised methods (Kean *et al.*, 2006).

Researchers however well trained and experienced they may be are still not persons detached from their own humanity. Unless they are working within their own communities in a social environment to which they are well adjusted, they are moving out of this into situations of which they will have had no previous experience. They will be moving out of the relative stability of domestic and university environments, a natal culture into which they have been well socialised.

They find themselves in social environments involving them in the stresses which come from living in situations characterised by social distance between what they are used to do and think and with what they are now exposed to professionally. No amount of reading and advice can prepare researchers for the realities of having to live and associate with people for long periods with whom they have little or nothing in common either in thinking or in their behaviour. There is certainly no mutual interest in the research work.

We know little or nothing about the range of these stresses on researchers. Even Malinowski as we read from his diaries found it stressful to live day in and day out with Trobriand islanders and looked on breaks with white traders as a relief as they were culturally nearer to him than those whom he was researching (Malinowski, 1967). He would certainly not have chosen to associate with such people had he been at home. We know little of the effect of such stresses on the dropout rate for researchers and their projects in which in their public and published form are no more than peer related records of success. In the 1960s a third of the non-African researchers associated with the Ugandan Institute of Social Research produced no known results.

Stressful it must be and a source of bias for anyone to be compulsorily surrounded by people whose personal habits, linguistic codes or languages are basically different to their own and who have a contemporary tradition of non-cooperation or at least veiled hostility to intrusive and socially useless outsiders, except as a source of minor employment. This is not just a European and possibly somewhat outdated reaction to fieldwork as we have seen in Malinowski's psychologically disturbed reactions to his isolation in the Trobriand islands during First World War. It also occurs with a middle class Asian woman researcher who gave up her fieldwork because of the lack of privacy (Dua, 1979) and another who as a Brahmin had multiple difficulties in fitting into village life once his caste became common knowledge (Srinivas, 1979). It needs considerable psychological and social ingenuity as well as strength of commitment in their projects to enter and cope with totally strange environments and moreover not to be biased from the experience.

We just do not know the extent to which these strains alter the conclusions of social scientists. There is also the personal rather than professional strain which comes from the prolonged exposure to widespread distress about which they can do nothing because of their low standard of living, cultural differences and political instability. To be confronted with these differences whether in Chicago or in Kolkata is a distressing experience from which researchers may find it difficult to isolate themselves.

Most researchers if not well-to-do are at least relatively well protected from the distresses of poverty in any personal sense. They can become mentally deadened from the multiplicities of misery which they are forced to notice among refugees, subsistence farmers, slum dwellers, addicts and the unemployed. Their recognition of their own uselessness as in their inability to prevent the death of a friend-informant (Bowen, 1964) or in the case of Bob Geldorf, the founder of Band-Aid who described himself as being deadened by the mass misery which he had seen. The drift into political considerations must be a constant source of both bias and role difficulties.

THE BIAS FROM PERSONAL RELATIONSHIPS

Fieldwork whether within a social scientist's own society or in another cultural environment is a break from any existing social situation and a personal insertion into another which can only be known intellectually from prior reading about allied societies. There are variations in the ways in which social scientists can become detached from their own societies and attached to others for intellectual rather than for personal reasons. It is only in rare cases that researchers detach themselves in any permanent sense from their own societies and attempt to become long-term members of another society which in terms of personal psychological and social well-being is a potentially dangerous activity.

Few social scientists are able to sustain long periods of isolation from the backgrounds into which they have been socialised. Even if they are somewhat dismissive if not contemptuous of the inadequacies of their own societies, few realise until they are separated from this background how dependent they are on their own cultural backgrounds and its bureaucratic support.

Fieldwork unless it is done in the congenial surroundings of their own social environments in which their participation is part of their own way of life, always involves substantial social and psychological disruption. A doctor researching a particular disease in the hospital in which she works or an American sociologist researching education in a highly mobile community in which he and his wife are not all that different to most of the couples there (Hennigh, 1981). Neither are going to experience much social and psychological disruption over their research work, and they do not even have to learn a new linguistic code; a drift into some aspects of complacency is always a possibility.

In almost all researches the social scientists have to form new social relationships not only to further their research but also because it is virtually impossible to maintain isolation from a wide range of individuals whom they need to make life if not pleasant at least tolerable. Whatever relationships they initiate or are initiated for them, the results are potentially biasing.

THE BIAS FROM BEING ONE OF US

The greater the social distance between the researcher and the researched the greater the need to look back at least to some people that link them to their own social backgrounds. Professor Evans-Pritchard found long periods isolated among the Sudanese Azande tiring and he wrote appreciatively about being able to get relief by staying with the British colonial administrator of those people who incidentally would have had to bear the costs of such visits as the researcher would not have been classifiable as an official visitor. There was probably no alternative if he wanted a temporary relief from the tiresomeness of research. He, just as much as Malinowski, may have wanted to talk English, have a bath and a beer free from the strain of living among 'natives' with which they had only some shared intellectual interests which in this case could only have been cattle. These contacts may have been influential in maintaining a social as much as intellectual distancing which social scientists need for the detached evaluation of their work.

There can be little doubt that there are no parallel emotional difficulties in studying bacteria or primates and that this makes scientific detachment easier. This is never so in fieldwork with humans. Most researchers never cease to be outsiders and they continue to have social and emotional relationships within their own cultures which remain deeply emotional and of indeterminate influence. In-bred biases which are regularly refreshed by this coming and going between the research area and the social world from which they came and more importantly to which they will return. This means that all social science researchers are not only seeing their work through their own socialisations but that they find it boring and stressful to be separated for long periods from their own backgrounds and thus seek opportunities to keep in touch.

THE BIASES FROM ATTEMPTING TO BE ONE OF THEM

It is one of the characteristics of fieldwork that the principal informants on whom they depend would see their employers for that is what they are, as socially unusual and often useful friends. The researchers go along with this while using them for their research purposes and indeed for their own personal and professional advancement.

Since this relationship in social science terms is relatively clear, it is a source of bias since researchers become dependent on perhaps no more than half a dozen regular key informants. It becomes a question of who is using who. Malinowski in his diary draws regular attention to particular informants whom he thinks are unusually clever. It seems likely that his recognition of the 'kula' of concentric circles of exchanging ritual objects and the intimate details of their sexual behaviour came from these men and through them came his professional eminence. Little is known about these key men and women with whom all researchers have particular relationships and there is always the thought that they may be using their particular talkative qualities for purposes that are not closely related to aims of the research. Why should we assume that they have suddenly developed detached views of their own society and the researcher's presence there?

The snag comes when these relationships develop from a professional need which in Malinowski's case was paid for with sticks of tobacco to the informants and who continue to provide information because of the fringe benefits which they get from associating in such a personal way with prestigious well-to-do outsiders. They end up becoming part of the personal as much as the intellectual life of the researchers, a little group with specialised needs and practices which in social terms belong neither to the society of the researcher nor to that of the informants.

Victor Turner wrote appreciatively of the intellectual perceptiveness of Muchona the Hornet, the Ndembu diviner (Turner, 1967) and ending up seeing him as something more than an extremely important informant. Certainly, Muchona thought of Turner in these terms as someone with whom he could discuss his work in the privacy of their relationship without weakening his local position as a diviner. In the circumstances of this dyadic relationship there was theoretical abstract thinking which would have been unlikely to have been shared with the subsistence farmers who were his clients. Turner comments that when he left that research project Muchona might well have felt greater distress from the breaking off of their relationships than he did. Muchona would no longer have an outsider with whom he could discuss the ins and outs of his own work as a diviner with someone whom he could appreciate as in some vague way his intellectual equal. This is an aspect of the relationships with key informants which social scientists tend to forget; the clouding of personal perceptions when it becomes entangled in a more personal relationship. They create close relationships with these men and women on whom they may have come to be intellectually dependent and then abandon them for that is what it is, when the research project ends.

The dividing line comes in such relationships when such people become part of the emotional perceptions of the researchers who are isolated from their own sustaining relationships. They become over-dependent on these few men and women who seem so ready to help them in their social isolation. The researchers have moved into the magical circle of personal feelings over cultural differences which should be no place in scientific detachment. The situation in which Laura Bohannan, the wife of an anthropologist found herself (Bowen, 1964: 156, 338). "I had allowed myself to become too absorbed in the personal affairs of the few households I knew best...I stood over Ameca. She tried to smile at me. She was very ill. I was concerned that these women could not help her. She would die. She was my friend but my epitaph for her would be impersonal observations."

There is thus the professionally dangerous change from using people as informants as a professional necessity as might be said of police informants and then finding that they have moved over a dividing line into a relationship which they interpret as friendship with its locally understandable reciprocities. The researchers would see them as professionally important but would shrink away from thinking of them as friends. They would not see these relationships in terms of obligatory reciprocities in which they appear to provide materially out of proportion to what they get in return. They may not realise that in many societies information is a commodity as negotiable as tobacco, goats and money. Perhaps we have to accept that personal feelings are always biased even if it is in practice impossible to avoid them.

BIAS FROM THE GROWTH OF INTROSPECTION

Most researchers are unprepared not only for social isolation which comes from going to work for long periods in another cultural and social environment and for the introspection which is likely to develop in such social isolation. Most people have experienced package holidays or gone to work for their pre-university year in an environment strange for them. These experiences are always like moving from one social nest to another. Researchers are always moving out of a circle of known people on whom they can bounce off ideas and loneliness. Without this facility matters can get out of proportion in the solitary mind. We do not know whether Malinowski was an extreme example of this when he writes repetitively in his diary about the possible fluctuations in his own health and the relationships with his prospective wife and others.

While it is possible that contemporary social scientists are better prepared for and aware of social and cultural differences, this does not cover the sense of isolation from having to live in a strange community as an intellectual but necessary requirement which might indeed be no more than a few geographical miles from 'home'. Powdermaker wrote 'This was my first night in Lesu alone. I asked myself, "what on earth am I doing here, all alone on the edge of the world",' (Powdermaker, 1966:51). The title of this study of fieldwork in many different environments including her study as a white researcher of race relations in the southern United States in which she details that she had more problems than in the Pacific environment of Lesu.

THE BIAS FROM HAVING SERVANTS

Most researchers come from social environments in which their domestic needs are catered for by the institutions in which they belong; there are canteens, washing machines, electricity from a switch and water from a tap. They think in terms of their individualism and yet they are totally dependent on the institutions which maintain them or on what is provided without question by their families.

The fieldworker moves out of this carefully cushioned taken-for-granted social environment into situations in which little is provided. They are now isolated particularly in subsistence communities whether in agriculture or slum economies, in which they have no prior connections; they now have to look after themselves or make arrangements to get water, firewood, lighting, laundry and food. For most this is a totally new experience in the practical necessities of living. They have to do it all themselves and waste time from what should be spent on their research when they cannot stay there indefinitely or employ someone else to work for them as domestic servants.

This may not be a new situation for an Indian social scientist but for Westerners with perhaps a student background of political involvement with socialism this is now. Now they are in fact incapacitated from their primary task unless they become employers of servants as in most societies there is no appropriate role for a man to do the cooking and fetch water or for a woman to employ someone else to do this. They learn soon enough that domestic work is very time consuming.

So we have social scientists who in their research role only have their professional hierarchy and seek no other status enhancement, find that they have upgraded themselves in their own eyes and that of the surrounding community by having at least one servant. Whether they accept this or not they might find it difficult to maintain their predominantly leftist views. This servant is a channel of information about the surrounding community as well as a provider of information about the researcher. An additional personal relationship detracting from the researcher 's need for taking a detached view of the community. This servant as a particular person having very specific local roles is no more a detached source of information than any other informant.

BIASES AND THE PROCESSES OF RESEARCH

There are no people in any culture at any level of education and intellect who do not have likes and dislikes for which there will be limited rational reasons. Similarly, we have to accept that social science researchers either consciously or unconsciously are just as likely to have likes and dislikes which will affect how they see the people and the social environments in which they are working. In fact it would be irrational to expect any individual to so detach themselves from their own psychological background and the processes of socialisation to which they have been subjected in their childhood and in the processes of higher education, that they have taken on the characteristics of a recording machine.

All human beings attach themselves by choice with those they prefer for innumerable reasons of which they may not be aware. These commonplace preferences are associated with ethnicity and kinship, age, sex, education, occupation, and religion as well as quite trivial behavioural characteristics which have no rational basis at all. Bias has to be assumed to exist in all social science research work rather making fruitless attempts to prove that there have been no biases in any particular report.

It is essential to accept that whatever the biases that any particular researcher may have as in the case of Colin Turnbull's dislike of the Ugandan Ik which indeed may well have been shared by those reading his description of their crude survivalist way of life (Turnbull, 1973). His suggestions for their future might just as well have been written by a colonial administrator. It works both ways as the researchers and the researched may both have reason to dislike each other; the Tanzanian Ssonjo may dislike the long-term intrusion of an anthropologist just as the Irish academic community would dislike an enquiry into the political connections involved in the making of appointments. Both bias and attitude are bilateral processes in which knowingly or unknowingly people react to each other. We worry about these deviations from scientific rectitude which can be attributed to the researchers while forgetting that those researched are reacting in similar ways to those who intrude however peripherally into what they experience as the stabilities of their own lives.

BIAS AND THE FACTOR OF CHANCE IN THE SELECTION OF RESEARCH

In clinical trials it is possible with care to avoid biased selections of participants that are going to be compared by randomized choice but even then the web of professional gossip may influence those chosen. On the other hand social scientists in their fieldwork are ostensibly randomized in what they do and with whom they do it, but they have little control over this process. Researchers choose what they want to do but they are often directed to or accidentally come to certain locations and topics which have little to do with rational needs or the particular choices needed for the verification of data by comparison.

In practice it seems likely that there is little randomness about what is chosen and in the circumstances in which research is undertaken since it is likely to be predetermined by social, political and economic factors. It can only be called random for the ideological convenience of the researchers who might not like to have their theoretical hopes modified by factors which may have little to do with their methodological needs. Malinowski 'did' the

Trobriand Islands because as a nominally enemy alien he could be allowed to go there where he would not be considered as a problem. The writer studied three areas of Tanzania because he was sent there by his employers.

It may even be rare for a researcher to actually go and research what he or she hoped to do in the first place when considering their options. All manner of issues will make for choices governed by time, funding, entry permits, personal willingness and the internal politics of research institutes and funding organisations. Much of the selection is out of the control of the researchers who may only have the option of acceptance or refusal but it is not a random process.

BIAS IN THE USE AND CHOICE OF KEY INFORMANTS

There are other aspects of biased selection once the researchers have started their work. It may well be that they are chosen by potential informants rather than that they have been carefully chosen under some process of randomization. There cannot be any process of randomization because these are socially constructed choices. They come to work for researchers because of self-interest, availability, economic and social needs and personal preferences. It cannot be maintained that these important relationships are anything other than the result of a whole range of channelled coincidences and chances (Tanner, 2001).

Just as Victor Turner benefited from his association with Muchona the Hornet, informants certainly benefit from working with an outsider of superior status since obviously he or she would not be doing this work or just being there unless they got their income from somewhere; they have sophisticated minds which are well able to calculate their own interests. The writer at one time had two kiSukuma and one Swahili informants who certainly benefited from these dyadic associations and like all social relationships it is impossible to know the extent of the bias in this, even if they might in fact be better classified as research associates.

Informants whether it can be proved or not, provide doctored memories of what may have happened in the past for that is what they are passing on to researchers. Memory is an unreliable means of passing on information unless it is of some cultural events retained in the memories of specially trained individuals. Information is likely to be inaccurate as what is passed on may be related to the informants sense of enhanced status and what they might gain.

BIAS FROM SAMPLING

When social scientists study a community in a village, university or hospital, they may start from street maps, telephone directories, electoral rolls or lists of hospital admissions but such lists will often produce such large number of people that no thorough study can be made in the time available. So samples are taken from such lists which are assumed to be accurate even though not all people have phones that work, participate in the teaching for which they are listed or all those suffering from a particular disease attend hospitals so that limited workable number in terms of the researchers assumed capabilities are approached.

This sample cannot be a true reflection of the universe from which it is taken if only because it is a small minority chosen by accident; we just do not know what the left out overwhelming majority may feel about the matters being researched so it is an act of professional faith that one reflects the other, despite the clear knowledge that of individual variations and behavioural change.

In addition, there will always be drop-outs from the sample of those who do not want to participate for what may well be valuable reasons, move away or are absent repeatedly when the researchers look for them. In a parish survey in Guyana by the time that the recorder of family details reached the end of the community list, the composition of those recorded at the beginning had changed. In Western societies between 10 to 20 per cent of most communities move annually. The larger the community or universe being researched, the larger the number of people who will be excluded or exclude themselves from such randomized choice of doubtful validity.

Outside the institutional controls built into the care of disease, it may be that people cannot be randomized in anyway that can conform to the requirements of 'hard' science. In a Tanganyikan district a leprosy specialist more than doubled the number of lepers in a short visit. Most senior police officers would claim that they know more than half of the murders committed in their areas. The concept of a firm social universe from which people can be sampled is a nebulous one.

It is not so much that people drop out of these contrived research universes in which they are placed for the convenience of the researchers and their time and motion capabilities, but that this is seen as a handicap and a matter of regret rather than as a reflection of how social life usually proceeds. If societies and human behaviour are organised around constant change then it seems a noticeable shortcoming of social science methodology that it puts enormous effort in creating a theoretical stability which can never have existed.

So researchers are inevitably caught in the dilemmas around the accuracies of their results taken from mathematically correct samplings or the accidents of limited associations that are possible in any community or field of enquiry. A large sample involves inevitable inaccuracies between the broad and indefinable categories used in the analyses to which many different factors can be fitted.

On the other hand a small one for which detailed information is available may well be too specialised for any general application as there will be different views of events even in a single family. Had a sample been taken from participants in sample of a long ceremony as in a Sri Lankan Buddhist ceremony at the Katagarama pilgrimage centre in which about half of participants were lying down asleep. Any work on such as sample would not disclose the realities of their participation.

In all samples especially in clinical ones there is the possibility of contamination as would be the case of detailed studies of a single family. Once comparison comes into social science research influences on one sample may affect one sample but not another and it would be much more difficult to detect in two villages or two branches of the same trade union.

Small samples may not get the wide variations which are certain to exist in even the smallest and least developed of societies and the larger samples will get the variations but not the small scale implications.

THE BIASES FROM INTERVENTION

It is probable that the harder the scientific issues involved in research the more that the researchers can be isolated from the social rather than the intellectual influences on what is being researched and the results.

How do we know what the researched community was like before the arrival of the social scientists? There is no reason to suppose that the provided memories of what may or may not have happened previously are accurate. The writer attended the initiation ceremonies of the Buchewzi 'secret' society on two occasions ten years apart. On the second occasion he was assured that the ritual was the same as he had seen before and photographed; there was nothing in common between the two sets of ceremonies except the blue and white beaded headdresses of the leaders.

Social scientists in their fieldwork are always participant observers and as such whether they like to admit it or not, they are their own principal informants. As such they are not isolatable from the social environment in which they are operating; they are always intruding socially and indeed they are always likely to be intruded upon by those not directly involved in their research; the shut door is in some ways a middle class Western characteristic; the rest of the world lives under conditions of social openness in which privacy is not particularly valued.

So researchers intrude on the social environments in which they come to work and it is only after some time and in some small ranges of involvement that they can become part of the social furniture so to speak and no longer be experienced as something extra to the social environment which has to be explained. The Saudi Arabian woman social scientist found that it took some time working in families other than her own but of the same social level, before these people carried on their daily lives as if she was not there (Altorki, 1982). Where the social distance is far greater as indeed it must be in most research situations because of ethnic, caste, education and sex difference it is much more likely that the researcher will never be accepted as more than a tolerated outsider.

The researcher can enter a community in a role already known and accepted by these people such as teacher or nurse but it is still intervention. The role of researcher is not easily accepted by any community or institution without some modification of their behaviour. The South Indian Coorgs had been visited so often by anthropologists that some of their intellectuals used English anthropological terms in discussions with visitors (Varadachar,

1979). The American anthropologist Cushing tried hard to become an American Indian Zuni without attaining anything more than being accepted as a rather unusual well-meaning 'white' persistent visitor to a small community within their resentment at white American overall dominance of their lives (Gronewold, 1972). Margaret Mead (Mead, 1956) had such a long-term relationship with the Manus that some elders publicly mourned her death but she had materially benefited them.

In 'hard' science the researchers cannot influence the materials on which they are working except by recordable procedures and aside from their intellectual capacities to interpret them in deliberate ways or by chance, their personalities and social behaviour have no influence over what is being researched. Of course their 'otherness', personal habits, marital status as well as their mental and physical stamina have an influence but not on the base lines from which they are working. Their being on or off stage can only have a minimal bearing on what is being researched.

However, in the social sciences there is a constantly variable distinction between the off-stage behaviour of the researchers when they are their 'normal' selves and on their on-stage actions when they consider themselves to be at work. This on-stage behaviour (Goffman, 1969) is their formal presentation of themselves as professionals, but even when they are not on stage their presence remains with those being researched.

At an earlier period this distinction was kept clearer. In Malinowski's diary (Malinowski, 1967) he records more of his relationships with the few Europeans he met, the weather and the scenery and little beyond some irritation with the natives. Without retrospective knowledge of his eminence as an anthropologist there would be little in this diary of sociological interest except for the fact that he was an expatriate Polish intellectual wandering about in an Australian-cum-British social environment. So we know that the fieldworkers had two quite distinct roles.

While social scientists have inherited a professional distinction in these two roles in their minds, it is perhaps now seen as socially and politically unacceptable to underline this difference. Thus we have social scientists at work with a form of on stage behaviour which has some analysable distinctiveness but not as clear as that maintained by doctors and judges.

It is only occasionally that this distinction is muted when the degree of participant observation is so extreme as to obliterate the distinction as must have been the case with the Canadian woman anthropologist who lived in the same house with Eskimo family throughout the Arctic winter (Briggs, 1970), in which she tried with difficulty to maintain some otherness in order to write up her field notes. Her influence on this family must have been so overwhelming as to exclude any possibility of drawing conclusions independent of her prolonged presence there; she was in effect the creation of her own biasing presence though we can admire her fortitude. But in terms of involvement there is very much a minority of the time in which they are an influence on those researched. Social scientists move in and out of their field of research in a constant change of roles.

THE INFLUENCE ON THE RESEARCHER

Is it possible for social scientists not to be seriously influenced by what they are experiencing? In the quantification of data their reaction is likely to be one of boredom in collecting and codifying such data detached from its humanity; it is a dull activity only relieved by the rationing of time involved and the satisfaction of seeing some results mathematically expressed. Apart from the suspect nature of the data as to how it was collected and the meaning of replies, there are difficult issues in the codification of replies and the numerical accuracy of replies relating to human behaviour expressed to decimal point definition and boredom may well be a factor in such predetermined accuracy. A form containing data about or provided by the 18 years old Maria Idadi provides no identity to which the recording social scientist can relate to; she is just a statistical unit in a population universe not all that different to what might be recorded of a group of chimpanzees.

With qualitative data the experiential reality of what is happening to social scientists in the field must mean that a whole series of reciprocal influences are going back and forth between those involved. The researcher influences the field in which they are operating whether they mean to or not and sometimes it is just pure personal emotional indulgence. There is the picture of the English woman anthropologist dancing with the Ndembu in their Hunter's dance (E. Turner, 2006:153). Such an, outsider stranger woman would have no recognisable place in such a public male activity. The people watching would not have reacted neutrally to her breaking of convention although she intended these actions to be a demonstration of her goodwill and emotional involvement in their lives.

It seems likely that Edith Turner in both her African and Arctic fieldwork and Verrier Elwin (Elwin, 1988) who had a long marriage with an Indian girl are extreme examples of social scientists who became personally committed to the ideas as much as the practices of the people they researched. With the former it was an emotional conversion to a new form of understandings and with the latter a commitment to the material and political needs of the tribal peoples of India of which he became a citizen.

But surely these two examples and the rarity of such autobiographical explanations of conversion and commitment should not be left isolated at that end of the experiences of social scientists doing qualitative work with small numbers of people. Anyone who has a long and detailed association with a group of which they are not themselves members is going to build strands of commitment without any intention to do so. A question of degree but there can be little doubt that all these outsiders do develop various forms of social commitment even possibly one sided affection.

This can be seen in the career patterns of these men and women whether they are nationals or non-nationals, most of whom will have had a particular community in which they have done fieldwork and this will remain a long term focus of their research interests. Kumar concentrated on Banaras (Kumar, 1988) just as Victor Turner did on the Ndembu and each concentrated on particular parts of those large social populations. Most social scientists do not change their interests in mid-career so that their professional and more specifically their emotional lives remain focused on their initial fieldwork.

Clearly researchers are influenced by what they see and experience which at the very least is a breaking out from the range of their own cultural preconceptions. This must inevitably happen whether it is the necessary association with homosexuals in prison research, the recognition of personal revulsion over animal sacrifices to the Goddess Kali or the excitement of seeing the wholesale possession of young Ssonjo men by the spirit of the deity Hambagau; the constant pull between structuralist and qualitative explanations.

A study through extended interviews of the ways in which three Chicago Americans dealt with theological issues in their past and present religious beliefs and activities (Bradshaw and Fitchett, 2003) highlighted the unique ways in which these three coped with such complicated issues. These two researchers will have empathized with them and cannot have remained not so much unchanged but unmoved by their relationships. Much the same can be expected to have happened with the six social scientists who researched quasi-traditional contemporary healers in Tanzania and provided their profiles (Gessler *et al.*, 1995).

Even if we accept that researchers influence the researched it is equally impossible to disentangle this from other influences entering the minds and behaviour of people and communities which come from the overall overwhelming processes of social change.

One suspects then that the social scientists must influence in some ways the social environments in which they work; some things will be told them just because they are outsiders and some things will be hidden from them for the same reasons. In every sense they take up some social spaces which were not previously occupied. A particular example would be the potential influence of the seemingly independent woman researcher as well as any young man assuming equality for his enquiries in societies socially dominated by mature men.

All researchers may well aim to be able to put some sort of social fence round their projects and hope to be able to ignore intrusions. Leaving aside those which may come from the outside private lives of researchers, the social environment in which they are working is always going to be interfered with by factors outside their control. Objections may be taken to their work by some powerful local figure, civil disturbances, epidemics, earthquakes and economic fluctuations.

It may be prudent to conclude that however probabilities are determined in regard to a community or institution in which the researchers have been in effect participant observers, this has to be accepted as a factor.

BIAS FROM THE INSIDER RESEARCHER

On occasions researchers will research their own institutions or ones into which they have inserted themselves in pre-existing roles. This is a comfortable situation as it cuts down the time which has to be spent in learning new patterns of behaviour with its linguistic code. But by assuming an existing role such a researcher will take on the social restrictions of that role and will be part of the internal politics of that institution.

If the researcher is already a member of that institution, their future relationships will be affected and in their own interests they may modify their observations. This writer published research on the European community in East Africa of which he was then a member which certainly modified his social relationships or were these conclusions no more than reflections of his existing and indeed his wife's viewpoints (Tanner, 1964, 1966).

There is certainly insider knowledge which has been gained previously from a particular position and the biases which go with that and this would be valuable in relation to the probabilities of that particular position. Overall there would not seem to be any identifiable advantages from such biased positioning for a study of any community or institution, except in terms of that one role.

IMPERSONAL BIASES

In quantifying research involving large numbers of people about whom nothing is known in any personal sense, the dangers of bias may come from commitment to some theoretical hypothesis to which those involved may have already committed themselves by training and previous research work. This can be seen in rather numerous recent examples of academic fraud of which the cases of Bruno Bettelheim and Cyril Burt are well known. The motivations for committing scientific misconduct have been given as career pressure, pride believing something to be true because of their professional standing without going to the trouble of actually proving it and finally, the ability to get away with it (Goodstein, 2002). Overall the sheer quantity of published material makes it unlikely that anyone because of the time it would take, is going to check particular sets of figures, even misprinting of data with no intention to defraud is common enough and apparently unnoticed by readers.

Physicians have connections with the pharmaceutical industry whose products rightly or wrongly become not only part of their professional lives but also influence them in their wider professional lives; this degree of influence has become so widespread in the United States as to give rise to both medical and political concern (Choudhry *et al.*, 2001). We should assume that in the creation of probabilities there are hidden somewhere preferences for particular assessments; personal hopes are a particularly insidious form of bias, however much it may be disguised professionally.

Whether it is detectable bias or the perceptions of attitude which are reflected in the subtleties with which we all observe the behaviour of others, social science researchers are probably no better than other less qualified people, in the accuracy of their observations and perceptions just as the researched are not themselves static reflections of any social realities.

Perhaps the most persistent and pervasive bias comes from the researchers sense of their own intellectual superiority, a three-fold consequence of the selection processes in Western type education, their high standard of literacy and overall cultural exclusiveness. Their sense of being more or less in the know or approaching the knowledge of how society works, may make it difficult to accept and give equal value to the ideas and practices of at best marginal literates.

Political thinking is always part of any researchers understandings even if they have no personal political affiliations. If social scientist were to be politically categorized as likely to be socialist, while the communities they study or at least their leadership are broadly conservative in the sense of being appreciative of what they think they may have done traditionally.

There are other forms of bias which may creep in from the nature of the research itself. A researcher working on the social behaviour on a small island off the west coast of Ireland found that their political behaviour was based on the basic fact that they were almost entirely dependent on subsidies as they had all been defined as officially blind. He found it safer to study kinship than to find himself tied up in the inevitable intrigues in the maintenance of this duplicity (Fox, 2004). So researchers are likely to shy away from topics which socially and politically are too dangerous as well as too difficult to study. Green published the economic implications of corruption in Uganda but published his conclusions after he had left (Green, 1981).

Research into kinship, agricultural practices and traditional meanings of key words in an unscripted linguistic code might involve researchers in an understanding of individual animosities but they might thus be able to avoid becoming involved in wide-ranging disputes which have split communities. Unless they are relying entirely on their own observations, an inevitably biased approach, they will always be dependent on informants who will present their information in terms of the roles which they have in their own communities; their newly achieved role of informant to an outsider would be a minor and temporary role in comparison to this.

The researchers will always and perhaps inevitably have to rely on biased information. Indeed there may not be any such concept in the semantics of many languages as it is assumed that whatever is spoken will be based on the speakers own interests. Most would see the oath taken in a court to tell the truth to be a particular form of Western legal hypocrisy except in the rare occasions of not having any knowledge or opinion of the case.

PERSONAL BIASES

It is obvious enough that any detected bias in research would prevent its probabilistic predictions from being accepted even if they did manage to get published or at least placed in departmental libraries. Biases are usually not only part of every researchers socialisation but also at least in part the consequences of the research itself. Margaret Mead's original study of adolescence in Samoa (Mead, 1928) was influential in making intellectuals think of the possibilities of human nature being much more malleable than had previously thought to be the case. The fact that she may have been mistaken or rather misinformed (Freeman, 1983) is now quite irrelevant in retrospect as it was valuable at the time that it was published. Few academic conclusions about human behaviour have survived half a century of intellectual change and continuing research. It was a tribute to her importance that a subsequent social scientist took so much time to seemingly disprove the data on which she based her conclusions.

A woman researcher coming from a university environment in which sexism is not only politically incorrect but institutionally avoided, is not likely to view impersonally what she might see as the subordination of women to male interests in non-Western societies generally and not just in Islamic ones. In much the same way most researchers who are predominantly male and have been socialised in patrilineal cultures and would not see matrilineality as an equivalent system of seemingly equal pragmatic rationality.

Most social scientists trained in Western patterns of evaluating social behaviour are secular in their thinking and social practices. Very few psychologists are religious believers. There is a tendency to assess religious and spiritual practices at whatever level in reductionist terms and this failing to accept as evidence that the people who are thinking and practising in these ways have created a form of seemingly non-pragmatic reality.

Social scientists nor any other type of person are without a range of personal biases for which there are no logical foundations. They are not likely to recognise their existence unless required to do so in some therapeutic session or sociology seminar. It seems likely that while there may be a minimum amount of bias in studying agricultural or fishing practices, it is likely to be much more in working on patterns of thinking which are infinitely more complicated linguistically and psychologically to understand once we leave the safe preconceptions of our own ways of thinking.

All social scientists will have some sort of a commitment to some social group which they feel has some special and unusual characteristics which they themselves have interpreted. This has little to do with the impersonal detached standards at which they are professionally aiming; this bias is both unavoidable and perhaps natural. It is another important factor affecting the possibilities of predicting behaviour.

10

Social Science as Contemporary History

Many social scientists collect their own data or use data collected on a national basis to establish an accurate picture of some nearly contemporary situation. They then work out the reasons retrospectively and indeed convincingly to show that these contemporary situations are an almost logical consequence of a series of pre-existing factors.

In the United States a panel study of income dynamics and a health and retirement study were analyzed together which suggested that retrospective reports of childhood health were of sufficient stability to warrant their professional use in population research and that retrospective reports of overall childhood health were fairly reliable over time (Haas, 2007). This is a standard well ordered piece of research but can it and others like it be acceptable as valid scientific evidence?

The main drawback to such assessments and connections is that the recent analysis of all preceding data are dealing with a completed picture as they are looking at what is currently happening. Professor Evans-Pritchard has called the work of anthropologists who were studying the present were in fact recording what had happened. While historians may be prepared to accept the factor of chance in what had come about, they find it difficult to accept that there may not be any linear progression in providing dependable connections. There is much more likely to have been a pervasive cloud of lateral chance happenings for which there can be no logical use or understandings. Historians who are by the nature of their work also social scientists can only guess at the motivations if indeed there have been anything so clear, as to why individuals have taken the direction they have in their social behaviour. Social scientists in this context are in a similar position to those who read the last chapter of a detective novel and then understand how it all fits together.

However, there are significant drawbacks to such retrospective analyses since we know the current position and it would be virtually impossible not to connect past data as being consistent with the last available information. Whatever the degree of personal involvement of the researcher with the current data which is being presented, there is a tendency to support the more recent data by making such connections. There must be doubts as to the validity of such retrospective data when such self-rated categorizations of childhood health are recorded on a scale of excellent to poor. Well-intentioned memory is an uncertain basis for any statistical comparison which in its numerical presentation will always suggest accuracy.

However, examining the same contemporary data sources without making categorizations from memory, the pathways between past and present can be made more exact as connecting the absence of a father and growing up under adverse economic conditions can lead to an elevated risk of heart attacks for women (Hamil-Luker and O'Rand, 2007). This surely is always an individualised issue and we cannot know without detailed small scale analysis what the absence of the father means. We cannot just imagine that this refers to divorce and ignores the possibility of hostile but maintained marriages and the absence of the father for most of the time because he is an air-line employee or a professional soldier.

All such studies involving large numbers in the sample are a necessary prerequisite for statistical analysis. This obscures the individual pathways for each member of such a sample between the alleged but quite unproven childhood circumstances and their present health status. We can always assume quite rightly that the past affects the present but to turn such obvious connections into the rigidity of statistics is an improper methodological assumption. It was stated by Beveridge the founder of the proposals on which the current British welfare system was based that "more discoveries have arisen from intense observation of a very limited material than from statistics applied to large groups, for only by being familiar with the usual can we notice something as being unusual and unexplained" (Beveridge, 1957:105).

There is the implication in all such studies retrospectively linking the present with data collected in the past not necessarily for the same purposes but for a different objective. This approach connecting different sets of data collected years apart or referring to the memory enhanced past rather resembles the approach of transferred ogives to deal generally with unreliable demographic data from developing nations (Carrier and Farrag, 1959).

Just as we have to accept that "the past is a foreign country, they do things differently there" (Hartley, 1953) and that there are thus inevitably many gaps in the patterns of information required for watertight statements connecting the past with the present. This is even more so for any assumption that any such connectedness might apply to the future events and behaviour. For instance, a study of Dutch young adults leaving home (Billar and Liefbroen, 2007) could be of value for future projections if and only if the proportional hold of quasi-traditional norms could be quantified and in any case had remained the same as when this study was made. Any such projection would have to know the individual marketability of each young person for employment, the availability of housing in their natal neighbourhoods and whether they wanted to live there, the willingness of parents to provide financial backing for any moves out of the parental home. All such and many more factors are rather more individually based than can be based on national statistics; such studies as this are more in the nature of time-based history.

THE DOMINANCE OF RETROSPECTION

Probability is often if not usually a retrospective evaluation with the carrying forward of data which has already been collected and categorised. These research results are often given in percentages which suggest with the methodological authority carried by printed numbers and that certain behaviours are likely to reoccur in these proportions.

This exactness is often provided in medical research results for the assessment of risks (Jabara *et al.*, 2007) and for the successes of treatments (Honkonen *et al.*, 2007). These are in effect historical studies which may have little relationship to what may or may not happen in the future even accepting that their use for such predictions is a necessary if not inevitable part of quasi-traditional, alternative or scientific medical practice. This is not an unusual research situation since there is always a substantial time lapse between the time when the data was collected and when it is publicly available. For professional reasons researchers are inevitably not in a hurry to present the results of their work without delaying thought and consultation with their colleagues while keeping an eye on parallel research results. The gap between field work and publication if they are published at all is often five years unless the matters are of immediate public interest and are reactions to social and political interest. Scientists may delay publication of their results as they feel the need for additional clinical or experimental evidence. A classical example was Long's seven-year delay in publishing his use of ether as an anesthetic in order to be assured of his results (Long, 1849). Now-a-days the delay in publishing the results of social science research may be due to shortage of journal space, editorial policy, peer view processes and the ever growing numbers of researchers wanting to publish as a career necessity rather than as a public obligation.

It is not unreasonable to suggest that realistically for one reason or another relating to the behaviour and social factors involved, most results are out of date by the time they become available to the professional community.

Secondly, these research results relate not only to a predefined and thus restricted field of study as for example being connected to particular people in a particular part of India or the United States, so they can make no claim to wider applicability. There are no scientific reasons that can lead anyone to assume that there would be reduplication of initiating factors and results in other areas under different social and environmental conditions.

Since we have to accept that social science research has two time based handicaps, the nature of the way that so-called contemporary data is in practice out of date from the moment that it is recorded so that in terms of assessing future probabilities it has diminishing accuracy. Then there is the delay over writing up and completing a report and more particularly getting it published and we know that a high proportion of research is not completed or refused publication for reasons that have nothing to do with the academic quality of the work.

THE DOMINANCE OF CONTEMPORARY THOUGHT

Social scientists, however, well-trained in the requirements of professional detachment are dominated by the present into which they have been socialised and the plain reality of whatever they see and hear and record as coming from their contemporary social environment. This dominance of their contemporary surroundings may mean that they alter their understandings of the past to fit into modern needs which has occurred with the rewriting of Russian history so that it conformed to the political needs of the authoritarian Soviet system. It is an almost 'natural' attempt to make sense of the past in terms of what they interpret as lineal logic; contemporary thinking can obscure understandings of the past.

It has been suggested that historians cannot avoid making moral judgements (Fischer, 1970) on what has gone before whether it is in connection with Ruanda, Darfur, Nazi or Serbian forms of genocide. Social scientists do not set out to write history although indeed they dupe themselves into thinking that they are professionally trained mirrors of contemporary events.

It seems likely that they cannot avoid 'chronological snobbery' (Lewis, C.S., 1955:206) that present current thinking with its long recorded history of development must be superior to what has gone before because to think otherwise would be in part a denial of their own sense of achieved and perhaps even ascribed intellectual superiority.

In any analysis of proto-contemporary behaviour in which there is not only substantial social but cultural distance between the researchers and the researched, social scientists are faced with ready-to-hand personal interpretations provided subconsciously as much as consciously by their own cultures of which they assure themselves that they have a competent understanding.

The alternative of gaining a knowledge of the researched culture and how they think about the issues which have been recorded is an extremely difficult process. There is never an accumulation of wide enough data to make this even vaguely possible. The understandings and thoughts embedded in another culture are not likely to be any more uniform than those of the researchers' own societies. Thus the ideas of Bengalis and Bantus about witchcraft are going to vary with status, education, age, sex and intellectual capacity. So these social scientists interpret with the intellectual capacities provided by their own education and mental acuity. Few if any social scientists are going to state that they do not know enough to even attempt such an exercise in cross-cultural understandings so they fall back on their own culture bound interpretations.

Presentism often seems to merge into relativism which admits the real diversity in human understandings but such social scientists wish to get it evaluated in terms that imply or assume that that there can be some equality in the values used in such assessments. This leads immediately to the problem of what is the meaning of any abstract term used. Any use of the term 'equality' leads to difficulties in its application to societies outside the Western pattern of thinking, a substantive clash of values. It seems doubtful whether many other cultures accept the individual as having a persona which is divorced from his or her social roles. There is not only the difficulty of finding what are the relative values and explanations of people in other cultures whose views we attempt to obtain. Alternatively we write that the Balinese do not accept an individual as having any characteristics independent of their social positions. "The Western conception of the person as a bounded, unique, more or less integrated motivational and cognitive universe, a dynamic centre of awareness, emotion, judgement and action organized into a distinctive whole and set contrastively both against other such wholes and against a social and natural background is, however, incorrigible it may seem to us, a rather peculiar idea within the context of the world's cultures" (Geertz, 1975:48).

So this reverts to the problems of presentism as to what opinions and views are we going to attempt to detail and in relation to what? Most people give no thought to the reasons for their own behaviour however well developed their social system and thinking patterns may be. Their explanations would be provoked by the question or they reply that this is how they and their likes have always behaved as it is part of their traditions. In many cases such enquiries end up as the opinions of atypical elites as something approaching a Western lineal and logical one.

THE HIATUS OF PROBABILITY

The best situation for assessing future probabilities must be contemporary data and looking at its immediate implications for what might happen in this immediate future. As we have seen most data is in effect no more than recent history and it is this gap between then and now which is of significance.

There is the assumption that probability is a linear exercise and that it can be narrowly defined in such terms. However, any human behavioural action is affected by lateral events and it is these which dominate any attempt to connect even the recent past with contemporary probabilities. There are firstly a range of non-human events such as epidemics in a community as the effects on family life of AIDS in Uganda leaving many children in the care of ageing grandparents without resources who had anticipated being cared for in their own old age. A further example would be the effect of a smallpox epidemic on the Indians of north-western coastal America. This resulted in a dislocation of the social system such as the absence of marriage and remarriage partners thus lowering the fertility even further as there was now a shortage of women and the appropriate categories of people for working parties and ceremonies. As status positions were now more readily available there was an increase in competitive ceremonies with fewer taking part (Boyd, 1999).

Then there are the lateral effects of climate change with prolonged droughts in Australia and in Africa south of the Sahara which have forced change on many families. Suicide bombers have certainly affected social life in Iraq and the generalised effects of civil unrest in Zimbabwe, Pakistan and Palestine.

Then there are the lateral effects on individual and family life of accidents, bereavement and family troubles from economic change which are known to occur as part of the general background to human existence but which are not expected to happen here and now to individuals. In this time gap between when the present data were collected and there are inevitably accumulations of factors altering the circumstances in which the original data were collected assuming that it was accurate in the first place. It is surely unwise to assume that there are enough exactnesses in human behaviour to justify any assumption that history repeats itself.

11

The Problems of Communication

There are few problems in communicating on scientific matters as there are hard definitions and the problems are likely to be limited to degrees of ignorance and lack of attention to the required detail. Communication in whatever form it takes between people is a behavioural event over cultural, social and personal barriers made difficult by social distance factors and cultural and personal egotism. Everyone of these differentiating factors makes the assessment of future probabilities to be based on little that can be called exact.

There is firstly the basic fact of individual differences in their genetic make-up, their socialisation and current social environment. Even with identical twins who may have different social experiences, one person is communicating with another who is different. This can only be modified to a limited extent when people have been in a relationship for long periods and have grown up in a community whose behavioural traits are well known and widely observed. Even in this there are limitations from chance and uncertainty as there are always differences of interpretation over what has been said and what was meant.

The factor of social distance means that as this increases the possibilities of misunderstanding may increase proportionately. At the extreme boundaries of such differences are when those communicating are of different ages, sexes, cultures, education, intelligence and speak different natal languages, communication is not only difficult but often virtually impossible without serious misunderstandings. This must be a regular feature of social science research when the researchers and the researched have almost nothing in common except a short-term shared social environment and a shared but not well disguised need to take advantage of each other.

Whatever position one takes on the Sapir/Whorf hypothesis as to whether languages modifies behaviour or behaviour modifies languages, it would seem more likely that both occur at the same time. The basic factor must be that languages, while clearly binding in the sub-cultural environments, are the major barrier to effective communication and even more so when there is no help provided by accompanying understood body language and environmental clues.

There are thus the two parallel barriers to effective communication. Firstly, language and this means that once communicators go outside their own language and more particularly the linguistic code of their profession or community into another one which does not belong to their linguistic family, there are bound to be ongoing difficulties in understandings. There are problems over the translation of words that do not relate to materials and in grammatical forms which have no parallels to the major world languages which themselves may not easily interchange as is certainly the case in translations between Mandarin, Hindi, Arabic and English. An example would be the tonal sophistication of Cantonese which cannot be translated into French or French into Cantonese without substantial semantic losses.

Then there are the problems of cultural distinctions. The difficulties of communication between people of different cultures should not be seen as one of contrasts between the major societies of the Eastern and Western worlds and small peripheral ones in which only specialized social scientists are likely to be interested and which have very limited global significance. Examples would be the Dinka of the Sudan (Lienhardt, 1967), the Ganuku-Gama of New Guinea (Read, 1967), the Kwakuitl and Hopi American Indians (Postal, 1965). There are built-in communication difficulties between individuals in call cultures and at all social and intellectual levels.

Our interest should be in societies which are close to national developments and the main trends of social change which have not lost their specific psychological and social traditional patterns of thinking and behaving. An example would be the Taita of Kenya (Harris, 1978) living in a block of hills a few miles south of the main rail and road link between Mombasa and the capital Nairobi.

Even more specifically we have to be interested in the

difficulties of communication within the city boundaries of Banaras and Mumbai as well as the linguistic codes which differentiate doctors from lawyers as well as the Hindi speaking literary elite living in Delhi and the dialects which distinguish the French spoken in Paris from that spoken in the south and west of France.

The difficulties of effective communication have to be accepted as a constant problem in contemporary life and likely to be experienced by everyone, not just social scientists, who are communicating over relatively minor social distance differences within their own societies. It is not just a problem that comes up in communicating with people who look different to oneself and who are obviously cultural strangers to the local majority.

BIOLOGICAL DISCONNECTIONS

It seems a natural assumption that the processes and aims of communication are shared between people who are more or less equal if only in their wish to communicate with some rational equality. This is an illusion based on the stereotypes which we develop about perceptual averages as in fact few people conform to any such biological averages. In any population there are many who cannot hear adequately enough to recognise the changes in tone in which they are being addressed and few languages if any are independent of these slight changes in sound which have these important differentiating meanings.

Much communication depends on body language and in many societies there are large numbers with defective eyesight so that they would find it difficult to pick up these necessary clues to the meaning of what is being communicated. There are also many who have movement impairments which means that they cannot use any adequate range of body language to accompany their speech.

DEMOGRAPHIC DISCONNECTIONS

Again the demographic profile of any population shows that on average there may be little in common between the two people who are communicating as they are plainly different. There will be basic differences over age, sex, place of living, ethnicity, citizenship status, examinations passed and employment. In subsistence societies for example everyone may have the same characteristics of being married and farmers but that cannot mean that there are not just as wide variations in individual characteristics. The crudities of demographic classifications even if they were reliable may miss out all the subtleties of status differentiation around the functions of all such seemingly egalitarian communities.

THE PSYCHOLOGICAL AND SOCIAL BACKGROUND

While it is possible that an informant can provide information in a detached manner approximating to the requirements of 'hard' science, there is no reason to suppose that this is a common factor. Any information that is provided by an informant comes from a social and psychological environment of which in many cases we have no knowledge and which it might well be impossible to acquire.

We are perhaps able to accept that we ourselves have crises and moods that may affect how we see the situations we are examining and the ways that this may affect how we interpret data; we have our 'bad' days. It is more difficult to accept and allow for these types of differences affecting the provision of information by our informants. The straightforward anticipation that we should be told their ages does not allow for that fact that this is a question answered in a social environment which may make the raising or lowering of admitted age to be a social and psychological necessity.

There is no information coming from an informant that is not likely and indeed is most probably affected by the mental state of the provider and their social situation at that particular time. Information which is provided by an informant whether in a face to face interview or in filling in questionnaires come out of a particular behavioural situation in contact with an outsider or outside institution for a short period of time and then they return to the social and personal situation with which the social scientists have no contacts or influence. Two social and personal circles which overlap only when they are communicating.

Social scientists may be able to find a broadly correct interpretation of the ways in which a society may be working which their colleagues and some members of the researched community may accept as correct. However, the instability of the social and psychological environments from which this information comes, makes its most unwise to express such results in narrowed figures suggesting an accuracy which is just not possible in behavioural matters.

INTELLECTUAL DIFFERENCES

Without considering whether it is possible or not to measure intelligence within any society much less by methods that can do the same thing cross-culturally, any community and thus any sample of a population will contain people who are highly intelligent and those of very low mental capacity. This is independent of education and any ability to read and write.

Within one's own social environment it may be possible to spot the differences in these intellectual capacities because there are social clues which show this up. Outside this rather narrow social and professional circle, much less over cultural barriers it becomes much more difficult. Those who communicate may not know the correct way in which to communicate. The responses which these researchers and other communicators get are not due to stupidity but the inability of the speakers to say what they mean in linguistic codes of which they have only a limited knowledge and very little social experience.

It is safer to assume that both the Mishmi and Mumbai populations have much the same proportion of highly intelligent and low intellect men and women. This may have little to do with whatever education they may have had the good fortune to acquire. Since the majority of education is probably no more than primary, this probably means that what they are able to write will not reflect the complexities of the language which they speak. On average both parties communication may have knowledge of their own specialised vocabularies but not that of the person with whom they are communicating.

PROBLEMS OVER THE SOURCES OF DATA

Leaving aside any assumptions that social scientists can or cannot make accurate observations of what they see and experience, there remains the question as to the extent to which information from informants can be considered accurate enough on which to base probabilities. Can we accept that there is any shared accuracy between what is intended and said by informants and researchers.

Surely the desired accuracy in which both parties are on the same wavelength of communication is always going to be questionable apart from the plain fact of their individualities. The social scientists are collecting and recording information for their own purposes so why should informants share the interests of these outsiders rather than align themselves to their own social circle. Both sides are to some extent deceiving each other as to their real intentions even if they do actually understand what each is intending and saying. The receivers of information certainly assume good intentions on the part of their informants and this is no more than an act of social faith.

Even within a single culture or social environment there are likely to be variations in the ability to express themselves and it is often assumed that the researchers are likely to be relatively sophisticated in both intelligence and education. It is always an uncertain social environment in which both parties may well be operating with different intentions and abilities. It is clear that to base the assessment of probabilities on information provided by people unsupported by harder data is bound to cause doubts about any potential reliability.

LIMITS OF COMMUNICATING IN ANY LANGUAGE

Verbal communication is always assisted by the social environment in which it takes place and any learning of a second language is not accompanied by any tuition in the body language which parallels much of what is spoken. Even when a new language is learned by total immersion only a few of the necessary cues will be picked up. The situation is even worse when there are written communications and nothing is shared except marks on paper which have grammatical and dictionary significances of which the communicators may have limited awareness.

Demographic and social inequalities exist in every society and this is reflected in what is communicated and how it is done. It is likely that understandings are more frequent when two professionals are communicating about a finite issue in 'hard' science but not whenever there are more abstract issues involving interpretation. Communication is certainly aided by substantial professional training, shared backgrounds and the need to reach agreed understandings by negotiation. Even in this a traditional elder with limited literacy may be a more proficient communicator in a wider range of behavioural affairs than a social scientist.

Most societies if not gerontocratic in structure are likely to be overtly dominated by middle aged males. Thus there are built-in problems when the researchers seeking information are young adults or indeed women. This is made even more difficult when the language itself involves sexual and age discriminations. Some indeed may not wish to communicate because of personal circumstances which are too disturbing to relate to outsiders (Mayaram, 1996). Obvious or implied non-compliance should not be interpreted as stupidity or just hostility to the researcher.

The meanings of much communication can be inferred by body language and this is restricted in interviews and absent in the completion of questionnaires. Much of this is related to commonplace communications in everyday affairs. But once communication involves more complex matters with abstract meanings, information will be heavily soaked in cultural, ethical and personal understandings (Tanner, 1993).

It is always necessary for the researchers to ask themselves what is the purpose of this particular communication and who gets what out of its successful completion. More particularly the extent to which the information relates to their professional intentions.

THE IMPOSSIBILITY OF SHARING A LANGUAGE

Most communications are around commonplace situations and involve the use of restricted vocabularies. Talking about agricultural work practices may be relatively easy but discussing spirituality and political tensions is much more complex and difficult to interpret because what people think and what they can express are inevitably different. Key words and phrases have fans of meanings which will fluctuate in their uses.

The well-educated speakers of a Bantu language will have just as much difficulty in understanding a Nilotic language from the southern Sudan as a German or Japanese researcher; the fact that they are both African languages has no relevance except as a sentimental obstruction to understandings.

Even within a single language which communicators share there will be a mutual process of interpretation rather than any process of translation. The deeper the researchers penetrate into another culture and learn the language, the greater the possibility of misunderstandings as they go beyond the more material aspects of a culture. We are all subconsciously committed to our own personal and cultural understandings.

Once communication involves words which are abstract rather than clearly material it is likely that shared meanings are not even marginally aligned. A Western European researcher who is overtly secular in his thinking using the word 'God' will have monotheistic assumptions which will certainly not be shared by his Asian colleagues. According to the 1993 United Nations Conference on Human Rights 'female empowerment, perhaps the key concept of the conference has no meaning in Chinese without knowing which kind of power is being discussed—personal, political or physical' (Ankerl, 2000:xiv). Difficulties over the meaning of even the simplest of words is going to be commonplace at all levels of communication.

Many languages, dialects and linguistic codes have not been committed to writing and some have had only a century of such centralisations. Few have had any development of abstract scholarship as has been the case of Hindi and Bengali. Even in such works of scholarship the meanings of key words used by their distinguished authors will have changed over the years of their thinking.

Nor is there any reason to think that any language is superior or inferior to any other. Some of the Australian Aboriginal languages are incredibly complex in comparison to the major global languages and often grammatically different to that spoken by their immediate neighbours; sometimes these languages make English seem relatively impoverished.

THE CATEGORIES IN WHICH COMMUNICATION TAKES PLACE

Unlike law, medicine and inorganic chemistry, social scientists have no professional vocabulary of agreed definitions between those coming from different cultures and different schools of thought; whenever communication takes place there will be a clash of semantics. Contemporary communication is likely to involve if not different languages certainly different linguistic codes as most of us are not consciously aware that we talk in different ways to different categories of people who are demographically and socially different to ourselves, just as our informants are probably using a linguistic code which they only use for communicating with strangers.

Firstly, there is the language used by informants. There is no reason to suppose that in listening to a Baluchi, we are getting something approaching standard Baluchi. The natal speakers of a major language may not realise how fortunate they are in not having to learn different languages for different layers of the society in which they live. It is not just that everyone is personally varying how they speak their natal languages (Aarts and Aarts, 1982).

Members of subordinate subcultures or societies may learn different languages as a social necessity. A Tanzanian Roman Catholic priest learnt in succession his tribal language kiHangaza, then the national *lingua franca* kiSwahili, then English in his secondary school and then in the seminary Latin and finally French. A Ruandan bishop regarded French as his natal language. A Muria in India might well know Hindi and Urdu from military service as well as some English.

Thus it seems that informants whatever their natal language may have been, may be passing on information which has a confused semantic background which is likely to confuse the meanings of abstract matters. Informants are not passing on undiluted and to some extent natal language meanings.

Then there is the researchers' knowledge of the community or the field in which they are working and however much hard work is put into learning about this it will never be comparable to natal socialisation. The national researcher may have advantages in this but they are still internal expatriates although they can still get greater emotional access by assuming classificatory kinship roles such as brother's wife which had sacred connotations in that Indian society (Dua, 1979), but linguistically there are always problems. This inadequate knowledge will always give away the fact that they are outsiders. Their professionalism will always lead to some discrimination as in the use of Mandarin in which an average farmer or urban worker might know at the most some two thousand ideograms while the researcher would know more than ten thousand.

What is certain is that these researchers learning a second language have an understanding of grammar which the national does not need to know from their socialisation. This rather narrow learning approach may give little understanding of the fluidity of a language in its social context.

So for many there is no single linguistic environment in which they wish to use or are compelled to use by the particular environments in which they are working. One language in the home, another in school or while shopping and yet another talking to outsiders and government officials. A Goan researcher (Mascarenhas-Keyes, 1987) will have been receiving information in four languages, Portuguese, English, Konkani and kiSwahili. So we have polyphonic informants talking to social scientists who may not know so many languages.

Thirdly, there are the understandings which informants have of the person with whom they are communicating; the social framework within which information is being passed. What is their perception of the researcher such as their wealth, age, sex, status and political and social influence in that social environment.

Fourthly, the social environment in which the information is being passed from the informant to the researcher and *vice versa*. The formalism of a one to one interview, picked up in passing as they walk together and information collected in a group setting or when conversation is likely to be overheard. Indeed the information is likely to vary between chatting, being written down, photographed or recorded.

Finally, there are the languages or rather linguistic codes in which the researchers present their findings and conclusions to their professional colleagues or back in the vernacular so that it can be read by members of the communities from which the information was obtained in the first place. Thus there can be no simple equivalence between whatever the data may have been in reality is likely to be obscured by the varieties of language with which it is communicated.

THE IMPOSSIBILITY OF LOGICAL INTERPERSONAL COMMUNICATION

Communication is always a behavioural event and is thus unstable in all the factors involved. The exceptions may be the exclusive sentences of formal logic which even are formed in a particular language and the quantifications of 'hard' science.

In the situation of social science research it is always to some extent cross-cultural communication even when researchers are working undercover on some aspects of their own community or profession. Over these cultural boundaries there may be very basic difficulties in understanding what the others in communicating are trying to say or the framework of thinking in which they are operating. Marriage to a westerner has some connotations of singularity and permanency but this same word would not be interpreted in the same way by well-to-do Saudi Muslims nor by the Tanzanian Sukuma who have no less than eleven different types of marriage linguistically distinguished (Cory, 1953).

A Western social scientist or one trained within the Western framework of thinking would approach individual behaviour within a concept of autonomous individualism. This personalized self is seen as inviolate and of supreme value in and of itself; a particular incarnation of abstract humanity, a nomadic replica of general humanity (Dumont, 1970). On the other hand Indians have a concept of autonomous individualism but in order to be this they would see context and social relationships as a necessary precondition for behaviour; the ideal state of individualism can only be reached by dropping out to become a religious *saadhu* (Shweder and Bourne, 1992).

Such communications are attempts at connecting the undefined variables sent as undefined messages within undefined social environments. Thus there are three sets of varying and variable factors. The fact that the communication may be in writing or more specifically in print or broadcast from scripts creates a somewhat bogus suggestion of stability and indeed accuracy but which can still be interpreted in innumerable ways by receivers; indeed there may be little or no coincidence between what the communicators intend to send and what is thought to being passed by the receivers. There will always be a mixture of overt and covert factors in any communication and this behavioural mixture makes the use of communicated information an unstable basis for any formal assessment of probabilities; we now turn to the more formal problems of translation.

12

The Problems of Translation

In any communication there are translations of meaning between the communicators but in most situations this is an almost instantaneous process, a whole series of interpretations as the conversation, listening and viewing progresses. Once matters of importance are committed to writing and more specifically to print and it is thus provided for the understanding of others, then the processes of formal translation take place. This process may take place within a single language as when a religious text is produced in standard English or standard American as has occurred with the Christian Bible. It is when the translation is made between different languages and different cultures the problems of understanding then multiply.

Except when there are the informalities of personal letters which in many cases are not meant for keeping, translations are made of documents which have been written formally. This is often the result of prolonged scholarship, in which there is repeated redrafting at different institutional levels which has been worked over and produced by committees. They are thus usually group productions and the work of combined intellects.

Obviously all research depends upon the transmission of information through language supported by body language and social supports. Except for a limited range of material matters; talking about a cup or a knife does not usually involve cultural problems of interpretation. Almost everything in communication involves symbolism. This means that it requires interpretation by the receiver which may or may not have ideas that coincide with what the transmitter intended.

Since language started with the sounds of interpersonal communication, it is only recently that it has become detached from this with writing. So language to pass a message and for it to be interpreted in ways that are usually understood by the receivers, is always accompanied by sight, body language and intonations. In its social uses language has none of the simplicity of numerals which are themselves symbols for something else.

So in all research involving the use of language whether in personalised or impersonal print is threaded with serious difficulties over what the producer intended and what the receivers interpret as the intended meanings. These are particularly difficult when there are language differences and when language is used for quantitative analyses.

We can presuppose that when there are translations from one language into another there will always be difficulties. In a study of the religious involvements of nurses in Taiwan (Yang, 2006) a Chinese researcher took the Wolmer Psycho Matrix Spirituality Inventory (Wolmer, 2001) translating forty nine items in Mandarin which was back tested by a panel of five professional bilinguals. It seems highly unlikely that words such as the term 'divinity' as used by a Western professional is going to have the same meaning for these nurses of whom only a small minority had had university education and who may not have had any course on English related spirituality.

There are many such examples in which translation is not so much between two languages but between the core values of two widely different long established cultures using their languages for symbolic purposes. Other than some material coincidences, surely we have to assume that the American psychologist constructing such an inventory after long clinical experience in that culture will have little in common with Chinese nurses socialised in their thinking in a culture antedating the American one by several millennia. It is widely accepted that it is virtually impossible to translate abstract words into and out of Mandarin Chinese and this is the natal language of some one billion people.

There was this same difficulty in the work of a Tanzanian Jesuit translating the Spiritual Exercises of Saint Ignatius into kiSwahili (Mkenda, 2005) the national language of Tanzania and the common language of the East African coast from Somalia to Maputo. He had the same difficulty in having to explain at some length the use of certain words for which there were no comparable ones in kiSwahili, a composite language involving Bantu and Arab cultural heritages with a long literary history written in Arabic script.

Bantu languages from South Africa to Kenya have the same grammatical structures so that translation and understanding between them may not be all that difficult. These different tribal languages have the same sounding word for God which may or may not mean that they have the same general understandings of Divinity. However, it is difficult to even hypothesise that Saint Ignatius as a Spaniard writing in Latin can have had the same understandings about God as modern Bantu intellectuals and subsistence farmers. Even between languages in the same linguistic group such as the European Romance ones, there will be difficulties over translating terms which have had independent cultural developments.

There are also problems within a language when it covers a large area and is spoken by large populations so that there are dialectical differences between northern and southern China. The semantics of professionals will always be different to that of more practical people. In missionary work in China the Protestants tended to learn the Mandarin dialect used by the low ranking people at whom they were aiming their Evangelism. The Jesuits on the other hand learnt the Mandarin of the educated power-holders. The result was that the Protestant missionaries assumed the low status associated with the linguistic code which they had learnt to speak.

Socialisation must always mean the partial confinement of thinking patterns to what their language provides. If the Kenya Kamba have no indefinite future tense in their language, this does not mean that they have no understanding of the undefined future but that they will have difficulties in discussing such abstract concepts as the Second Coming in Christian thought; it would mean long circuitous explanations. Just as in Meru it is not possible to state that they believe in God as that implies the possibility of non-belief which they do not consider to be rational.

The greatest of all difficulties in translation lies in matters for which there is no provision at all in the other language. In Japanese there are wide ranging differences in the ways that men and women speak (Suzuki, 1978). Western thinking and practices give a special isolating status to 'I' but in Japanese its use is always related to the relationship in which it is used (Smith, R.J., 1983). It would seem that all sentences in Japanese are relational (Kondo, 1990:31). So to translate this into English which has no such divisions means that the English translation is missing the deeply felt meanings implicit in the Japanese. Similarly Burmese has status reflecting pronouns, an important aspect of everyday relationships for which there is no provision in English. We can conclude that English has poor resources in which to express many other languages.

The Roman alphabet has twenty-six characters plus a few special accenting signs which provides some languages with many combinations which have to be individually interpreted in social situations perhaps a particularly Western difficulty. Chinese on the other hand has no alphabet but over forty thousand different ideograms which restricts literacy to feats of memory and specialised needs.

There are also difficulties because some languages do not have capital letters as in Arabic and Mandarin. There is an enormous differences between describing Jesus Christ as the Son of God or as the son of God which is clear in English and cannot be shown in speaking. This is a major theological issue in discussion between Christian and Muslim theologians (Tanner, 1979) when they go beyond speech into written agreements.

In the choice of words to mirror the ideas of other cultures there are moral choices in what words are used in translations. Many tribal societies have complex metaphysical ideas which are translated as 'magic' with their professionals described as 'witchdoctors'. If the translation was done in reverse for turning the Christian liturgical handbooks into Mandarin would Christians feel that the Roman Catholic belief that the ceremony of the Mass creates the presence of Christ in that church would be properly described as 'magic'? By this choice of words the whole complex understandings within a culture may be relegated to the status of overall cultural inferiority. Many words have hostile meanings which make reasonable understandings difficult particularly when there are numbers of alternative words which can be used (Tanner, 1993).

THE FIXING OF INFORMATION IN WRITING

Except when there is verbal translation and there are no transcriptions of what has been said, the words once spoken are lost. Once something is recorded in writing and even more particularly in print, there are major built-in problems. Communication is essentially a behavioural event and as such will always have nothing in it which cannot be the subject of change. This rigidity and its restrictions on change occurs almost from the moment that anything has been recorded in writing.

Writing is a unidimensional medium affecting the intellect through the eyes only. It is no longer a behavioural event affecting those involved through their eyes, ears, nose and mouth. It is a limiting medium turning an enormous range of social information into a series of static symbols which may have no compulsory or defined meanings. These symbols can be interpreted in any way that the reader likes from something which is incomprehensible for cognitive reasons to something unknown or unknowable reasons. These may include elevations of the spirit which may have nothing to do with the highest standards of intellectualism which can be attributed to that language. Writing is socially dead except in whatever ways the individual can bring it to life in their minds. In some cases religious writings have a value which comes to those who possess such documents which they cannot or do not wish to read. Much Chinese and Japanese religious writings are purchased at shrines and then have to be translated for them by experts. For most of the time these printed religious writings have a parallel significance to protective amulets.

Much of the documents which have to be translated involve dominant international languages in which social scientists have to publish if they wish to attain international recognition and in this English leads. In this respect little acclaim can be achieved by publishing in Russian, Mandarin or Arabic which in their own areas have large readerships. So much translation fixes information in English, the second languages of many who wish their information to be read widely.

TRANSLATION BY ELITE BILINGUALS

Translation in one form or another is constantly occurring in all social communicating because of the social and intellectual inequalities between communicators and those with whom they are trying to communicate. Since most communication is verbal, this process of translation is more or less instantaneous in which success in understanding is assumed to have occurred whether or not this is a social reality; while listening communicators watch the faces of their respondents.

Most verbal communication is between people of limited or limiting education who have no particular interest in linguistic niceties. Even among populations that have a high proportion of people classed as literate, this should be assessed in the UNESCO's definition of literacy as the ability to receive and send a simple message.

We have to remember that most literate people would prefer to talk than read which is a time consuming and laborious process and to write is even more so as writing provides few of the social benefits which come from conversation. So writing is a very small proportion of what is being communicated in even the most literate of societies.

Translation in any formal sense involves reading documents in one language and transposing it in writing into another which is a slow and intellectually taxing process. The only exception to this would be the professional translators at international conferences and legislatures who manage to provide verbal translations of what is being said while listening with the other half of their brains to what is being said in another language.

These documents which are seen as valuable data by social scientists and which have to be translated have been formally written and not in the literary style which would occur in verbal communications. They are the work of professionals and make no pretence to be written in the more ordinary forms of language. Even without the need for translation, speakers of that language would often require a knowledge of specialist vocabularies to understand what has been written since documents which are considered to be important are written in special linguistic codes common enough in law, philosophy and theology which are of particular interest to social scientists which are ignored as incomprehensible by the commonality of mankind.

Translation from one language to another rather more than the simplifying of professional linguistic codes within a single language, is usually the work of bilingual professionals. The formality of thought which goes into translation is a recognition of the importance which is attributed to what is being translated.

The more important the document, the more specialised the language used and the number of people involved. The translation of the Christian Bible into kiSwahili took years of committee work involving specialised bilingual Christians and natal speakers of English and kiSwahili. The result has been a literary production which most people literate in that language would find difficult to read.

In the need for accuracy there is not only the professional translator but the time involved in trying to work out equivalences for abstract terms which would seem to have no equivalences in the second language. The spoken word can always have emotional consequences and it seems unlikely that the translation of the Japanese 'haiku' poems and a parallel in the brief verses in Sukuma dance group songs can have any emotional equivalent in their English translations.

These formalities and specialisations probably mean that there is a filtering out of everyday realities which might have some significance for more ordinary people. An interesting aspect of translation is that bilinguals probably have a better grammatical knowledge of the second language than they have of their own natal tongue for which they often have to use a dictionary for exact meanings.

THE DIFFICULTIES OVER WHAT LANGUAGE IS BEING USED

No known contemporary community has its members using a single language or linguistic code throughout their everyday lives. Even historically this may have been rare with only the long isolation of the inhabitants of Easter Island being an example of the continuing use of a possibly unchanged language free from external influences. The distribution of blood groupings shows that there has always been social contacts between widely distributed populations.

Even the widespread use of an official language does not involve its use outside official processes and international business needs but there is little equivalence in the exchange uses of any language. Many thousands of Chinese and Japanese speak and read high standard English but the numbers of Westerners having an equivalent knowledge of Mandarin must be numbered in the low hundreds. With the disappearance of colonial occupations and the widespread restrictions on missionary activities, the numbers of Westerners with a colloquial understanding of African and Asian languages must have diminished.

The imposition of an official language in many states is a political measure attempting to unify a country in which most of the inhabitants have nothing in common and is a bureaucratic necessity. Mumbai, Kampala and Berlin will each have dozens of languages in current use and the translations of these vernaculars in the popular press will often be crude approximations of what originally may have been said in the street. In a Kampala housing estate (Parkin, 1971) English was used to show status, kiSwahili to show companionship, tribal languages to show exclusiveness and Luganda to show deference to the reality of local political dominances. None of these linguistic differences would involve the literary effort of formal translation and translators.

So whatever is written and translated will apply more specifically to certain people in certain social environments. We cannot assume that what is recorded in writing will have any day-to-day applications. In terms of social science analysis much written material might rather more be described as codified inaccuracies and as such is providing valuable behavioural data of questionable accuracy rather than representing any social accuracies.

Most written translations are underlining some social exclusivities rather than any generalities of communication. The documents of any importance will show in their translations the preferences of the specialist group which may have worked together for years.

The language in which data is recorded and presented in writing is rarely the language in which the data was originally expressed; it goes through a series of translations. Firstly, the data is interpreted into the language of the researchers as it is put into writing followed by further translations as it is put into the professional language for final presentation; a process of linguistic discontinuities. Many ideas may have been semantically dominated out of consideration because of the mind-set created by the socialisation of the researchers (Asad, 1986).

Most data is verbally communicated to researchers and putting it into print will appear to systematize the thinking of people who are essentially if not predominately non-literate at least at the intellectual level of what is being talked about and recorded (Douglas, 1966:91). The intricacies of their lives predominantly spent in primary groups is reflected in the complexities of their languages. Literacy almost inevitably changes this into crude simplicities.

We must conclude that there are destabilising factors in writing and translating into languages in which those involved have not been socialised from childhood so that there is the very real possibility of inaccuracy. "The telling (of the story in this novel) has not been easy. One has to convey in a language that is not one's own the spirit that is one's own. One has to consider the various shades or omissions of a certain thought-movement that looks maltreated in an alien language. I use the word 'alien' yet English is not really an alien language to us. It is the language of our intellectual make-up like Sanskrit or Persian was before—but not our emotional make-up. We are all instinctively bilingual, many of us writing in our own language and in English. We cannot write like the English. We should not. We can only write as Indians" (Rao, 1938).

We should also conclude that translation and the general consideration of written texts are doubtful sources for accurate data with Ricoeur's conclusion about the meaningfulness of any text that there is only the beginning of a dialectic of guessing and validation (Ricoeur, 1971). Thus it would seem that written documents involving translations may be an uncertain basis on which to assess and to use for the creation of probabilities.

13

The Dominance of Applied Social Science Research

It is necessary to remember that while educationalists and politicians see education as a right to which all people are entitled, the reality is that education particularly in the developing world is always seen as a way out of subsistence poverty and not as the way to wider intellectual understandings. Nevertheless as the proportionate number of educated persons increase in any society the qualifications for employment continue to rise and such higher requirements become necessary to lower down the employment scale. Whereas in the immediate post-War years primary education in East Africa would be adequate for clerical employment by the time of political independence secondary school qualifications became necessary and this rise in what is necessary for employment has continued to rise while there has not been any corresponding growth in the job market matching that of the population. In Uganda at the time of Independence the national University was producing twenty sociology graduates per year and yet the Manpower Survey estimated that in next twenty years there would be foreseeable employment for only two people with such qualifications. However much we may feel that education and the gaining of professional qualifications in the social sciences is part of any planning for the betterment of society it is in this situation that we have to look at what research opportunities there are likely to be in any society. How social scientists are likely to view and use such opportunities as exist are likely to be important factors in what data is obtained and how it is used. It is prudent in this context to remember the English saying that whoever pays the piper calls the tune; social scientists are as subject to market opportunities and restrictions as builders and cattle herders.

THE NECESSARY FINANCIAL SUPPORT FOR RESEARCH

Research is costly. The only exceptions to this are situations in which the social scientists are paying their research expenses out of their own private money or they are researching some aspect of their current work as doctors, teachers, social workers and librarians can do so without any call on their employers or outside agencies for support. In these situations much valuable work can be done covertly or overtly as such employees have long-term access to data and particular insights which may be only partially changed by the biases built into their roles. It is common enough for employers to ask some interested and qualified employee to look into a problem and provide their conclusions. When compulsory stock reduction was introduced in Sukumaland prior to Independence the administration was surprised that there were no hostile reactions to this required 10 per cent annual reduction in number of cattle, sheep and goats. An anthropologically qualified junior administrator was asked to investigate this; he found that stock holders were selling, giving in bride-wealth or eating more than this required 10 per cent destocking.

It is likely that this cost-free research or research paid for by job-specifications of employees is extremely common but with the restriction that such results are not publicly available. Major business organisations, educational institutions and government departments must have their files full of such confidential internal research and indeed many have their own departments who have just this research function. It is felt that it is worth the expense to have such internal research specialists with much of their know-how already paid for by the conditions of their employment. However, this expense may be justified in the developed world but not so much in developing societies such as sub-Saharan Africa in which the market may be large but the amount of money available as incentives is severely limited.

An enormous range of social science research is carried out internally and kept confidential by the conditions of employment because in the case of non-government institutions such information might be of value to rival institutions who might profit from using it for their own advantage. Estimates of consumer demand for any product whether tobacco, central heating, clothing and care of the growing numbers of elderly in Western societies,

Japan and China must always be the subject of continuing internal social science research projects which are aimed at increasing profits or reducing losses.

It would seem that only institutions of higher education would feel that the making available to the public of all research information which they have sponsored or passed for high degrees is an ethical requirement. Even this use is always restricted by copyright laws and in some cases universities have formed business corporations so that they can profit corporately from what has been discovered from the research that they have financed.

Financial support for research covers two areas. Firstly, the topic itself may require money in order to get access. Records and behavioural data have to be recorded so there are office expenses, computer use for access to journals may have to be paid for and in the larger projects there may have to be secretarial help.

Field assistants and interpreters and translators as well as principal informants have to be paid or at least given some material encouragement as they may often think with some justification that the researchers are better off than themselves.

Then the researchers themselves have to be paid in proportion to their professional expertise and personal adaptability; a married older researcher is more expensive to put into and keep in research work than a less qualified younger one. Younger post-graduates may work on research projects below what might be called national minimum wages because they need research success as a necessity for career advancement. If an employer is not covering the research expenses it is a relatively harsh and highly competitive environment in which the aspiring social scientists start their hopes for research support. In addition university appointments in the social sciences are few and far between.

Whoever is employed as a researcher have to be transported to where they are going to work, housed and fed, visa applications have to be made if they are non-nationals, insurance against ill-health and there may be preparatory work to cover if problems have to be read up prior to the start of any active research.

THE FORMS OF FINANCIAL SUPPORT FOR SOCIAL SCIENCE RESEARCH

Research even if done internally has to be paid for but if done externally then sources of support have to be found. This support is not so much limited in amounts available as perhaps overwhelmed by the numbers of potential researchers wanting money to do work which they feel is worthwhile and to which they are personally committed. An American foundation which advertised for applications to do research on the connection between spirituality, religion, health and well-being had over four hundred applications with proposed research programmes attached. One suspects that every source of research funding has thousands of applications annually which have to be reduced to fit their financial limitations.

Research in the social sciences takes two forms. Projects which have no particular relationship to any foreseeable or immediate human need as far as is known to contemporary thinkers and which perhaps does no more than contribute to the accumulating knowledge of human behaviour. University gazettes in countries with well established funding and research reputations fund work by their better students for higher degrees which will enhance the institutions reputations for high quality scholarship. Examples would be research into Australian Aborigine languages which are dying out, the relationship between Islamic thinking and architecture and prison policies and their colonial precedents. These have no connections with the assessment of active probabilities for funding.

Western universities are better able to support such seemingly 'useless' research in terms of contemporary needs because they have their own funds accumulated from benefactors, their own investments and property, the fees from wealthier students and government subventions.

Similarly the major funding foundations are often prepared to subsidize such seeking for knowledge research but they will be less likely to do so since they will feel the need to provide parallel funding for research into contemporary human problems such as the social consequences in sub-Saharan Africa of the HIV epidemic or the influence of advertising on smoking in Third World countries and related disease ratios.

We must conclude that support for research is more likely to be provided by foundations and governments if the projects are relatable to matters of contemporary public concern even though there may be no more than possible rather than immediate connections.

Overall the quantity of research if not done by Westerners is paid for by Western institutions which have the surplus funds available for purposes which have no immediate relevancy to contemporary problems. Such topics are closely connected to the personal career advancement of a limited number of post-graduate applicants. However, this will always be limited by the distributors of funding being aware of contemporary social needs so that so-called applied research will directly or indirectly predominate in successful applications.

IMMEDIATE NEEDS AND RESEARCH IN DEVELOPING COUNTRIES

The position is different in developing countries in which there are no funds available for research which might augment the stock of general knowledge as well as a general feeling that such research would be a luxury which limited national finances should not allow.

More particularly elite power-holding opinion thinks that social scientists who have been sponsored and indeed had their early education paid for by their own country, should repay this debt by working for their own nation rather than becoming part of a brain-drain emigration.

The position on the ground is different. First university salaries are low and so university employees either have to moon-light in other work to pay their living expenses or seek applied work which their own governments or aid organisations are prepared to subsidize research related to their immediate needs.

But there are snags to this involvement. Social scientists do not have much political power and their use in such research may be largely decorative for decisions which have already been made. The politicians and civil servants involved are living in an uncertain social and political environment and thus had little or no interest in the results of much research which is largely decorative.

Researchers who take on applied work are in practice often devoted to lessening the impact of decisions which have already been made to benefit other people. They have to balance the concrete situation of personally needing the money, the comparative needs of 'us' the researchers and their employers and 'them' who are being researched. Fahim in his work on the effects of the flooding on relocated Nubians when the Nasser high dam was constructed (Fahim, 1979) perhaps not entirely because he was paid by the authorities, found it hard to reconcile their continued complaints and unwillingness to cultivate part of the land provided for them with the amounts of money and effort put into meeting their needs in a country with serious financial problems. At the same time he was sympathetic to the fact that their whole lives had been seriously disrupted.

So social scientists may seek applied work to augment their salaries and at the same time this may lead to the neglect of the work which related to their official university positions. The solution to the ambiguity of their positions as employees probably lies in how necessary it is for such researchers to get and retain paying short-term contracts from their governments or outsider agencies.

As receivers of money from organisations which they cannot control and over which they have little influence they are to all intents and purposes employees. There is the illusion of academic freedom which probably does not amount to much when these researchers are over-dependent on such contracts for survival. There are public and private codes of conduct which do not have in new, unsettled or dictatorially dominated nations any built-in institutional support. Since these researchers have accepted this funding for work which they may be ordered to do, they are no longer in any position to question the stated intent of their employers since they are employees and even their reports are the property of their employers.

THE SOCIAL SCIENCE UNDERSTANDINGS OF APPLIED WORK

Civil servants and their political masters like to be provided with facts in a form which they can appreciate and which they assume to have some accuracy in relation to which the researchers have applied themselves. It is perhaps something of a political dogma that any conclusion backed by printed statistics has a value quite independent of the possible accuracy or inaccuracy of the data on which these figures have been based.

So a report on housing which states numerically what the

researchers have found to be the occupancy rates and their demographic characteristics have provided information in a form which civil servants consider to be appropriate for accuracy. There is also the factor that they may not pay any attention to such conclusions because they have other more urgent priorities. If such a report states that occupancy is highly fluid and at any one time it is not known how many and who lives in any house or apartment as well as the fact that whatever details have been collected they are now out of date because of the time gap between fieldwork and reporting, it is even less likely to be acted on. Thus quantitative research may well be self-defeating as a means of influencing power-holders.

If on the other hand social science researchers report that in their opinions as a result of close and prolonged contacts with the people they are researching they feel that there is a trend towards certain types of change, then the receivers are given the same uncertain type of information which the politicians get anyway from their own contacts.

A study of how crime prevention might be integrated into ordinary living produced a theoretical model which involved situational characteristics, crime and disorder, fear of crime, physical activities which were themselves moderated by psychological, demographic, environmental and other factors (Loukaitou-Sideris, A. & Eck, 2007). Such a published study showed the impossibility of the social sciences producing anything more than speculative probabilities for which the factors potential involved were listed as if they could be estimated from such data.

It is thus often questionable whether the expense and effort of collecting data for quantification and the resulting conclusions can ever be applied to a mass of people in the constant ferment of inevitable inter-personal change in the hope that it might influence their behaviour in the desired direction always has serious drawbacks. It fails to recognise that whatever the numbers involved whether or not change can be organised or pushed in the desired direction, depends on those individuals making decisions in situations which are now very different from when the research was carried out (Yeo *et al.*, 2007).

It is perhaps rare for social scientists to criticize their own work (Thumboo *et al.*, 2003) rather than this to be done by others. Apart from the conclusions that there were economic and ethnic differences between Chinese, Indian and Malaysian populations and their self-assessed quality of life which probably did not require the work of nine authors. They also drew attention to the limitations imposed by environmental categorization, the use of English for all interviews, multiple factors and the unwillingness of quite a number to provide personal details. The culmination of these criticisms applicable to many other pieces of applied research must stress the cumulative effect of chance factors modifying the statistical calculations made through multiple linear regression models of adjusted influence.

The conclusions must be that in applied research we have to be suspicious not only of quantitatively expressed data but of the social, economic and political pressures on the social scientists doing such work. Overall it is rarely if ever possible to verify the accuracy and consistency of replies to questionnaires and interviews and more particularly of official records. In Hong Kong there are police records of road crashes and medical data of hospital treatments. It was found that only 58 per cent of road accidents resulting in hospital treatments had been recorded by the police and in particular there was a one-third under-reporting of accidents to children and cyclists (Loo and Tsi, 2007). Applied research resulting in quantitative data is a suspect source of information on which to base probability assessments.

Part–B
Chance affecting the Nature and Outcomes of Research

14

Chance and its Predominance in Behaviour

Social science bases itself on the necessities of logic in how social scientists undertake research and how they present their results. This professional need does not recognise the fact that human behaviour does not usually base itself on linear thinking although it may primarily present itself in such overt ways and in retrospective explanations and understandings. Human behaviour is usually based on the covert or overt use of lateral factors of which linear thinking may be just one. The inconsistencies in human behaviour from one day to the next and in what they decide to do occurs because of variations in the framing of what they are thinking of doing, contingencies and outcomes and the characteristic non-linealities of values and decision weighting (Tversky and Kahneman, 1982). No one knows enough about the backgrounds to the matters on which they make daily choices to be sure than they are logical and the predominating factor in this inability must be the inevitability of chance affecting all human behaviour including the presumed realities of social science research. A soldier puliing another out of a burning tank remarked latter that it seemed to be the right thing to do at the time.

THE DEFINITIONS OF CHANCE

The Oxford English Dictionary defines 'chance' in four ways; entirely accidental events which happen out of the blue, an event or events which one expects to occur and which one comes across within the circle of the 'to be expected', and an occurrence which one comes across by accident, the unexpected and meeting someone by accident.

A scientist (Austin, 1977:78) divides chance into four

categories. Chance happenings, 'blind luck' in which nothing is directly attributable to the person involved so that no personality traits are needed. Secondly, good luck as the result of general exploratory behaviour; the Kettering Principle that chance favours those in motion and events are brought together to form 'happy accidents' when the researchers apply their energies in activities which are typically non-specific; curiosity about many things, persistence, willingness to experiment and to explore. Kettering, an engineer himself wrote "keep on going and the chances are that you will stumble on something, perhaps when you are least expecting it. I have never heard of anyone stumbling on something sitting down" (Kettering, 1977:72).

Thirdly, the Pasteur Principle which is generally accepted by scientists as part of their explanations as to how they made their own distinctive discoveries. Chance favours the prepared mind; some special receptivity coming from past experience permits the researcher to discern a new fact or to perceive ideas in a new relationship. A background of knowledge based on the abilities to observe, remember and quickly form new associations.

Finally, the Disraeli Principle that chance favours individualised action and that fortuitous events occur when individuals behave in ways that are highly distinctive; distinctive hobbies, personal life styles and activities that are far removed from the area of expected discovery.

It would seem that chance is either pacific in which something happens to individuals with which they have no ascertainable connection and chance which occurs to the individual who by being active creates the opportunities for something to happen when looking along a line of books in a library but unrelated to any deliberate intention. Chance has to be assessed against the hope of humans and indeed researchers that orderliness is the hoped for characteristic of all behaviour.

CHANCE AND THE HOPE OF ORDERLINESS

All social groupings aim to achieve orderliness in their personal lives and as far as possible in their neighbourhood relationships. They do achieve a degree of stability in their current lives and attribute a higher proportion of this to their traditional or familiar ways of behaving. In the developed world which has achieved some bureaucratic stability and efficient systems of social welfare, the people anticipate a reasonable proportion of the misfortunes which might happen to them; they know that they and their nearest and dearest will die and that there are going to be illnesses and prolonged old age which are mainly coped with by these institutions rather than by any personal and family efforts. Disasters are read about in papers and are not thought to have any immediate significance to their lives; as to how and when they occur is not so much a matter of probability as chance and the political activities surrounding them.

But this awareness of orderliness is a relatively modern way of thinking about the social environment in which only a minority of the world's population currently live. This assumption that social life can be made stable seems to be a combination of factors. Firstly, the results of the European Enlightenment which aimed to show that the physical and social world was subject to laws and after Comte's positivism that human behaviour would be as subject to and potentially controllable as any organic or inorganic matter. This became the basis of political and personal optimism that misfortunes would eventually be solved by science and political activism as had been the case with many mass diseases. It is only now that such thinking is less optimistic since many scientific findings have had only short-term benefits and have left an enlarging residue of even greater number of unsolved problems.

The fact that certain Western nations within the freedom provided by democracy and capitalism have achieved without the largely futile dominations of autocratic political regimes whether Fascist, Communist or just plainly personal or military dictatorships, high levels of reasonable living for the majority of their populations. This blanket of achievable well-being has set the pattern for private and personal ideas and ambitions which have gone far wider than what might have been achieved in the past and could be maintained in contemporary social environments.

Let us look first at the newness of any reasonable stability rather than having life dominated by chance disasters. What is known of the historical past is overburdened with details of the lives of the well-to-do and powerful who either left records or had their activities recorded by church and state; little what is known about the majority of these populations.

Some details are known of pre-Revolutionary France and the conditions there which only improved in the last half of the nineteenth century (Robb, 2007:80-5). In 1789 the towns and parishes of France were invited by the predecessor of the national parliament to list their grievances and sixty thousand of these records survive. "The desire of most people was not to have their rights enshrined in a glorious constitution. They wanted freedom from poor soil and bad weather, from gales, hailstorms, fire and flood, from wolves, cold and famine." These details show that keeping just alive was the preoccupation of these people and that they were in effect at the perpetual mercy of chance disasters.

To what extent is majority of the modern world's inhabitants marginally better off than the majority of the French in the late eighteenth century since the majority are subsistence farmers, seasonal and daily workers or low paid factory workers. In addition there are still continuing political instabilities which have made millions into refugees in the Sudan, Afghanistan, Darfur, Ruanda, Georgia, Serbia and Pakistan and made others in Zimbabwe dependent on international aid. In some situations as in Somalia it is not even possible to provide aid because of unlimited violence. It is a horrendous record of wide-ranging political instabilities creating human suffering.

There are still disasters over which humans have no control such as hurricanes in southern United States and Myanmar, tsunami flooding from sub-oceanic earthquakes, earthquakes in China and Pakistan, mud slides in Peru and flooding in Bangladesh as well as a ten-year drought in parts of Australia. The probability assessments of social scientists have to be based on the chance occurrences of massive natural or human created disasters.

The hand to mouth existence of most of mankind is related to the annual cycle of farming in which there is adequate food for the months following harvesting and then a progressive decline in quantity and quality until the next harvest. It is estimated that the Gogo in central Tanzania will have at best one year of famine in every five years. Most subsistence societies have traditional systems by which individuals do their best to create networks of reciprocity in good years such as the Sukuma system of loaning out cattle surplus to domestic needs to people in other areas. This way of insuring against chance misfortune has been disrupted by population growth and internal migration. It is not surprising that some languages such as the Kenyan Kamba only have a future tense to cover their immediate futures and do not have the indefinite future one which is available in English. For the urban unskilled the future is even shorter and more uncertain and the future for which they have some resources may be not as long as a week. Urban standards of living may be lower than rural ones and malnutrition common in the socially 'septic' fringes round many rapidly expanding towns. The necessary facilities for basic living have not been provided by local authorities which have been overwhelmed by the flood of incoming migrants in Mumbai, Lima and Accra. In such situations it is not difficult to anticipate crime and riots of dissatisfaction fuelled by persistent political illusions that these conditions can be changed.

We have seen that in the past that whole populations have been at the mercy of chance beyond those that they would have expected in the natural course of events; disease, broken marriages, abortions, the failure of rain on their fields and accidents with poisonous snakes and rabid dogs. It is not surprising that they spend a considerable element of their rational activities and non-rational, not irrational, assumptions in attempting to anticipate and control future chance events.

There has been little change in this preoccupation and the expanding cities of developing societies have large number of quasi-traditional diviners and controllers or explainers of the unexpected (Gore, 1998). Even in 1973 it was estimated (Harrison, 1974) that there were over fifteen thousand traditional 'medicine' men in Lagos with a population of two-thirds of a million. In Dar es Salaam the capital of Tanzania it has been estimated that in any one day these quasi-traditional men and women are treating more sufferers than all the official and non-governmental agencies put together. Delhi is estimated currently to have some forty thousand 'fringe' providers of help for self-diagnosed miseries.

The many chance events which have made individuals psychosomatically or physiologically ill, whatever their pragmatic causes since being hit by a car or losing one's job are considered undeserved realities. They are felt to have been caused by personal or created for malevolence of neighbours, fellow employees, relatives assisted by witches and wizards over employment, well-being, the dislike of ancestors for their own or their dead relatives misbehaviour, the jealousy of aborted fetuses and the inexplicable waywardness of free-standing spirits and minor 'gods' and the indifference of the 'great Gods'.

While the elite may believe in the inevitability of positivism for the fulfilment of their social, economic and political hopes but this has failed to enter the thinking of the greater majority who soon forget how the great leaps of science had benefited their predecessors. They have and remained at the mercy of chance for which they have developed their own rationalisations. While they certainly applied logic to the range of limitable and definable physical objects, most had parallel systems of restraining the metaphysical.

It does not mean that many people have accepted any range of cause and effect beyond what their traditional understandings have ensured for their survival. They still consider from their own experiences and what they see going on around them that chance events will continue to be the most likely disturbers and preventers of the hoped for regularities in their lives.

These adaptable and adapting systems may well have coped with the pervasive nature of the chance events which would have occurred in any case in their lives. Such occasions have increased enormously as a result of ongoing and rapid social change bringing together large number of people in tertiary 'touch and go' relationship and the absence of any understandable social relationship between workers and their work.

In practice through the media it is repeatedly brought home to them that they are likely to be affected now by even more well-publicised chance events than remain in their folk memories over which they can have no possibility of controlling. Of course pragmatists can always explain that these events have happened for explicable reasons both tsunami tidal waves, suicide bombers, diseases spread by tourists and the high rates of AIDS among long distance lorry drivers in India and collapsed buildings. The shared component is always chance.

Research shows that in many so-called developed societies with high rates of literacy and education engage in various forms of fortune telling in large number (Aphek and Tobin, 1989) and that it is probably just as common there as in sub-Saharan African ones (Peek, 1991). This concern for the possibilities of avoiding the overwhelming occurrences of chance in their day-to-day lives and the explaining the reasons for their hitting individuals rather more than communities. This accounts for the proliferation of men and women who have developed successful ways for dealing with new forms of social and psychosomatic distress as well as ones for which there are traditional accepted explanations.

Pragmatism has become so much a part of research methodologies that produce regularities leading to a framework of thinking that such certain behavioural regularities can be anticipated to continue. The absence of regularities and the predominance of chance events preventing any possibility of foreseeable regularities has not received sufficient recognition. The point must be that chance is the predominant factor in the uncertainties of human life and, therefore, it is just as likely to occur in research work as elsewhere.

15

Chance and Social Science Research

Social scientists have to plan their research well ahead in order to get the approval of their superiors and those involved in that area whether at home or in another country. They have to produce well worked out proposals if they wish to study anything beyond what they can do with their own resources and as a by-product of their present employment with much the same care that they would approach a bank for a mortgage. What they hope to do and what eventually gets the necessary support do not necessarily coincide.

CHANCE AND THE CHOICE OF RESEARCH TOPICS

Hortense Powdermaker had prepared herself to study an inland New Guinea mountain community (Powdermaker, 1966:55) but for reasons of her personal safety as a single woman in an area that had little contact with outsiders much less single white women, the authorities made her study the coastal Lesu instead. Much the same happened to Colin Turnbull in Uganda who had considered four other communities until he was more or less left with permission to study the Ik by default; his ill-disguised dislike of their way of living by brutal individual self-interest may well have been in part the result of this enforced choice (Grinker, 2000:160-1). So chance for a start may dictate where researchers will work for some time ahead.

Unless researchers have committed themselves to one topic and one only and they are not prepared to open their minds to other possibilities, chance may also dictate opportunities which as it were fall into their laps. Social scientists in Indonesia faced with the killing of so many coastal women by the recent tsunami, would certainly have seen this as an important research opportunity. The forced adjustment of men losing their wives and having to run their whole lives in ways not acceptable traditionally for adult men. It may not have been the main interests of such people but it would have been an opportunity too good to miss.

The writer produced a cabinet paper in Uganda which showed that unless the numbers of police were increased to match population increases, the number of reported crimes was likely to decline as a result of the absence of police rather than any decline in crime. The Commissioner of Police found this helpful and gave him access to the homicide files for a year which resulted in a published study of the results which showed that even in 1956, the year of choice, the murder rate was higher than New York (Tanner, 1970). Without the opportunity provided by the paper on manning levels it would have been unlikely that he would have got open access to such files.

About the same time sitting in his office in the University compound he heard rifle fire coming from the town in what turned out to be a coup to remove the Kabaka, the then traditional ruler of Buganda. Since it was obviously too dangerous to study a coup in progress, he made a study of the gossip circulating in the coffee shops in the town using four sociology students (Tanner, 1978).

The lesson from these cases must surely be that it would be unwise for any social science researcher to specialise to the extent that it might be difficult to get funds and indeed to find the needed subject matter might just not be available. In the latter two cases the writer responded to opportunities which happened to occur to him. It was not too difficult to read up the necessary background publications on murder (Wolfgang, 1958) and rumour (Shibutani, 1966). The planning of research beyond immediate needs leads to difficulties from inevitable chance events.

CHANCE AND THE FURTHERANCE OF RESEARCH

Since human behaviour is always changing what the researchers see and hear and indeed records however well planned is likely to be dominated by chance. Human behaviour is so volatile that it may well be that any form of categorisation is imposing a non-existent behavioural stability on socially fluid activities. The coincidence between the researcher being at a particular place at a particular time when something unexpected happens which provides new understandings. There is a difference here between the accident of a particular encounter and a particular event which was an accident.

The writer while researching agricultural practices among the Tanzanian Sukuma noticed people going into a wooded depression and on following them he came across a rain-making ceremony about which he had heard nothing as it was not yet a time in which a drought was happening. On another occasion a government servant whom he knew had been killed in a lorry accident and he was able to attend the Muslim funeral as a participant rather than as an onlooker. Sheltering from the rain and being watched by a group of Zigua children in coastal Tanzania provided the opportunity to ask them to demonstrate their games.

In the thinking of the researcher attending these two events there would be the important consequences of having events which were probably already known from discussions confirmed by the realities of physically being there and absorbing the atmosphere.

It may be that some social scientists do not in fact plan what they are going to do except find out but not what they are trying to find out in any detail. It was Malinowski's approach to his fieldwork in the Trobriand Islands that he never planned what he was going to do on a particular day as even a short walk out from his tent provided him with something or some activity that he needed to understand. This may have been something of an exaggeration since there would obviously have been seasonal changes in communal activities and his informants would surely have alerted him to some matters for which he would then have been on the look out.

THE INEVITABILITY OF CHANCE IN SOCIAL SCIENCE RESEARCH

There are successive divergent aspects of social science research which are inevitably influenced if not dominated by chance. Firstly, they choose a topic and the physical universe in which they want to carry out this investigation which is delimited as accurately as possible.

The choice of what has been studied is retrospectively described as a logical progression from a defined need but we have shown that what they do and where they do it may be unplanned and in some cases actually against what they had aimed to do. Malinowski at the time of his Trobriand research during First World War was an enemy alien and the government wanted to keep an eye on him.

Initially there is the individual choice to do research and this divides between projects to earn them career enhancing degrees or publications or the straightforward need to earn money from being employed to do applied research.

Most higher degrees require the carrying out of approved and supervised research and this is divided between sedentary and active projects. The former involves working from existing data with lower costs and may not involve the researcher in the collection of primary material. The arrival of computers has made access to sources easier and indeed has made huge quantities of data available making such research easier for people who may be physically handicapped. This writer is wanting to get his military record accurate for his autobiography received from the Army records over two hundred pages of documents in which his name was mentioned over his six years army service. To have found this amount of material by hand if not impossible, might well have taken a year with heavy travelling and living costs with no guarantee of success.

There is, however, a downside to such computer availability. A computer search for data linking well-being, religion and health over the last ten years written in English alone turned up about ten thousand references linking these three words in some medical contexts. To read this amount of material constantly added to by new publications is well beyond the capacity of even the most enthusiastic researcher so what is read is likely to be a matter of chance or directed to something by a chance remark of a colleague. It might be done by a committee approach or through the interest of an institution but not by an individual.

The alternative is to move out of the university environment and to carry out primary fieldwork research but of course this is much more costly than leaving off a student grant supplemented by part-time employment for which there are many openings in service industries. Working for the McDonald's chain is something of a rite of passage for American students.

Those wanting to do primary research have to get funds from their university, government or foundation and this is a competitive matter involving applications supported by senior academics.

There are several aspects of chance in this as to what these senior academics support and why in which there will always be a mixture of what they consider to be of public value to the world in general, their department in the internal politics of the university and what will be of value to themselves in their own areas of expertise weighted against what time and effort would have to be used in supervision.

Little is known as to the reasons for support or the rejection of applications but chance again favours some decisions rather than others according to the relative powers of committee members and their professional evaluators as to what they consider to be worth supporting at that time.

There are of course ways round this by joining the American Peace Corps or British Voluntary Service Overseas and being able to work in the areas or topics connected to their longer-term interests; wanting to work in Botswana or India need not involve any disclosure of academic interest in low rainfall economies or the handicaps of caste for the progress of women.

The choice of what to research involves a complex of interests in which chance as much as pragmatism may be involved. The sensing by the potential researcher that a particular topic is so to speak vacant. Then to convince a number of potential referees that it would be in their general and specific interest to back this on the basis of the candidates known record is indeed a chancy business. For a researcher to be successful in the confines of a university may not be any guarantee that such abilities carry over into the isolation of research in widely different social environments. Their ability to run their own lives may prove much more difficult than they anticipated and at one time one-third of the foreign researchers in Uganda produced nothing.

So all of the stages which lead an individual to enter research on their own account rather than just as an employee for an organisation wanting information are ill-defined. In such situations their decisions are rather less likely to be based on pragmatic factors than circumstantial theoretical and atypical ones. Individuals joining a bank or the civil service in a well-organised society will find themselves initially on a staircase of career progress which will be related to training experience, the passing of related professional examinations and the assessment of general aptitude by a succession of senior members of that organisation.

None of these commonplace bureaucratic processes apply to social science researchers. While this type of research can be seen as the practical application of theoretical skills, there is no parallel practical testing of potential researchers except perhaps in biological anthropology, to guide them in the application of intellectual skills to fieldwork situations dominated by chance.

Sociology and anthropology as well have no professional associations to whose standards it is necessary to conform and which have legal powers of incorporation and exclusion comparable to the medical profession which controls training and the legal power to practice. These observations should not be seen as criticisms but to underline the fact that in all the stages before the researchers start their work, chance appears to predominate.

16

Chance and Fieldwork Practice

Once the social science researchers enter the actual practice of fieldwork however much they may want to apply the logics of methodology to the human situations with which they are confronted, the basic influence is likely to be chance. The choice of the actual site of their research even to where they may live, who becomes their main informants and what key events they happen to encounter, even the literature which they find relevant to what they are working on are all going to be dominated by chance rather than impersonal scientific factors. Of course, there are logical factors as well but the completed research is a retrospective construction of logical coherence which in reality may have been largely the result of a prolonged series of fortuitous accidents. Not only is the factor of chance not mentioned in this sense of positively enabling an acceptable result but there is rarely any mention of the adverse effects of chance in situations that they missed because of chance. They did not hear of an important event until after it had happened and they could have gone to an important ritual but their bicycle wheel broke.

THE ACCIDENTS OF ASSOCIATION

Who do social scientists actually meet from whom they get the data on which their publications are based? Unless they use people who have been listed as having certain desired characteristics such as patients in a particular clinic, those who are cared for in special institutions for the blind or handicapped, prisoners in a gaol, those accused in criminal trials or sued for debt or are part of a student body who are studying a related topic and agree to participate in a connected research project, this is a matter of chance.

Even when the universe is known as in research on Roman Catholic priests, nuns and brothers, there were some who avoided being interviewed as in other research projects. We do not know the extent that these absences were chance or deliberate for some unknown reason. Leaving aside such semi-controlled situations, researchers who have to make contact with people in an unknown universe, are entirely dependent on chance.

The wife of Raymond Firth who wanted to do research in Malaysia within her primary role as wife (Firth, S., 1972), sat by the path outside their house and just waited for passers-by to stop and ask her what she was doing. Except that they might have the shared characteristic of being curious as to why a European woman should be seated by the path, these connections were chance. She could not even presuppose that those that stopped came from nearby and were in effect her neighbours. They may already have known something about her from whoever was employed by them domestically.

Such an approach may not necessarily work. Kumar records going to the same tea shop in Banaras on a regular basis, but it was a male environment, she was served but none there other than the proprietor ever spoke to her (Kumar, 1992). In an Indian village inter-caste meetings could only occur in certain predetermined localities, where inter-caste meetings were acceptable so chance encounters can be predetermined and limited by the location in which they occurred.

Where the researchers are working on a topic which is very soon known as the reason for their presence there, such as trying to learn about traditional healing, we cannot know the reasons for them approaching the fieldworker which have not been governed by chance rather than by any shared interest. In fact no researcher can know in advance with any exactness the people whom they will encounter of whom some are more likely to occur than others.

THE RESEARCHERS' BASE FOR WORKING

The temporary home from which the researchers will work from their point of view would appear to be a matter of chance but what actually happens in placing them somewhere rather than just anywhere. Do we really believe that the village in which Srinivas had decided to do his research could do no better than find him a place in a cowshed? (Srinivas, 1979).

Malinowski pitched his tent for his Trobriand fieldwork near to the house of the headman not by his choice but probably because that man wanted to keep an eye on him and get what benefits he could from such close association. Kondo, a Japanese-American researching a Japanese factory got tired of lodging with a Japanese family which expected her to behave as a classificatory daughter, rented a house in order to live alone and found herself involved in the role requirements of being a neighbour in a community of which she knew nothing (Kondo, 1990). Abrahams with his family came to research the Tanzanian Nyamwezi (Abrahams, 1981) and in consultation with the villagers they had built for them a mud and wattle house and its location which decided for him by chance who would be their neighbours and helpers.

From the point of view of researchers from where they work may appear to be dictated by chance while it may be determined by others over whom he or she has no control. Researchers wish to study a certain activity or community wide range of behaviour and where they actually go and observe may appear to be dictated by chance as regards the methodology which they hoped to apply to their work.

CHANCE AND INFORMANTS

In a business encounter we can be reasonably assured that anyone they may meet will have a shared interest in pharmaceuticals or whatever their interests are. Unless a researcher uses a sample from their own university with a known interest in social science research, there can be no certainty that there is any sharing of interest. A shared interest would also mean that whatever sample is chosen will have a biased interest in what they are involved as well as biases from that particular type of environment. The researcher's range of social involvements will be within their degree of specialisations so that much of their understandings will be departmentalised by the topics they are studying.

However, in the fieldwork situation researchers may wish to use methodologically sound samples but the people that they have contact with as informants are not really chosen systematically but by chance. Researchers who go to study a particular community or activity may well have some lead in from people with the same interests who will provide some real or fictional reason for their presence so that they will not be thought of as police informants or political spies.

In practice no researchers can know in advance what individuals they will encounter to further their work and moreover they will never know with any exactness why these people have become informants. From the point of view of the researchers it is certainly a matter of chance governed by the fact that they are social intruders and are offering the bait of being socially different. Many people particularly in subsistence communities lead very dull lives and a stranger in their midst is a break from monotony as a matter of attraction rather than as someone to avoid. Dutch villagers found it quite stimulating to gossip to an Indonesian social scientist as it was better than watching television and they could talk about local matters knowing that such an outsider would not pass it on.

So a major factor which may make some people become informants is having the time so the elderly are more likely to be available as will be farmers in the season in which there is little fieldwork to do and cattle herders at night round their watch fires as during the day they are always on the move. Long sentence prisoners have plenty of spare time and may even make the most willing of all unreliable informants as they are just that by the nature of their lives they are certainly readily available (Tanner, 1970b). Even that may be a biased value judgement as we do not have any easy method of assessing the reliability of any informant about whom the researchers may know very little.

It is inevitably a matter of chance who become informants governed by such indefinable characteristics as the gossip about the researcher's behaviour and personal appearance becomes known. More importantly some people assess the advantages open to them by the presence of such strangers there. These outsiders who are not really in much of a position to pick and choose and their informants will come forward for a combination of factors; getting material advantages which may appear insignificant to the researchers such as giving away ball-point pens, extending their influence locally, having the time to spare, showing off and the excitement of working with a stimulating outsider as was the case with Turner's Ndembu diviner, Muchona the Hornet (Turner, 1967).

Unless the researchers are going to be their own principal informants as might be the case when they are working in their own social environments or rely mainly on their own observations and cannot disclose their research by any direct questioning or following lines of enquiry not directly related to what they are doing, they need informants to extent the range of information which they can gain for themselves by systematic observations. This puts them in a weak position to select informants who cannot be chosen by the same procedures as would be the case with potential employees wanting paid work. It is not as if there would be a queue of potential informants and the researcher has no real means of knowing whether anyone is going to provide data or not. Certainly they have to be ready to talk and be informative but the latter can only be known when the researchers know something about what they are looking for. By that time they may be committed to use someone who is unsuitable and yet is very difficult to get rid of in a researched community on which they are dependent.

THE ACCIDENTS OF EVENTS

Sometimes researchers are largely static through idleness, inertia, dislike of dirt, illness or nervousness over making relationships. Usually they will have to walk about which may or may not be planned in advance and even when it is planned there are always limits to what can be anticipated. The regularities of social life can be to some extent anticipated; grain has to be harvested, cattle have to be taken to water, cities have in and out rush hours and public entertainments are well advertised in advance. But all of such anticipated events can be affected by chance; thunderstorms can prevent grain from being harvested, drought, disease and cattle rustling can affect the movement of cattle and after the suicide bombings in London's public transport large numbers of people walked home.

Certainly many contemporary societies are run by the clock and even Margaret Mead's society which chose to go 'modern' introduced an eight hours working day regulated by bell ringing. Many societies, however, are run by the sun and the weather. An overcast day means that work will start latter and storms mean no fishing. There are certainly patterns to much of social life but this patterning may be over-emphasized by the methods that social scientists apply to their work and how they record their data. While there are gross patterns which ignore small scale realities, what individuals actually do within these social patterns will be affected by their intentions and the unexpected. Social scientists soon accumulate an understanding of what is likely to happen and then become interested in exceptions which will show them the range of social behaviour.

We know that with even established procedures what happens is likely to be only broadly similar and so researchers have to try and attend these social regularities but what they see, when and where is a matter of chance. The more traditionally minded Sukuma when they have difficulties often propitiate their ancestors and informants provided data on the ritual which entered field notes as expected procedure. After attending a number of propitiation rituals it became clear that there were only very broad underlying themes in such rituals and that in terms of what was actually done, there were as many different rituals as ceremonies. Such themes as were identified may have come from the subconscious of the initiators of these ceremonies but they were only given form by the researcher. Indeed how could there be any overall similarity when there are no regularising written liturgies and any one propitiator is not likely to see the private as much as public ceremonies of other people to whom they are not related by blood or marriage.

This need breaks down social patterns into probabilities some of which will always occur such as births and deaths but not of course where and when while others are matters of chance which are common enough to occur but their form and timing cannot be anticipated. Whether the researchers come across probable events depends on chance. Some researchers are lucky in the chances which they encounter and of which they take advantage. Others may or may not have had just as many chances which for a variety of reasons they do not see or do not make use of when they occur.

THE OVERRIDING PRESENCE OF CHANCE

It would seem realistic to state that the application of scientific methodologies to the analysis of anything organic particularly human behaviour depends on the extent to which what is being examined has more or less static qualities. It is possible to apply a method to an object which has some permanency in its substantive characteristics, particularly ones which are not likely to be affected in any disorderly way by the methods of examination. A geological or biological specimen can be changed by this examination but what has changed would be part of some orderly quantifiable process. Once the object of examination is out of the control of those observing it, as must be the case with human behaviour then the application of scientifically based methodologies with any hope of getting comparable accurate results becomes tenuous.

The observation of primate behaviour in the wild is comparable to the problems in working on human activities outside of laboratory conditions of control. The animals concerned are elusive and much of their behaviour is out of sight much the same as with humans. Being out of sight and a dislike of being observed except in situations of their own choosing is a shared characteristic of humans and apes. When they are observed or make themselves observable it may well be that their behaviour has changed as they are 'on stage'. We can only guess at what changes have occurred and that it has happened and the constancy of chance in what we have seen and know about from informants.

It is likely that primates will come to a certain tree in a certain month because it is in fruit just as we know that relatives and friends of both families will come to the celebration of a Western type wedding. What happens then in both cases is outside scientific quantifiable methodologies on a scale between the probable and the unexpected. Even this will be handicapped by a multitude of ungovernable factors; clarity of view, spans of attention and the inability to take in multiple divergent activities This is an altogether chance dominated business. It may well be that the animals concerned and the bride and groom in the wedding are under the observation of the researchers for only five percent of the time that they were looking and recording. An illusion of method and the dominance of chance.

In fact in many situations researchers are making up a behavioural pattern from scraps of information collected by chance, very substantially less than might be the case for patients in hospital wards kept for dangerously ill cases. Even then there would not be total coverage as the nurses would not be watching the behaviour of bedside relatives unless it was retained on security cameras. These hard working researchers can only retrospectively impose something which they choose to call method in describing their long hours of observation. Mechanization may have meant an increase in the quantity and coverage of data but even this will require the recognition of the existence of chance because some part of an event had the camera or microphone working in that direction just then.

What seems to occur in most fieldwork in which the watched for behaviour cannot be limited or controlled, is a series of accidents in which the observers happen to be there by chance at what they subsequently interpret as the right place at the right time which they hope was not to be influenced by their presence. In fact a situation of chance in which the odds against anything of importance happening are very much longer than in any horse race and yet they have to be waited for.

THE PERSISTENCE OF CHANCE

In the study of human behaviour the social sciences have persisted in finding or perhaps rather created order out of the disorders of individualism and group interrelationships and chance events from research work on behaviour which has been completed. So the question to be asked is why the social sciences ignore the fact that all human behaviour and indeed approaches to the study of behaviour in general are subject to unquantifiable chance rather than what can be called quantifiable probabilities.

The model for human social behaviour is dominated by the ghosts of Comte trying to impose the orderliness of hard science to human behaviour which few if any social scientists apply to their own behaviour. This search for orderliness may be due as much to the persistence of bureaucratically efficient societies which have their citizens categorised under a variety of headings for their mutual convenience. It may also be due to the political dogma that with proper regulation many of the ills affecting society can be reduced or at least regulated.

It is a situation of seeming and indeed admitted chaos because whatever society is examined from the Bushmen in the Kalahari desert to a major Indian company there is an obvious orderliness which participants as well as observers think and indeed exists. But for the former it is an illusion and for the latter the formalism with which the company carries out their overt functions still covers the fact that there is in that company as much as in any school, prison, ship or factory a parallel less consistent adaptive secondary structure.

So all these institutions, social groupings and indeed families at whatever level of social complications and structure are in a continuing and constant state of reacting to unforeseen events and then to try and plug the hole in what they hope to be a watertight system. As we have seen subsistence communities have developed over many unrecorded generations the best possible ways of coping with the consequences of chance. While they have ways of burning off their surpluses brought by chance in various forms of combined material and social investment, chance events are overwhelmingly seen as hostile to their optimistic hopes.

Individuals and societies at whatever level of social complication are always going to be hit by chance events despite their ostensible orderliness regularly discovered by social scientists. Some societies and individuals may have an optimistic frame of thinking which has been reported as the Danish sense of the world although this may have been occasioned by such a small nation winning the Football World Cup. On the other hand Buddhist and Hindus would appear to have a sense of pessimistic nihilism which they have countered by creating forms of practical individual religious actions but these mental attitudes will not affect its frequency but only how it may be interpreted.

As chance is such a persistent occurrence in social life it will have to be similarly a part of the researchers own approach to their work and what they encounter so as to avoid the illusion of stability. No social scientist is professionally or personally happy to accept that their work is dominated by chance rather than having an underlying orderliness which they hope to be able to find.

17

The Instabilities of Social Science Research

Social science researchers are professional observers and recorders of human behaviour but at the same time they are individuals with their own social experiences and what they see and hear and indeed write is filtered through at least two decades of social living. We have already discussed the biases that may affect their observations which can be objectively discerned. What may be forgotten in the context of the individuality of the researchers and the researched is that they have to have their contributions assessed in terms of their individual life histories. What they see and how they react socially and psychologically to the new experiences in the research environment will be a compound of the pivotal and chance events which have preceded this involvement and in how they react to events disclosed by the research. However well trained and professionally committed they are not impersonal recorders of behavioural data.

PIVOTAL LIFE EVENTS

Those involved in research have not had their lives as an even progression but ones that hinge on pivotal events. The primary one of importance may be the exposure of the potential researcher to the intellectual possibilities which occur in their first weeks at the university. This is not a generalised opening up of the mind to which the university is committed but its exposure to the segmented thinking of the departments into which they have recruited themselves. The social science students have tied themselves intellectually to the excitements which will come from this specialisation.

It is not that their minds are closed off to the possibilities which would be provided by the study of medicine, philosophy or ecology but by committing themselves to one specialisation, there just is not time to take on the intellectual excitements of another specialisation. An example would be the practicalities involved. The Oxford Diploma in Social Anthropology over 24 weeks of lectures, seminars and tutorials had reading list of 120 books; so even a cursory look at these on top of what else was available would have meant reading at least five books per week. While the restrictions on thinking may well lie in individual psychology, in reality it is a question of severely rationed time. The initial pivotal event is the commitment for whatever reason to a particular topic and the intellectual closures which come from the limitations imposed by time. Napoleon said to his chief of staff, "ask me for anything but time".

Then the potential social scientists find themselves exposed to an enormous optional range of books and people. We can only speculate on what goes before in the minds of these people which would lead some to be attracted to Durkheim's *Elementary Forms of Religious Life* (Durkheim, 1961) as opposed to Rappaport's *Ritual and Religion in the Making of Humanity* (Rappaport, 1999). Neither of these books are easy reading but potential researchers are always going to find some books more attractive to their thinking and read them thoroughly but others will go back unread onto the shelves. There cannot be any social scientist who does not have a list of books which they feel they ought to read but never will because they just do not have the time. So most come under the influence of what they personally consider to be pivotal books quite early on in their careers and are time rationed out of reading more widely. We have already pointed out that some important subjects will have related reading lists running into thousands.

Next come influential individuals in the university isolated by their academic status who provide the stimulus for many students to continue with some particular aspects of their specialisation. This is very much an example of 'on stage' behaviour in which they present aspects of their own understandings from long specialisations. The potential researcher is bound to be impressed by the way that one professor rather than another presents their understandings and this is always detached from their private persona which indeed may well be much less attractive. These academic stars attract satellites.

Although the relationship may be bilateral it will still be pivotal as the junior may become attached to that person's pattern of thought and use it with the professor's approval in the attempts to get financial backing. The professor may also find it useful to have promising students who want to be researchers as satellites to their own interests; a mutual self-serving relationship.

Beyond these intellectual pivotal events there are also social ones. The move to the university puts each potential researcher into a more varied environment than they would have had at home or in their previous school. This means that they meet individuals socially and indeed excitingly different to themselves. Pivotal relationships will be formed which may act both as a stimulus to effort for a career as well as a handicap by making them unwilling to engage in research which puts them out of social range of maintaining such relationships. When the opportunity for research in Banaras is offered to a Bengali it may not seem a socially acceptable opportunity.

It is even more of a handicap if such relationships become formalised and the researcher is emotionally torn between the obligations built into such relationships and the requirements of time consuming research at some distant locality. The importance of these pivotal commitments is shown in the fact that fieldwork away from home and family is largely confined to the younger unmarried adult with less mature experience of their chosen speciality. Of course there are advantages in the use of these less committed minds but special relationships will almost inevitably be of pivotal significance.

A further pivotal event is the researchers' exposure to their first fieldwork environment. They themselves will have commitment to go to Rajasthan to study the social aspects of agriculture in areas of low rainfall but they end up in a particular village or in other situations a particular slum area in Mumbai or a particular Muria hamlet. Even if they do not actually express it in personal terms, they will think in terms of 'my' village, hamlet, slum community or tribe.

Doing fieldwork in such personally intermittent circumstances for so long and the unusual experiences which come from this association which may have gone on for months stretching into years becomes pivotal. Whatever they do later mentally it may well always be compared to what they first experienced in that distant Rajasthan village which will have very little to do with what they are now doing in Mumbai or Manipur.

There may be other pivotal considerations such as career issues which might have to take priority such as a book contract or the offer to participate in a television programme, the inheritance of property, the birth of children or the incapacity of parents which may all become pivotal constraints on what the researcher can consider doing.

CRITICAL EVENTS

While it is a reasonable assumption that there is an element of regularity in all human behaviour which probably has an ethological background onto which has been superimposed the bureaucratic regularities of modern centralised societies, any tight personal orderliness is probably an illusion. The keeping of a diary shows the extent in which every individual is in the process of constant minor changes.

Such regularities as we have are likely to be minor behavioural ones while the major patterns are likely to be interrupted or diverted by unexpected occasions which become critical in reordering subsequent behaviour. Some critical events are almost part of the normality of living such as rites of passage and the initiation processes of some traditional societies through which young men and women pass which change their social status and cope with the inevitability of illness, death and accidents.

A Canadian national survey showed that of 5,877 cases of suicidal behaviour, some 82 per cent had been involved in traumatic events (Belik *et al.*, 2007). It seems certain that in any person's passage through life there will be critical events which will have altered behavioural and thinking patterns. Iris Chang who researched the Nanking massacres of Chinese by the Japanese army in 1937 as well as subsequent atrocities was so affected by what she found out that this was thought to be the main reason why she killed herself (Chang, 1997).

So we see that research can disclose such shocking events as to alter the researcher's whole understanding of what human behaviour may entail. The lives of university students in the context of extreme behaviour is still a relatively sheltered existence which may not prepare them for the extremes of deprivation in refugee communities or in the famine areas of Ethiopia.

In some cases these critical events have been so extreme as to have altered every aspect of their lives such as the survivors of the Holocaust of the Nazi organised killing of several million Jews (Reulbach *et al.*, 2007). There is no reason to suppose that social scientists are exempt from the experience of critical events and that will have an influence on what they can do and what they think about the social situations with which they are confronted in research. They may be confronted in a very personal way with death and disease, corruption and political violence as well as what they see as the public subordination of women and situational morality of which they have been socialised to disapprove.

However outsiders may interpret the severity or triviality of critical events they are certainly turning points in the lives of social scientists working on human behaviour as much as any other persons although the Chang case is extreme and we do not know what other factors were involved. At all levels of behaviour critical events can change behaviour as we can see in the stopping of smoking and pregnancy (Ortendahl, 2007), and we can presuppose similar changes in researchers and their partners should pregnancy occur.

It seems unlikely that social science researchers will be able to separate purely personal critical events from ones that are the consequence of exposure of what to them are extremes of behaviour encountered in fieldwork. It may even be that the researchers sudden exposure to different cultural situations isolated from friends and family are extreme enough for them to suffer some form of post traumatic stress disorder. It may equally be that such extreme experiences have little effect. The receiver of a high decoration for bravery wrote 'you must believe me when I say that it was just another day in the life of a soldier. I did what needed doing to help colleagues and friends' (Watkins, 2007).

STRESS AND SOCIAL SCIENCE RESEARCH

Social scientists who undertake research for long periods whether this involves mental commitment under what might be called the normal conditions of bureaucratic employment or one that involves their physical separation from social environment which to some extent they have chosen for themselves and are accustomed to, is bound to be a cause of strain to them and their partners. The wife of Alfred Kinsey remarked that she had seen much less of her husband since he started his ground breaking quantitative research on American sexual behaviour. How much time the researchers may spend away from their normal social environments depends on their sense of commitment and the ways in which the research can be carried out. When a researcher is studying Hindu religious behaviour with temple events lasting a week or pilgrimages such as the Kumbh Mela or the Hajj to Mecca, he cannot work on a shift basis for fear of losing key events. In most research situations there is bound to be an element of stress.

This is bound to be worse for those separating themselves from their usual social environments to which they have grown accustomed so that they are thrown back on their own resources. It is not only this but that they are compulsorily forced to associate with people and their activities with which they have nothing in common except the fact of research which may be disguised. One can choose friends but the research environments to which individuals are committed prevents such choices.

So this is made worse by the fact that much research is done with people or about people with which the researchers would have nothing to do with in their usual life. While there is a need to research groups which are deviant to the average known and generally accepted norms of a society it is stressful for researchers who are outsiders to these deviances to work on or rather with drug addicts, the homeless, attempted suicides, murderers, sexual deviants and those who do not wash to their culturally based standards of cleanliness.

Research, whatever its intellectual attractions, may well be monotonous and prolonged so that there is an attraction in working on the sensational or at least what is unusual to the socialised thinking and behavioural patterns of the researchers. By choosing topics which are 'strange' and different to the social environments of which they have some marginal knowledge, they put themselves into stressful situations.

By the width of the social distance between what they have personally experienced and have some knowledge of, there is a proportionate increase in the possibilities of failure. We have already noted that just under a third of foreign post-graduate researchers attached to the Ugandan Makerere University failed to produce any results. The recognition that isolated fieldwork in a part of the country foreign to them with an inadequate knowledge of the language is very different to supervised tourist visits.

Social scientists enter fieldwork after several years of involvement in a particular form of social life in and around universities combining hierarchically organised as well as unstructured intellectual stimulus. There is the association with professional colleagues, a surrounding social environment providing many alternative forms of stimulus, entertainment and relief, fast-food outlets, laundries and lavatories, and all the physical comforts to which they have become habituated.

So in their fieldwork these researchers are experiencing for the first time the multi-faceted cultural and personal loneliness "which is not simply a desire for company, any company; rather it yields only to very specific forms of relationship" (Weiss, 1973). Of course one can be lonely in the middle of Mumbai or Manchester but in field research researchers are thrown back on their own resources in social situations for which they have had no anticipation or training. This situation has no parallels to the discomforts of back-packing with friends in a foreign country.

This isolation can lead to a form of behaviour which will influence the type and variety of information that they receive. There is always the premature choice of informants as they need someone to talk to on a regular basis. They need other people right from the start to help them survive socially in their new environment and to help them avoid the embarrassments of inappropriate behaviour paralleling them to improperly brought up children. Of course there are some people who are content enough with their own company but these would not be social scientists committed to the study of others and not their own introspection in isolation.

Many researchers create and maintain a sense of special relationships with the people they research which may not be bilateral at all. The researchers may refer to 'my' tribe, community, village or family and to their principal informants as 'friends' rather than professional acquaintances thrown together by mutual and probably divergent needs. Although there are cases in which those researched are referred to as 'our' researcher, the use of such a personal pronoun as 'my' suggests a need which may come from their social isolation.

The social scientists at work are no different in their humanity to others in society; they need to belong and they have often put themselves deliberately in situations in which they do not and this sense of social absence is certainly likely to affect their work (Baumeister and Leary, 1995).

This situation in which researchers are caught between their own persona and of being outsiders in some other strange social environment is bound to affect their access to information and their professional understandings and capabilities. There are always personal handicaps in which the researchers are under situational strains for which they are unprepared particularly as their actual work in contact with people in time and motion terms may take up only a small proportion of any day. This leaves long periods of social emptiness which they may not have the resources to fill. Malinowski spent some time reading English classic novels.

CULTURE SHOCK AND THE RESEARCHER

Any piece of research except in social environments which the researchers already know well or are part of themselves involves the anticipation and acceptance of the unknown. This may start a mile from their homes just as much as from a thousand miles of geographically based difference. It is not necessary for an Indian researcher to go from Nagpur to study the American Indian Navajo when they would find as 'strange' social behaviour not far from their own front door. Liverpool has a Chinese community boasting the largest ornamental road arch outside China. There are Bangladeshi and Orthodox Jewish communities in London which are as 'tribally' distinct as anything likely to be found in Orissa or Manipur. One does not necessarily have to go and live in a knowingly different society to experience culture shock (Milstein, 2005) and it occurs not as a result of anticipated differences but on chance.

Any researcher moving out of the cultural environment in which they have been accidentally rather than deliberately socialised, is going to be confronted with an almost infinite range of sudden social experiences for which they are emotionally as much as socially unprepared. Facial marks of caste and initiation, carpet-like body tattooing, betel nut stains on the pavement, not being allowed to touch a Hindu's personally owned religious picture, blood sacrifices, a Muslim washing a Koranic quotation off a board and drinking the water, the wedding party in Madeira after the priest had left clustering round the altar for photographs, and Nirad Chaudhuri's surprise at the ease with which he could get money from an English bank. The nature of the experience of multiple chance exposures to differences in the behaviour of fellow human beings is overwhelming.

In a personal sense these unavoidable confrontations have the individual moving from denial, defence and minimization in a form of social as much as ethnocentrism to acceptance, adaptation and in the growth of understanding and integration (Hammer *et al.*, 2003). The final situation is never going to be any elision of conscious behavioural and subconscious understandings between divergent cultures for which the learning started in early childhood.

Whatever the process it still rests upon chance, a prolonged series of unexpected encounters with 'strange' people with 'strange' ideas and even stranger practices. There is the dominance of chance encounters affecting the understandings of even the most theoretically 'liberal' and well prepared researchers.

When the researchers come and go into their research work almost as if they were commuters culture shock may be minimised. On the other hand when they are involved as far as they can as participant observers then these continuing chance encounters must create personal anxieties as to who they are. There is almost a form of cultural schizophrenia and in some the creativity of new patterns of thought from chance induced dialectics. The sudden realisation that the Sukuma did not have any conception of a loving intervening God but hoped that 'it' would just keep out of their lives and leave them to negotiate stability with disgruntled ancestors, spirits and the malevolence of their neighbours came as a shock to the researcher socialised into Christian thinking.

OVER CONCERN WITH THE EXTRAORDINARY

Much of human life is a matter of loosely constructed rather than absolute routines as without habit, regularity and normality human life as we know it would scarcely be possible (Rescher, 1995:34). Social scientists in this are no different to others and in their on-going lives there are formal and informal patterns of normality.

In practice the social scientists are not all that interested in 'normal' behaviour and in the studying of communities there is certainly going to be more attention paid to deviance, witchcraft and sexual behaviour rather than sanitation and ritual cleanliness which probably takes up more time than the former activities. Their research is concerned with exceptions to some theoretical base lines of normality.

On the other hand, since most if not all social scientists come from bureaucratised environments, there is often a tendency to apply these same forms of categorisation to others. To be concerned with the numbers of people who are married and avoiding the reality that this is a particularly Western legal state. A Tanzanian Sukuma unless they had gone through a legal ceremony recognised by national law, would find it difficult to state when a couple had become married rather than answering such a question by stating that they are more or less married than they were in the previous year.

Social scientists may be interested in such crude quantifications because they are easier to cope with than the intricacies of individual behaviour which are more expensive and time consuming to investigate but there is still the lure of the extraordinary. Homosexuality is to be expected in prisons but not that one dominant man had in practice a polygynous union with two other inmates whom he maintained with smuggled supplies of cigarettes and sugar. 'The rogue factors chance and luck now come to the fore' (Rescher, 1995:35).

The overall conclusion about the social scientist being a reliable medium for the recording of data which can be allied to the procedures and results of 'hard' research must be negative. They are rarely if ever sufficiently detached from their own personalities and social backgrounds to be included in any such classification. It is not that they do not try to be scientific but these personal factors in combination with their experience of uncontrollable and often exciting chance, may make their attempts at probability beyond the immediate proximate future no more than guesswork.

Part–C
Probability—Professionalized Guessing

In the study of human behaviour and the social environments in which it operates it is necessary to base our understandings on two basic factors. Firstly, that most data on human behaviour is only accurate in so far as it relates to factors which have been defined in advance and so exclude innumerably other undefinable factors. It should be assumed that most of the available data are both inaccurate or inadequate to some extent and that by the nature of its recordings is in fact now evidence of what may have occurred in recent history. Secondly, whatever be the efforts that the social science researchers make to become impersonal their work as scientific observers and recorders is imperfect because of conscious or unconscious biases. For these reasons attempts to provide probabilities as to what may or may not happen in the future is scientifically flawed in comparison to the parallel processes in 'hard' science.

18

The Need for Prediction

THE IDEA OF A FORESEEABLE FUTURE

In general humans as far as they are able to live orderly lives act on the assumptions that the seasons will follow one another with ordered regularity and that the trains will run on time and of course generally they are right and indeed right enough to run their lives on these predictions.

As far back as history provides data people at various levels of professional competence have planned their lives on the assumption of repetitiveness as in the organisation of grazing and the planting of crops on various types of soils. In this they have been remarkably successful as a major contribution to the survival of organised human life. In addition social life has pre-organised itself into cyclical and linear stages marked off by rites of passage which if not repetitive could at least be anticipated.

Ethnology provides a general scheme of seasonal regularities tied to food provision and in the case of chimpanzees out of sight and relying on their memory. It would seem that this working out of the future has at least an almost quasi-genetic element with repetitiveness as a survival necessity.

People in most if not all societies have tried to fend off the uncertainties of the future by the organisation of predictive systems since repetition obviously works and in many cases this is ascribed to the regularity of moral and religious factors.

There has been a steady increase in the popularity and forms of prediction because the rate of contemporary change has seemingly led to the growth of uncertainty on top of the accepted uncertainties of being bitten by a poisonous snake or having their crops destroyed by an unexpected thunderstorm. Being hit by a car or being unable to sell cash crops at what is seen as an acceptable price because of world changes in standards of living and in commodity prices has no part in traditional thinking whether in Manchester or Mumbai.

While there may be some increase in preventive action against uncertainty, it is certainly not appreciated by those flooded out in Bangladesh, the civil war in Darfur, political incompetence in Zimbabwe or famine caused by drought in Ethiopia. This growth in predictive planning is a necessity for organisational change as in the forward planning of the General Electric and Tata industrial complexes and the organisation of events. It seems doubtful that the Indian government did plan for 70 million pilgrims to attend the last twelve yearly Kumbh Mela festival on the banks of the Ganges rather than for a 'mere' twenty million based on previous estimated attendances.

The larger the organisation the greater this involvement in formal prediction as was the case with the Chinese planning for their hosting of the 2008 Olympics. We must surely accept that there were some unanticipated failures such as the unseasonal deluges of rain. In any such planning there are always the uncontrollable individual differences and the ever persistent eruptions of chance. From this prediction of factual realities emerges the difficulties of what can be reasonably predicted. There is always the division between this and what cannot be predicted as so-called 'acts of God'. In this context there has been an enormous amount written as to whether the United States could have anticipated the attack on Pearl Harbour even when they were able to read the Japanese coded messages. Some have concluded that in this, as in other situations, there were so many chance coincidences, that unpredictable elements will always be a major factor.

Nevertheless, it is from these observed regularities that there came the conviction that if these were so many both in the present and in the recorded past then the regularities of the future could be similarly calculated. This thinking was aided by the fixed and calculable odds in gambling in certain games which have a long history in card games, Mah Jong dominoes, roulette and that if ten horses are in a race one is going to win.

People do not like the uncertainties of the future and the

predominance of chance although it is a constant feature of every life. They have always hoped by careful attention to detail by professionals rather than the people themselves it would be possible to reduce the odds and to be able to plan the future with some certainty. There is always some unwillingness to accept that it is only in fixed situations that the odds can be calculated mathematically and that such a method is somewhat dehumanising. Even the concept of odds is uncertain; there are only fifty-two cards in a pack and its innumerable permutations can be very unsettling.

It is just not possible with any exactness to calculate the odds on any event involving human behaviour being likely to occur or not in even the simplest events because although a number of factors may be known and even be definable, there will always be innumerable unknown ones. In addition there will be the possibility of chance events which as far as one can assess after they have occurred are one-off events which are never likely to occur again in such specific circumstances. Any one can list hundreds of events which have happened in their lives which could not have been foreseen and certainly are not likely to be repeatable in their own lives or in the lives of others, but these limited situations cannot be replicated in behavioural situations. The innumerable permutations affecting everyday life must inevitably be very unsettling.

The insurance industry bases its calculations on the assumption of repetition in specific circumstances and outside this it covers the uncertainties of what it can know, by pushing the risk on to its customers by the size of the premiums that they require to be paid, and this cuts out for them most of the dangers from chance. Many calculations are mathematically presented and are based on factors which have been similarly presented in more or less the same situation which can never be a reduplication. It is equally obvious that the insurance industry makes a profit from the premiums charged rather than on the accuracy of their calculations about particular events. They miscalculated the recent flooding in Britain for the premiums on housing on low lying land despite the obvious correlation between low lying land and extremes of rainfall. The Indonesian tsunami as it affected tourists was covered by the fact that the majority of tourists make no claims.

So there is a difference between quantitative calculations which are almost inevitably inaccurate because future human behaviour cannot be based on any assessable combinations of individuality and chance except by boxing in what is being calculated. On the other hand the compromise probabilities can come from qualified assessments by professional understandings that certain trends in the more immediate future may happen. But why should we put so much effort into trying to produce accurate predictions about the future when from the earliest recorded times men and women have had many examples of their costly inaccuracy.

THE PERSONAL COMPULSION TO PREDICT

It may be that people have always felt that there was some repetitive pattern in how their social and physical environment on which they could rely for which there may be some ethological quasi-genetic background. Chimpanzees move to annual feeding grounds and to new water sources for which they have some 'inherited' or taught memory since the places to which they move are well out of sight.

People want stability and from pre-literate times they have organised their future options with as much care as any Western building society does over the granting of a mortgage. The Tanzanian Sukuma attempt to weave a network of potentially supporting obligations by providing help to neighbours and loaning out their cattle. They also attempt to control the future by seeking explanations for their current misfortunes.

So planning in a socially and ecologically unstable environment is a necessity for personal survival, in order to further their own interests within the primary groups created by birth and marriage. There is also the competitive nature of small group living in which individuals and families try to better themselves at the expense of their neighbours with whom they have to live in peace. In addition we are all socialised to predict what we are going to do next year in planting our crops, planning our holidays or it is often the case that the date for modern marriages are carefully planned for the advantages they might bring in tax with little concern for sentiment as is certainly the case in the many millions of arranged ones. Lawyers make a living in providing against the unexpected in pre-marital agreements.

Planning ahead is commonplace in all societies at whatever level of intellect, economic status and education whether it is done on paper or in the mind or by taking the advice of knowledgeable elders and specialists of whom there is a range in all societies. But while most individuals can guess-estimate what is likely to happen in their immediate future, going beyond this may involve expensive consultations whether it is to a professionally trained expert or a reputable traditional foreseer of the future. The Greeks were much concerned with divination and there are at least sixty named artificial methods of divination (Cohen, 1964:193-4) and in the opinion of some experts some modern methods of prediction are just as accurate as traditional ones in the cleverness with which they cover the possibilities of inaccuracy (Taleb, 2007).

THE INSTITUTIONAL NEED TO PREDICT

Any building work or event requires planning and chance is limited by the nature of what the institution is trying to do. Certainly the building of the Pyramids in Egypt required planning and the success of those projects showed that the planners assumption of building conditions were correct. They were able to assume political stability and the absence of any records of earthquakes as well as their ability to rely on the Nile's annual floods for which they kept accurate records. It is clear that their work was planned accurately enough to insure completion.

However, the World Trade Centre was built to last according to the 'hard' science conclusions about the life of the materials but they did not plan for these twin buildings to be hit sideways by modern air-liners. This surely was a failure of planning because the nearby Empire State Building had been hit by a large military aircraft and had survived. San Francisco is built on the San Andreas fault and has suffered a catastrophic earthquake and it is reasonable to anticipate another but there is no reluctance to build there despite the clear knowledge that this will happen not that it might happen.

So there is a distinction between planning for events which will happen sometimes such as an earthquake, death and disease for which mathematical probabilities can be worked out. But there is always the factor of chance which cannot be allowed for. The D-Day landings on the coast of France took two years to plan taking the prediction of good weather was likely in June when the tides would be suitable. They did not plan for the storm which occurred two days after the landings or that the Allied air superiority in early 1945 over the German Ardennes counter attack would be nullified by continuous cloud cover. Retrospective logic does not nullify the unexpected appearance of chance.

With literacy and organised as well as with organising governments come bureaucracy which endeavour on the basis of past understandings and confidence in their ability to control individuality, passes enormous number of regulations. It is not that these regulations are inadequate in their coverage but they cannot allow for chance events and the chance development of ingenuity by which individuals get round these legal requirements. The elements of bureaucracy (Weber, 1946:196-204) as the basis of modern social organisation are specialisation, hierarchy of formal offices, rules and regulations, technical competence, impersonality and formal written communications, are planned to avoid chance and probability and indeed standard textbooks on sociology make no mention of these possibilities. Such structures are features which bureaucracies have created on the assumption of regularity.

Bureaucrats are permanently involved in avoiding disorder with an handicapped inability to implement their own regulations not only because of a parallel growth in the bureaucracy of avoidance but because of chance and individual ingenuity.

THE EMOTIONAL NEED FOR CONTROLLING THE FUTURE

There is certainly a dichotomy between the fixing of some finite practical issue always tied to the hope that it will go right on the day as those involved have planned for as many eventualities as they can think of and can afford to foresee. In addition there are possibilities which are too infrequent and costly to provide against and issues which are minimally practical and are largely exercises in hope. This in terms of majority practices is tied to the need to simplify the worries over extreme events.

The Western system of thought which is tied to scientific experiments is one of binary alternatives. This is reasonable enough if we can see human behaviour in such simplistic terms as turning left or right at a cross-roads and whether to eat now or later. This of course ignores the social and psychological circumstances leading up to such choices and this complicates and makes impossible the simplicities of binary choice.

The people in most cultures think in more complicated if not more devious ways in which there is little acceptance of such simplicities and lateral thought predominates. The average Bengali or Bemba accepts the possibility that almost anything can be an influence on what happens to them and that they live in a real as well as metaphysical world in which uncertainty is a preoccupation. All human activities lie between straightforward binary extremes and a mist of uncertainties. It is not uncertainty itself which is worrying but the sheer range of the suspected and undefined eventualities. So there are on-going pressures and processes to cut down on uncertainty by insuring against the future. In this emotional need there is not much difference between the professional planner and the peasant farmer and they both have their own private and public 'charms' to promote success.

Those that organise the making of rain ritually and those that make the scientifically based weather forecasts probably if not certainly know that whatever techniques they use may make little difference. Both know when rain is likely to fall but not where and weather forecasters are no more accurate in local forecasts as opposed to general ones (Murphy and Winkler, 1992); my farm as opposed to what might happen to the area in general. There was the famous conversation between the explorer missionary David Livingstone and an African rain-maker who enquired if Europeans could be so stupid as to believe that rain could be made by the performance of rituals (Livingstone, 1857:23-5).

Except for the scientists themselves, a very small elite group who understand the processes which they are carrying out, most of those who use these procedures or accept the results, are accepting what has been done or proposed by planners and diviners on trust. They trust those who are officially accepted by public opinion in Delhi more or less on the same basis as the Tanzanian Sukuma or Hangaza accept a rain-maker who may have a parallel reputation for success. Whether the individual is an educated intellectual sophisticate or a non-literate quasi-traditionalist in a modernising environment they both have a shrewd awareness that their professional reputations depend on a web of gossip.

For most people the future is uncertain and there is an emotional as well as a practical need to reduce this uncertainty as much as possible. The insurance industry does well out of reducing some personal anxieties and well organised social welfare systems in Western states also reduce worries, but these never cover the whole frame of anxiety. It is not only in less economically developed societies but in developed ones as well that there is not only the constant stream of pilgrims to shrines in Hinduism, Buddhism and Islam but there are enormous increase in numbers going to shrines in Europe. Even if these petitioners in their millions do not succeed in controlling their future with the help of their gods, goddesses, spirits and ancestors, it helps them to come to terms with the inevitability of chance.

THE TWOFOLD APPROACH TO UNCERTAINTY

Everyone is faced with uncertain futures in every aspect of their social and individual lives. It would then be almost automatic for them to attempt to discover the probabilities for specific aspects of their future lives and then to work out the alternatives to the best of their abilities, often with the help of professionals.

Whom do people consult over their future probabilities? Firstly, there are professional estimators accepted by the scientific establishment as competent to make such estimates like doctors and insurance companies make them for individuals, social scientists make them for local governments and economists make them for companies. Almost every institution has official and unofficial projections about their future.

Then there are very large numbers of alternative system 'professionals' who are obvious enough in traditional as well as modern environments where their growth in numbers is proportionate to personal uncertainties and population growth. They are recognised as a necessary part of contemporary life. Whether they are defined as diviners, palmists, herbalists, witch-doctors or astrologers, they perform accepted roles as a necessary part of stabilising individual and collective lives within acceptable dimensions.

What is perhaps not recognised and accepted is the enormous number of comparable 'professionals' in developed societies. It is reported that 1,220 out of 1,750 daily newspapers in the United States publish horoscopes. Astrology there is an industry that can support some ten thousand full-time and seventy-five thousand part-time astrologers and that the industry as a whole has an annual turnover of $200 million (Aphek and Tobin, 1989:100). There may even a similar number of alternative full-time and part-time 'professionals' coping with personal uncertainties by other methods. We can be certain that people in all types of contemporary societies and in all situations continue to be concerned not only with the probabilities of their futures but for equally important retrospective explanations for their past misfortunes.

19

The Inevitability of Uncertainty

While the development of physical science has found 'hard' facts that create some of the realities maintaining human existence, this cannot be said to have provided human behaviour with any inevitable traits. Any human life and its social inter-relationships will always be altered if not dominated by chance, choice and chaos. The inevitabilities of heredity may not occur where there is Huntingdon's Chorea in the family as there is always the factors of infant, adolescent and early adult mortality from other diseases and accidents from traffic to terrorism. Thus it would seem that attempts to parallel human social behaviour to the rigidities of physical science despite the warnings to keep in mind its subjective aspects, is almost certainly a fruitless exercise in deterministic modelling (Harvey and Reed, 1996).

So we see that with Huntingdon's Chorea there will be a measure of harsh genetic reality but by no means inevitable because of pre-emptive chance; carriers may be infertile or not have sexual intercourse. Once we go beyond this individual level, how this tragedy is coped with by families, communities and institutions can never have any behavioural rigidity; all those involved will react in different ways in a long process of random variations. Professor Lambo, a West African psychologist has commented that judging from statistical results by modern methods of mental care are probably less successful than traditional African methods.

THE NATURE OF RANDOMNESS

It seems clear that ideas about randomness are confused between results in fixed situations and those in which the future cannot be foreseen. Firstly, the mathematically exact results in situations in which the odds are fixed without any unknowable factor being involved such as the mechanical throwing of the six-sided dice, the setting in motion of the roulette wheel, the tossing of a two-sided coin and the dealing from a fifty-two card pack. There is nothing here that is random as the odds are mathematically predetermined and in the jargon of card gambling there is no joker in the pack. "The break at the beginning of the pocket billiards game sends coloured balls rolling, ricocheting off one another and bouncing off cushions until they all finally come to rest in what would appear to be a random pattern. Yet physical law can predict the path of one ball hitting another, hitting a cushion, rolling on an inclined table... Given the particular initial condition and all the facts involved, their paths and final positions can be determined mathematically" (Bennett, 1998:152). In such situations the widespread belief in chance is mere ignorance of the initial conditions.

True randomness was recognised long ago by Cicero (Cicero, 1920: 2.6.15, 29, 24) in his writing on divination characterising chance events as those which occur or will occur in ways that are uncertain and events that may or may not happen in some other way. Random situations are those in which there is no possible way of foreseeing what might or might not happen because there are innumerable influencing factors quite beyond any possible human calculation either individually or collectively. It is not possible to estimate the examination successes of university students because there are many factors involved which are outside the control or estimation of the institutions concerned. With chance events there cannot be any question of knowing more or being better informed because indeed there is a 'cloud of unknowing'.

There are of course heightened probabilities on which actuaries make their decisions, shortening the odds that certain events may not happen or happen sufficiently infrequently for the costs to be covered by their successes in a predetermined sample. Such a blanket bet as regards any particular event is still going to be random as it may happen under chance circumstances.

The odds on death occurring from a particular cause can be calculated but not with any watertight accuracy since it depends on an initial diagnosis being confirmed by post-mortem examination. In some 900 post-mortems carried out in Yugoslavia the diagnosis was in total agreement in 49.3 per cent of the cases and in total disagreement in 9.9 per cent (Ermenc, 2003). We can see in such an example that the existence of scientific facts requires unscientific behavioural interpretation.

Traffic accidents are based on chance events but accurate statistics are often more accurate for such events as they often involve the police, the hospital and the insurance company, but not for stepping on a poisonous snake or being injured in an earthquake.

This is not a question of calculable probability as in horse racing in which it is obvious enough that one horse will win but the sheer fact that much of what happens to individuals comes within the boundaries of probability but in fact is entirely random. No individual goes through their lives without hundreds of chance events which they could not have foreseen even imaginatively but which played a key role. This applies as much to social science researchers as if does to Bengali subsistence farmers and Mumbai business women.

THE CONSTANCY OF HUMAN VARIATION

The calculations of probability when they go beyond what might be called enlightened guesswork are always having to deal with the fact that the issues for which they are making assessments are always in social, physical and psychological movement. Human behaviour can rarely if ever have the long-term consistency of inorganic chemistry. Human behaviour is always in a process of variation because that is its biological nature combined as it must be with similarly varying social environments. The objects of probability assessments are in fact moving targets always in the processes of radical or minor change. Hitting such targets is a matter of chance.

The probability of an individual becoming the subject of some medical situation is not just a question of proportional possibility of infection or accident as it will always be something particular to that person at that time. Making a statistical assessment does not alter this individual's personal and social isolation. Both may be common enough under epidemic conditions in which not everyone catches the same infection and not all riders of elephants or football players have accidents.

There will always be innumerable minor factors which will

alter statistical probabilities. Changes in life style such as the sudden availability of more water making washing more likely and with it the loss of some immunity, a change of diet, job opportunities in another field of work. Statistically calculated possibilities will always miss out the constant probabilities of the individuality of chance and these multiple in any assessment of complex situations. The depopulation of native Americans came from the chance loss of their protective isolation.

INSTABILITY

In all human behaviour what is expected to happen is likely to be a small proportion of what does actually happen to individuals as part of their total life experience. If this is so in relationships which are deliberately created for known finite ends such as taking up particular employment, a business contract, marriage, studying for a qualification, then there are likely to be an infinite number of shortfall categories in which membership of a category disguises the wide range of individual differences in interpretation and practice.

The social sciences are in particular difficulty when researchers are directing themselves to find out what is publicly unknown as if there could be any consistency in what might happen on the basis of what has happened in the past. This instability has multiple roots. The boundaries of what is being assessed involving human behaviour cannot be laid down with any necessary exactness. There is nothing that parallels the movements of snooker balls at assessable speeds and in the restricted environment of a pool table.

So we have to ask ourselves what are the base lines from which social scientists work in reaching conclusions from their research. There are laboratory reports which can be presumed to be accurate except for operating errors, deliberate fraud which is perhaps not all that infrequent and machine variations such as the finding that electric power fluctuated so altering computer calculations and the dampness from Ugandan afternoon showers which affected the machine sorting of punched data card.

Most if not all data whatever its source and method of recording apart from the inaccuracies which are built into any method of data collecting, becomes out of date from the moment it is recorded. Therefore, its relationship as a means of evaluating and predicting the future becomes progressively less possible as the past recedes.

However, in general we have to assume that these types of recording methods for social science data are probably as accurate as they are ever going to be because human behaviour is elusive. They are evidence that this type of information in that form has been recorded and nothing more.

But once the researchers enter the scene as interpreters of even the most exact of laboratory calculations much less public behaviour, then every conceivable human frailty comes into consideration. The range of knowledge and expertise, social awareness, intellectual acuity and indeed the preparedness of the individual's mind to receive both expected and unexpected factors. We shall see that there are wide variations in how professionals interpret the same sets of data and how the memory of events change quite quickly in their substantive accuracy. We can be sure that in working out the future probabilities of any human behaviour that there are no firm base lines from which accurate predictions can be made by any statistical extension. By taking past data to be accurate for the assessment of changes there is an illogical jump to assume that there are indeed comparable factors.

Human beings cannot be physically and mentally contained. The mind can wander over any boundaries unless it has been chemically changed and even in a prison there are substantial interchanges between those inside and the outside world. It has been shown that in France before the time of telegraphs, and railways, news of important events concerning the Revolution in 1791 and Waterloo in 1815 reached the most distant parts at speeds between 11 and 4 miles per hour which the French author Alexander Dumas found incredible (Robb, 2007:141).

Ideas have always travelled along with humans and their wanderings occurred extensively by sea and land long before travel became mechanically easy. There was substantial historical movement between China and India (Bagchi, 1950) and there was planned Chinese movement all-over the Eastern world (Needham, 1954), just as the Romans had trading posts in south India (Curtin *et al.*, 1984). While missionary movements have existed from the time of the Emperor Asoka, it seems likely that ideas have always moved independently and unexpectedly by seeing and listening.

The probability of a particular idea influencing behaviour is beyond scientific assessment.

Then there are biological changes in both the researchers and the researched such as seasonal changes, demographic ageing and the circadian rhythms which will affect both the interpretations of data and how inter-relationships are conducted. Whatever situation is being researched and probabilities assessed, the situation is a naturally unstable unit and its artificial stabilisation through restricting definitions, contributes to its inexactness.

MEMORY AND PROBABILITY

Much data on what probabilities may be based depends upon memory and that has been found defective often enough to make it a persistently unreliable basis for what may happen in the future. In 1962, a sample of Americans was interviewed and again 32 years later and the accuracy of remembered details which had been recorded in their adolescence was generally no better than chance (Offer *et al.*, 2000). A self-administered questionnaire given to a sample of Canadian physicians found major agreements on only three of the seven case definitions originally cited in a study of short-term memory loss (McKeown-Eyssen *et al.*, 2000).

Social scientists in researching the flow of social behaviour have difficulty in accepting that at the moment in which they record most of their data, they are in fact dealing with events that have already occurred. Further that how this past is reported will always be altered to some degree by self-interest (Shoemaker, 1970). Viewed in this way there can be little doubt that data when it is recorded by camera or on tape is rarely hard and of course only a minute amount of behaviour is so recorded. Even that is always divorced from the wider surrounding environment which would have formed the basis for much of that particular behaviour.

Unlike so-called laboratory experiments with a human sample in which the environment can be controlled to a limited extent and human thought probably not at all, this may mean that there will always be some conscious or unconscious alteration in how an individual reports or fails to report some event from the past. This difficulty covers everything which has occurred as few minutes before to their earliest childhood memories.

It is no longer accepted that the ability to remember will

necessarily be shortened by the introduction of literacy as people are always differentiated by their cognitive capacities and by what they need to remember. A Sukuma subsistence farmer will know the names and uses of hundreds of plants just as the lawyer and doctor will know the details of hundreds of cases. Students working for their final examinations will have to memorise massive amounts of information most of which will be forgotten within months. The fact that a Chinese will have to remember some two thousand ideographs in order to read a popular newspaper, does not necessarily mean that they will have accurate memories of what happened in their factory or village last week unless it involves their personal affairs.

This is not so much a moral issue as an inevitable behavioural one that no one has any reason to remember their experienced past unless they have a conscious or unconscious reason to do so. A limited number of high events from the past will be more easily remembered than trivia; most people will remember in some detail the circumstances of their first marriage ceremony but few will remember their own systems of personal cleanliness or eating in any detail unless they are neurotically involved. An isolated riotous event might be remembered but not tensions which occur repetitively.

Almost all social science researchers into human behaviour use informants on a scale from touch and go meetings to long-term inter-relationships who at the end of several years work might be better classified as field assistants. Leaving aside that they are the socially biased collectors of the memories of others, they also provide their own memories. We know little or nothing of their cognitive capacities except the researchers' own intuitions that the data they produce holds together about which similarly we know very little.

At the lower end of the scale the informants might just want to get rid of these social intruders and their questioning and in the latter case the informants know very well the type of information which their researchers want. The in-between informants will probably have memories in their details which will expand and contract with the advantages which they assess will accrue to them by keeping the relationship going. There will be parallels to the business interview in developed societies in which one party is seeking to get information from the other without disclosing too much about themselves.

The difficulties over memory are numerous not only because there are real possibilities of conscious and unconscious deception. What is disclosed depends not only on the environment in which listener and speaker are related but also because of many distant and proximate conscious and unconscious factors (Tanner, 2001).

We cannot know with any accuracy except by inference why individuals reply as they do to even the simplest of questions. There are no particular reasons for accepting such data as accurate except that the researchers have strong personal reasons to do so. Such a situation based on trust is not an adequate reason for accepting memory data on the say-so of informants as the bases for probability assessments.

It may not be possible for information about extraordinary or commonplace events to be corroborated beyond common knowledge. Informants will automatically produce information which are personal viewpoints whether they are key role-holders or just onlookers. There is little reason to suppose that detailed information is any more reliable in its varied facts than casual remarks.

Memory unsupported by similar information from other varied sources concerning something more than generalities must always be suspect. Researchers tend to consistently over value information provided by individuals while in fact they themselves are consistently unable to see and report anything in a manner approximating to the detachment required by the scientific approach.

It may be possible to build up the data about a single event in the form of a case study which may not be based on provable information but it will provide a qualitative picture of some inward looking accuracy for a small group. This approach would be of less value for larger social units because the researchers would not be able to accumulate enough personal corroboration to make their conclusions more than professional opinion on possible trends.

THE INEVITABLE UNEXPECTED

Let us look at the life of a single individual over a time sequence because its inevitable complications become multiplied in the probabilities involving many people interrelating over many issues. Whatever the length of time which is used, the individual is changing whether he or she is conscious or not of what is happening to their thinking and behaviour. In addition to this there are bound to be half expected pivotal events as they are likely to be ill from time to time, have close and broken relationships, and suffer the traumas of bereavement. All their interrelationships will inevitably change just as their physical, economic and political micro and macro environments will as well.

In addition there will always be abrupt pivotal totally unexpected events for which the society in which they live will only have developed partially successful cushioning. Serious accidents, business bankruptcies leading to sudden unemployment, unexpected deaths, house fires, becoming the victims of serious crime, premature births, stock dying and vermin eating crops even unexpected thunderstorms have time tested social behavioural reactions which have some continuing similarity. Nevertheless the social and psychological environment in which they occur will never be the same.

What can be certain is that there are no sequences in human behaviour which have anything approaching the steadiness and probabilities of laboratory controlled experiments involving organic and inorganic materials which cannot be described as socially responsive in ways that parallel human behaviour. The individual human experience consists of a series of partially expected and totally unexpected pivots as a result of which changes are forced on them by circumstances outside their control.

VARIETIES OF THE UNEXPECTED

There are firstly the expected and unexpected randomness. Much data is obtained from or collected by informants about whom researchers know very little and have no direct means of authenticating their information or indeed controlling their procedures once they are out of sight. One expects to change but not in the form with which individuals are confronted. The weather is rarely if ever consistent enough for people to act appropriately.

Then there is unexpected and expected randomness. The illness of researchers and their informants as well as disagreements and their proportionate occurrence in the wider world surrounding them.

THE UNCERTAINTIES OF DEPENDENCY ON THE RESEARCHERS

How any particular aspect of human behaviour is approached by social science researchers can be no more than an approximation to the methodologies required by 'hard' science. It is done in individual ways in the hope of accuracy. There is no quasi-statutory professional way of researching apart from the fact that it is always filtered through a personal perspective.

Its fundamentals are a combination of how and in what ways the objectives are open to investigation by a particular person or persons who will always have relative success and failures in what they are attempting to do. It is almost inevitably a social situation in which the researchers and the researched are tied together by reciprocal influences of which the majority may well be not assessable even if they were known. So how any behavioural matter is researched is restricted in some way by the limited ways that are open to investigation.

Then secondly the researchers have to have the ability to use methods which may produce results and to have the temperamental nature for working such methods. Some with outgoing personalities will prefer and get better results from personal approaches in small scale studies. Others with more detached impersonal abilities will choose methods quantifying some aspects of the behaviour of larger groups. So whether this or that method of researching is chosen and in particular whether the results are expressed in quantitative or qualitative terms is very much a matter of chance. This depends on the probabilities of personality and choice within the boundaries of social possibility.

THE FUTURE IS BASICALLY UNPREDICTABLE

Everyone knows even if they are not prepared to admit it for professional or personal reasons, that the future is unpredictable beyond some immediate possibilities. Even for these probable regularities there are always some covering phrase which allows for the possibility that something will prevent the expected from happening. These expected things will happen but are qualified by such standard phrases as 'if God wills it' or 'all things being equal'. In fact it is impossible to predict with absolute certainty that any human activity will occur in the manner anticipated. Further the larger the number of people who are involved in any future event, the greater the range of impediments which will prevent the event occurring in anyway that can be accurately forecast.

20

The Forms of Prediction

As far back as historical records go and for which there is some archaeological data people have been logical enough in their understandings of everyday life. However, beyond that they have persistently tried to find out the explanations for what has happened to them and what is likely to occur in the future. Since these attempts go beyond their logical capabilities, this has usually involved the other world of ancestors, gods, goddesses, spirits and directed evil in the forms based on each culture's metaphysical understandings. Efficient enough since it takes into account all the necessary current factors in those particular situations. In such explanations there are spoken rather than written ambiguities providing people with enough interpretable answers to reduce rather than to eliminate their anxieties.

THE FORMS OF PREDICTION

It is perhaps unwise to make a distinction between developed and developing societies or between social forms of literacy, illiteracy and non-literacy. These inevitably end up in discriminating between the pretensions of scientific thinking that they can foretell the future with the same accuracy as they can retrospectively explain the causal reasons for completed events.

In so far as there has been any historical development which has been largely confined to the Western world and its patterns of thinking, there has been a clear division between methods of explanation and foretelling the future using logically explicable information with a scientific foundation and defined base-lines and other methods without such bases. These alternative methods attempting to foretell and control the future have no closed relationships to existing knowledge beyond the intuitive understandings of existing social situations by these experts who may have religious connections or may be assumed to have paranormal abilities and understandings. The former are common in medicine, the manipulation of public opinion in political planning and economics while the latter with their wider and more personal coverage predominate in most developing societies and in all social areas for which there are large scale medical and welfare provisions. These cannot or do not provide solutions for those who have no settled lives in which there is little assessable stability. We have seen that these quasi-traditional or innovative alternative and parallel systems probably predominate in almost all societies and among people of widely different status, education and intelligence. There is indeed a difficult dividing line between the Christian and Muslim prayers to a monotheistic God, the polytheistic ones to Hindu gods and goddesses and Buddhist derivatives and the similar petitions to ancestors, spirits and saints which are classifiable as magical.

It is only recently in human history that finding out about the future has become a professional secular activity but principally related to economics and medicine. It has been in the selling of toothpaste, and such finite base lines that there has been much short-term success as well as some notable failures such as that of the Ford Edsel new car design. But overall it is only in short-term prediction that there has been success and whenever the base lines are left undefined or are in reality indefinable that the success rate drops dramatically.

In an estimate of future sales of phones for homes and businesses there was 95 per cent success (Williams and Goodman, 1971) and in another one month ahead covering 600 forecasts showed 93 per cent success (Newbold and Granger, 1974). These were all short-term forecasts in which the factors involved were restricted and in many cases static. Toothpaste or whatever have no say in how they might be used but it may not necessarily be used for cleaning teeth, just as Andrew's Liver salts was used by some Tanzanian Sukuma as good for venereal disease.

There were no obvious reasons for the new Edsel saloon car to be an expensive failure except that sales were affected by some sort of social contagion, a factor of chance which could not have been predicted. The ground nut scheme in Tanganyika to provide cooking oil for post-war Britain failed because of over-optimism and a failure to plan realistically in ecological conditions of which not enough was known.

PREDICTION

There are culturally and scientifically acceptable methodologies for prediction although in the end it comes down to a form of professionalised guesswork. The sheer number of unknown factors and the overall persistence of chance will always form the background to their use by communities, institutions and families. This is how they reach decisions about how to cope with unexpected eventualities and how they propose to arrange their behaviour to fit in with their predictions of the future.

There is a relatively new factor required of prediction in the making of binary decisions. The predictors are asked to provide hard information on which they can make decisions; to do or not to do a planned proposal. The social environment of highly developed sectors of society, they do not ask of predictors that the answers they are given should have the same range of ambiguities with which traditional societies have resolved their uncertainties.

So this new form of closed decision making which enables roads, bridges and buildings to be built always has a definable static element dominating one side of the equation and does not involve much behavioural probabilities. This would appear to be elitist in its origins and application.

Decision making in many social situations and not just in subsistence societies is made in open meetings of those involved in which the alternatives are argued out in public until all those who want to express an opinion have had an opportunity to do so. Something approaching a consensus is reached without the divisive probabilities of putting the matter to a vote which publicizes social divisions and leaves a publicly dissatisfied minority. The modern ways of dealing with future issues would seem to be a bias towards binary yes or no decisions or decisions by divisive voting.

Often the decisions over probabilities are made in secret by professional elites, whereas traditional ways have always been more public because of the absence of closable houses and the public nature of much subsistence living. In such situations in which a decision is sought as to what to do, there is no fixed agenda but the parameters within which decisions have to be made are known and self-restricting. While on the one hand this is a free exchange of views on the other there are social limits to its dialectic potential. Even the quasi-traditional diviner who may become possessed by the spirit of an ancestor is unlikely to put forward proposals outside the potential capabilities of those involved. It seems likely that even the modern professional predictor is confined to their own estimation of what those involved would be likely to accept unless they are independently funded and are not worried about their own future employment.

The ancient Greek oracle at Delphi was the predecessor of the methods used by contemporary quasi-traditional as well as professional providers of predictions (Rowe and Wright, 2001). The Oracle's method of decision making had experts reach a consensus amongst themselves through a series of rounds controlled by an anonymous summarizer, the hidden but publicly and politically acceptable Voice of the Oracle.

Modern committee making of decisions may well follow the same procedure with the chairperson gradually eliminating differences of opinion with the differences relating to the use of less publicly acceptable experts. In quasi-traditional methods of prediction the diviner, the expert, is subject to much more open public opinion influence since her or his future employment depends on being accepted as wise through community gossip. With the modern expert there is always the possibility of social ignorance since specialisation and relative social isolation from small community opinions can lead to barriers for the acquisition of new and surrounding information. These experts may be of use and make valuable contributions but in general they are giving opinions largely on unforeseeable factors outside the range of their professional expertise; success in fact may be itself largely accidental.

As we have seen prediction has been used extensively and successfully in sales predictions and particularly the Delphic approach has been used (Basu and Schroeder, 1977). It seems likely that the processes of decision making by the evolving of a social as much as a business consensus is not much different to how traditional societies reached decisions.

Most issues on which predictions have to be made do not have enough hard facts for predictions to be made with any accuracy because chance always intervenes, particularly at the level at which decisions are made. Individuals become ill, there is a fire in the factory or drought affects crops and personal differences between different levels of management are just as disruptive as those between families and in-laws.

DIVINATION AND POPULAR PREDICTIONS

Professional predictions may relate to those aspects of modernised societies concerned with the immediacies of sales and manufacturing and with public opinion and voting patterns. These are outside the resolution of personal difficulties and anxieties of those who spend their lives on the fringes of those modern communities which can be described as structurally well organised. It is there that divination in its many forms predominates as a response to popular need.

These diviners are well aware that there are scientific solutions to some but not all problems and they are even more aware that these solutions are uncommon, distant and expensive and thus are likely to be of a limiting influence on what they hope to do. Certain mass diseases may have disappeared but the reasons in oral history may not be attributed to science. Even more certainly the modern world has been for many a social environment of continuing disappointment rather than the realisation of personal dreams. For most there is just as much poverty, ill-health and the dominance of a corrupt elite as in the remembered past. This is the mental world in which many resort to systems of divination.

There is a marked difference in how divination is viewed and practised according to the degree to which they have been influenced by modernity. This split is typified by the distinction that some societies concentrate their concern over probabilities in explaining the past, while others have a parallel concentration on those of the future. For most of the world's population the influences of modernity over their thinking patterns may have been peripheral. Material change certainly but it would seem that people remain in the ideological community which implies a rooted belief in that 'past' system of thought (Malk, 2000:34-44).

These societies have patterns of thought correlated to the short-term range of the practicalities of their lives; no written sources of religious knowledge, an achieved priesthood from personal choice or inclination which has no collective institutions or training systems. They have languages which do not have any indefinite verb tenses which do not correlate to annual economic cycles. What they require from divination are explanations of what has occurred; who or what has been upsetting them and how it can be put back into social equanimity.

The societies which are more concerned with future probabilities appear to have long established religious ideas of complexity and ambiguity rather than specifics, specialised priesthoods with specialised training institutions; a substantial overall cultural investment. Both appear to have or used specialised linguistic codes which their priests rather than worshippers understand or interpret.

Rituals of divination for they cannot be seen as anything more than perceptive analyses of intuitively obtained clues about the social behaviour of those who consult them, are a global phenomenon in all types of cultures. In many less developed ones they are an essential public part of religion and of the individual's daily life, while in more developed societies they are carried more privately but probably no less frequently.

In Israel there has been an increased frequency in a variety of fortune telling and of visiting astrologers or having their palms read has become more than a merely casual entertaining experience. The methods used parallel to those in less developed societies; a dyadic relationship in which the diviner does most of the talking using language to provide a range of possible answers which are applicable to certain populations in given sets of situations. They use familiar rhetorical devices of metaphor, repetition, hesitation, pauses and silence. The diviner's remarks contain a scale of relativity into which the listeners have to fix their own position. Researchers attribute this increase as a reaction to the ostensible pragmatism on which Israeli society is functioning (Aphek and Tobin, 1983).

Divination expresses 'the inescapability of ignorance, pain and injustice in the human plane while simultaneously denying that these irrationalities are characteristic of the world as a whole (Geertz, 1973:108). Its uses should not be seen as an exercise in credulity by people who should have more sense than to rely on such pragmatic futilities. These consultations are more complex than any such simplicity.

These diviners usually have no prior knowledge of the people who consult them and many such people would prefer to go to a strange diviner who could have no prior knowledge of their personal details. The consultation usually takes the form of a monologue in which the diviner is attuned to the body language responses of those that consult them who will in effect decide which of the possible reasons for their misery are the most likely, which then becomes the acceptable diagnosis. It is this dyadic relationship in which more often than not those that consult them are confirmed in their own latent suspicions.

THE SHORTCOMINGS OF MEDICAL PROBABILITIES

We have to accept from the accumulations of medical data that a substantial number of diagnoses are either incorrect or partially so despite the prolonged training of physicians in scientific methodologies unless confirmed by laboratory analyses. Even then the diagnoses on which action is taken may be inaccurate because of multiple morbidities and related to degenerative diseases for which there can be only control and amelioration. This has to be seen in the context that these medical diagnoses occur in a minority of ill-health situations and to an even smaller minority of people in all societies.

For most of the world's population there is either no access or access only in relation to a few mass diseases. When there is access to a significantly competent medical system and in this context it is reported that in Delhi alone there may be as many as forty thousand fringe so-called 'doctors', diagnosis and treatment will always be qualified by non-medical factors. The absence of the appropriate specialist knowledge as well as work-study aspects of treatment related to time, place and cost. Looking at any list of medical articles it would seem that getting attention at the appropriate level of expertise and treatment is largely a matter of chance and has to be seen in the context of the probabilities of cost and specialisation.

So most human populations for most of their psychological, physical and social difficulties will continue to be coping with them in ways that their societies have devised over the past millennia and presumably have done so with a reasonably acceptable rate of success and thus have contributed significantly to human survival. These are the systems of guesswork and divination which in providing hope have allowed the human system to survive.

In such social situations there is a wide range of professional healers as professional they must be considered from their specialisations and the fact that without any professional backing they are still in business because of their reputations. These men and women have achieved talents and acquired unsystematic knowledge usually from long social live-in apprenticeships. They have worked out for themselves the probabilistic solutions to the problems of those who consult them. There is an echo here of the doctor who says, "there is a lot of this going around now".

These commonplace systems of probabilities are divided into two types of procedures. Those deciding the reasons for misfortune and their future solution. In its modern form this is a medical consultation and treatment based on a diagnosis and the diviner deciding on the social rather than on medical grounds as to what are the reasons for misfortune by processes similar to those of Western psychotherapists. Alternatively the guiding of future conduct by processes of prayer and petition such as the shaking out of diagnostic sticks in Buddhist or Shinto temples and having printed horoscopes provided there which have to be explained by experts. Here would be included the enormous range of private preventive behaviour in the West carried out to insure good luck.

DOCTOR OR DIVINER AND DIFFERENTIAL DIAGNOSES

One of the assumption of Western medical science is that there are scientific exactnesses relating to whatever illness their patients may be suffering from and that there is a connected appropriate treatment. While this may well be true that there are certain treatable uniformities as in the elimination of smallpox as an epidemic disease, these are limited. There are always variations in how certain medical conditions are treated. Eminent physicians create their own spheres of influence in which diagnoses and treatments are named after them. However, the whole process of scientific regularity is subverted by the individualism of those involved as to what is wrong and how it should be treated.

Medical textbooks suggest the best treatments for certain conditions in terms of the current state-of-the-art. A large scale study of American health care in which health records and treatment were matched found that just more than half of the participants had received the recommended care for their conditions according to a nine member multi-disciplinary committee of assessors (McGlynn *et al.*, 2003). This is not to suggest that these patients had necessarily received wrong treatments or that if they had received the recommended treatments they would necessarily have benefited. The factors here are chance and probabilities which are not necessarily removed by a finite diagnosis.

This is only to suggest that there are pervasive weaknesses in scientific medicine when its successes are self-evident but to suggest that there are substantial variations in how physicians see the data which reaches them and how they deal with the consequent probabilities. The distinction between doctors and diviners is also on another level as scientific medicine operates often without the patients involvement or any necessary understanding of the procedures and rationale. More importantly the diagnosticians are not directly dependent for their livelihood or their professional reputations on their patients. The diviners have to create their own reputations or they go out of business so much of their work is on a scale of part-time involvement with other forms of subsistence.

These quasi-traditional diviners know something of the epidemiology of the more conspicuous diseases and universally know the signs of advanced AIDS but they have no theoretical understanding of disease. They see most human misfortunes in terms of social rather than medical pathologies and thus have a larger number of satisfied and understanding clientele. They also provide from a local pharmacopoeia with often actively experienced results which may not have any relation to the affliction as far as is known.

THE DOCTOR AND DIVINER AND THEIR VARYING PERSPECTIVES

What are the functional parallels between doctors trained in explicit scientific medicine and the diviner trained in implicit quasi-traditional methods are perhaps too far ranging to have any general application. The diviner will usually accept that the doctor will often be successful in the reduction of certain misfortunes such as broken limbs. They will often refer their clientele to hospitals when they suspect that the misfortune has no social origin, but most doctors do not reciprocate. They do not wish to include diviners in their understandings of misfortune. They live in different social and professional worlds and perhaps also do not accept that diviners are indeed successful in the many malfunctions which have a psychosomatic origin. The highly educated do not take kindly to any proposed professional necessity to treat such people as having a useful expertise parallel to their own.

The doctor operates in an environment in which their knowledge of their patients is a short written record augmented by a brief meeting which is unlikely to be as much as ten minutes. These interpersonal contacts lead to no particular off-the-record knowledge of any patient's background; it is not so much that such details would be seen as generally irrelevant to particular medical problems and their reduction but the physician see themselves as scientific technicians rather than social workers for matters which can have no immediate solutions.

Doctors are in some sense dealing with predefined essential peripherals brought into practice by the immediacies for which the patient wants solutions but the physicians get no benefits for going beyond these immediacies. The numbers of patients which they see in their consulting rooms is dictated by their availability and hours of work rather than by public reputation. It is doubtful whether they would recognise more than a few of their patients because of their particular medical problems rather than because of their social backgrounds. The relationship is dominated by social distance factors and of time particularly when it is a free social service. They are trying to find solutions to specific medical conditions identifiable by scientific methods. A restrictive perspective in which there is a progressive reduction of ambiguities.

On the other hand the quasi-traditional diviner operating a private practice whether in Mumbai, Manchester or Meknes has a clientele drawn to them by reputation. But just as with the medical doctor they have very little knowledge of their patient's backgrounds except what can be gained from the consultation which is not governed by office hours. The consultation time spent is governed by the complexity of the personal problems presented to them.

The cost to the patient is related to their perception of the value of the consultation and this itself is dominated by the fact that the social distance factor does not greatly influence the relationship. It is a negotiable one which comes from traditional acceptance of the fact that these diviners come from the same social backgrounds as those that consult them.

The doctor on the other hand has a limited number of patients who come from the same social background as themselves and they feel professionally that it is better to retain social distance than to build up wider more social than clinical relationships. Similarly the diviner operating from within a neighbourhood environment or parallel communities as many would prefer to go to a diviner whom they do not know personally. They are able to assess the difficulties of their patients as they come from similar backgrounds and have a more personal understanding of what that may be but is more likely to be the cause of their distress according to their non-linear ideas of causation.

While it may not be acceptable to any Western understandings of contemporary life to parallel the doctor's consultation with a patient to that of a fortune-teller, we must not use prejorative terms to such people who also deal with human distress. They are both in their own ways attempting to confront individuals with the realities of their lives but they are also providing them with their estimates of their personal futures from two different perspectives.

We may well find this difficult to accept because the physician goes through a long period of professional training and base their opinions as far as possible on hard data. They have this trained confidence to interpret about which their clients may have little more than gossip awareness from newspapers and some knowledge left over from their own education. The key to their professionalism is the consultation in which both the physicians and the diviners attempt to put over convincingly their interpretations about the future in which there is certainly an element of intuition.

The successful fortune-teller may also have a learned professionalised cleverness. It is not only Turner with his understandings of the thinking processes of the Ndembu diviner Muchona the Hornet (Turner, 1967:131-151) but other social scientists who have been able to reach a close understanding of such men and women. A cultural anthropologist (Opler, 1936) has described the Apache medicine man as an intuitive psychoanalyst with an uncanny feeling for the symbolic and personal meanings of their clients' dreams. Another was just as impressed with the diagnostic acumen of Yoruba healers in Nigeria (Leighton, 1969). They use the symbols gained from playing cards to Coca Cola bottle tops as facts which similarly have to be interpreted and in this they could be described as professionally 'hard' as the Tarot card configurations have fixed values (Aphek and Tobin, 1986).

Both forms of consultation have the same structure and aims; the order, arrangement and presentation of themes. The overall establishment of credibility, the use of words and the framework of presentation which are accepted as particular to their professional explanations, attempts to downgrade the information to the level of their client's understandings. Although both would state that they take particular pains to make their explanations and suggestions conform to their client's understandings, much of the physician's phrasing will be formalised rather than vague and ambiguous.

Both types of professionals are using classes of knowledge largely unknown to their clients and they have to pass onto them a feeling of certainty rather than to suggest that their diagnosis is not conclusive. At the same time they have to suggest hope even when they may consider that there is none. Often their statements of probability have to do this and if it is not their primary role it is at least a pre-eminent one. They would lose credibility if they dealt only with misfortune which is probably no more frequent than good fortune.

It is only too easy to assess doctor and diviner however defined in terms of a clear cut binary opposition, almost an ethical division between the scientifically correct and the obviously fraudulent. In practical terms there is quackery on both sides of this functional divide. Any assessment in the context of their abilities to provide probability judgements should be seen in the context of individual abilities, qualifications, conduct, responsibility and personal professional development almost but not quite regardless of the form of therapy in question (Wahlberg, 2007). But such an understanding misses out the essential factor of the patient's self-assessed satisfaction; a probability that they diagnose as benign is more likely to be seen as correct than incorrect.

The physician gives a high proportion of exact information by excluding many knowable and unknown factors from their assessments. The parallel fortune-teller or whatever provides a wider range of scientifically questionable conclusions but reaches these from a wider range of potential data from which nothing accessible is excluded.

PROBABILITY AS GUESSWORK

Unless we are dealing with a situation in which the odds are fixed and predetermined so that the probabilities are mechanical and the odds on any particular outcome are not related in anyway to any social likelihoods, any social event which is related to probability is in analytical terms unique. Social scientists and analysts in general may reduce this uniqueness by excluding factors which contribute to this and thus reducing the options to what they consider to be manageable proportions.

We know that this approach is common enough in its legal sense over the breakdown of a legally binding contract and this does not take into account the reasons for such a breakdown unless such an eventuality was written into the original document. Such a breakdown might be due to as many factors as imagination can produce.

An analysis of divorce is likely to be related to the age of the partners, their occupations or status as recorded on the marriage certificate and length of the marriage. It could be suggested that almost every factor that might have contributed to the breakdown is excluded by such brevity of data either because it is not readily available or too expensive to find out for even a small sample of those divorcing.

So, however the probability of divorce or any other social matter is assessed, it is going to be done on the basis of relatively accessible bureaucratically produced data by those who are considered by training and experience to know enough to reach such conclusions. So the odds on something happening is based as much as anything on intuition. The building up of any probability conclusions about human behaviour is done with the materials that are available and this excludes much information which those analysts would admit to themselves as vital to any accurate conclusions and of course excludes chance.

Also any research which comes up with correlations between two or more sets of facts has not established that there is any necessary connections between them. It is prudent to assume that causation is not involved rather than to hold to such tenuous and unproven connections. A Chinese survey found no association between cigarette smoking and obesity (Xu *et al.*, 2007) despite some correlation just as the much tighter but irrelevant correlation between Indian murderers and tea-drinking. We have to accept (Taleb, 2007) that prediction in anything other than narrowed eventualities such as toothpaste sales, is more often than not guesswork dressed up as a professional skill.

21

Influences on Estimating Probabilities

As we have established that much social science information is both inaccurate and historical rather than having adequate current relevance and that in terms of possible accuracy probabilities have an appearance of professionalised guesswork, then we must look what are the influences dictating these assessments. What are the factors which enable well intentioned and professionally qualified individuals to make these assessments which they know will have little likelihood of being fulfilled accurately.

A social scientist making a statement of probabilities would have been required to follow an orderly process of thought following in sequence base line data, then comprehension, application, analysis, synthesis and finally evaluation (Bloom *et al.*, 1956), an orderly cognitive process but to what extent is this systematic approach followed.

PROBABILITIES AND THEIR CULTURAL CONSTRAINTS

Probabilities are like their particular sub-cultures whether they be communities of subsistence farmers or that of lawyers, doctors or geneticists. These are tight little social and emotional worlds with their own cognitive processes stabilised by socialisation and specific training. However, in the contemporary world it is unlikely that any culture or professional group is sufficiently exclusive and isolated to control practices much less thought in any overall way which would make the assessment of probabilities easier.

Certainly any form of specialisation whether domestic cooking in Bamako or the settlement of a bankruptcy dispute in Banaras provides both conscious and unconscious guidelines as to how those involved should carry out their functions. But the cook sees advertisements and the lawyer picks up professional gossip as to how she might get the better of her opponents. Culture may be king but today everyone is in a dialectical situation with invasive ideas from outside their particular social environments.

The scientific culture within which modern medicine operates and works out its probabilities is in some senses universal as vast quantities of information are potentially available 'out there' but that is not to suggest that it is 'inhere' to the doctor making diagnostic decisions. Of course she can index a key word on her computer and then be confronted with some hundreds of possibly relevant references. How much time can she spend on these references which are all potentially relevant. She has other patients waiting at the door and when she gets home in the evening her family obligations take over from any possibility of going through medical journals. In theory the base line data is there but in practice their availability to that doctor is a matter of chance; something may have caught her eye or a colleague may have suggested that she should read some particular report.

The treatment of a particular disease or physical condition if it has been diagnosed correctly is likely to be within known parameters whether in China or Canada. Their professionals are trained along similar lines and have access to the same journals. So in a general sense these professionals operate within a global network in which they are able to communicate with other professionals provided that the information is in a mutually understood language. In this sense English is an international language but Mandarin is not, so information in Chinese or indeed Japanese journals is restricted to the environments in which those languages are spoken should scientific data be published there.

This is a closed world in which what is communicated and understood does not go outside the socially restricted social environmental boundaries constrained by education and status. A British doctor on being asked how she communicated with a Bengali woman in east London who spoke no English replied strictly on a veterinary basis; the only means of communication was through body language.

Are social scientists any better situated for accessing knowledge about the base lines from which they are calculating probabilities; a bacteria has a certain exactness which can be evaluated, while human behaviour has none except by excluding possible relevant matters. Doctors and scientists may disagree about the interpretation of facts, social scientists are much more weakly situated since they are few in number and each one has far fewer contacts with their professional colleagues than doctors and lawyers. Comparatively they work in professional isolation meeting infrequently at conferences and social occasions but not usually in the circumstances related to their fieldwork about which they often maintain a high degree of privacy. In addition there is rarely agreement over the stability of data.

Social scientists although they may have some sense of corporate professionalism, it is not defined well enough to have the same effects as it has on lawyers and doctors. The label of social scientist does not carry with it any understanding of what that person might be like. But there is another difficulty with their collecting of data. Except when they are studying their own social world undercover, they are going to do their work in social environments of which they will never know enough to feel that they have a comprehensive understanding of that culture.

MULTIPLE AUTHORSHIP AND UNCERTAINTY

Social scientists will almost always be working alone and even when there are joint projects the inter-relationships do not parallel joint concern for a patient or the joint development of a particular experiment since cooperation will mainly be on committees or comments on the completed work of others. There is rarely agreement on the basic terms used so these are often compromises to enable inclusion rather than to create anything approaching scientific precision.

The majority of scientific papers and a substantial number of those written by social scientists have multiple authors and with this comes the assumption that they have been part of the research project throughout. Given that all individuals are different and may well see the same event in different ways, we cannot assume that such co-authorships means any constant measure of agreement except for the form of the final publication. Their work may have been in a standard form as with the use of a questionnaire or there may have been agreement about the theme for their joint research. Both of these approaches have their own difficulties in reaching any uniformity.

Firstly, the bringing together of the results of self-completed questionnaires apart from the difficulties as to whether the questions have been answered in the sense intended by the researchers and the simplicities of quantifying binary answers, which involve individualism. Anything other than this requires the coding of answers or their insertion into grades. This is a time consuming process involving hours of cooperative work in committee and the results are usually compromises over the wide differences between answers and their evaluation (Schubert *et al.*, 1999), particularly as in this study there was 84 per cent agreement on pass or fail from the 180 examiners involved, but such a binary decision would seem to be a simplification of a complex situation in which there may have been other explanations and needs. If the coding is done by a single individual we can assume some consistency in the results even if there is inaccuracy. If the coding is done by several persons then there will be substantial variation in how particular words and phrases are slotted into pre-arranged categories or much time has to be spent in attempting to reach acceptable uniformity.

Then there are multi-method co-authorship research in which the data is looked at from different perspectives as a study of parents of troubled children recorded their satisfaction with the mental health treatment received. The quantitative results varied with the number and type of sessions received (Rey *et al.*, 1999). With the rigidity of fixed answers we are still left with the interpretation of these quantities and the fact that these answers have been shown numerically, must mean that joint interpretations are likely to be questionable.

When five authors collaborate in a study of marital strain and risk of coronary heart disease in which there were 3,682 participants with a ten-year follow-up (Eaker *et al.*, 2007), there are bound to be problems. This study produced such probabilities as self-silenced wives were four times more likely to die than wives who spoke out raise serious problems over consistent interpretations and indeed there would be time changes in the five researchers themselves over the ten-year period of this collaboration.

There is another aspect to these problems over numerical accuracy. If researchers have been working together on an agreed theme or themes, then it would seem reasonable to assume that these individuals can through discussion reach qualitative conclusions from which reasonably significant probabilities can be produced. With just two authors we can assume that their approaches have been brought together with some authoritative cohesion as in collating the stories of high-risk adolescent mothers (Williams and Vines, 1999). But in other co-authorships the results provided different models with large differences in predicted scores for some individuals (Temkin *et al.*, 1999). It would seem that co-authorship raises a number of issues that complicate even further the possibilities of inaccuracy and bias.

Social scientists are inevitably creatures of their own cultures combined with the consequences of specialising but not specialised education so that their thinking and communications, and with this the manner in which probabilities are worked out, are culturally restricted. Of course there may be prejudices and biases involved, but this channelling is much commoner and less reprehensible and is indeed a factor in all forms of communication.

THE CULTURAL COMPONENT OF INDIVIDUALITY

However, well trained the social scientists may be, they will always be the creatures of whatever their cultures may predispose them to see in their fieldwork. The Japanese researcher who worked among the Zuni would not have been seen for long as a peculiar type of detribalised American Indian. Even if he did not put this into his assessments he would certainly have looked at their behaviour through Japanese eyes and no doubt that the form in which his views would be presented would have been a valuable difference to that of the 'white' Americans who have dominated this field for so long.

While it may be easy to see the differences in the contexts of Navajo, Ndembu, or Bengali cultures but what is the base line from which such differences are assessed? Are Bengalis different to Mexicans or the other way round? Also it has to be recognised that in each case a separate culture is part to some degree in some larger culture, even if it does not go so far as to presuppose the existence of Gaia with the globe as a single biological unit. Black American professional women (Freedman, 1988) state that on the one hand they have been brought up to mistrust the dominant white community including the medical profession. On the other hand the poor understanding by the white medical community concerning their black patients, beliefs and values relating to religion and matrilineality is in part the result of this.

So the assessment of probabilities will always be conceived within the constraints of their creators' cultures which are themselves ill-defined and ill-understood. In this respect the scientific world of medicine and the proto-scientific ones of economics and politics handicaps probability assessments by the narrow ill-defined nature of their field of factors.

INFLUENCES ON ESTIMATING PROBABILITIES

Probabilities are based on the availability of information and there is a personal factor in this related to the amount of physical and intellectual energy that any individual may put into finding out what they want to know. Of course the necessary information may indeed be somewhere out there but may not be retrievable because the topic is too difficult in itself or too difficult for those attempting it because it is private rather than public behaviour and the cost may be beyond the researcher's budget.

Imagination is also a factor which may bias certain evaluations as in the Castenada working up of his relationship with the American Indian mystic so that the more rational seeker for facts on which to base further work may be defeated since these popular books lack base line information and social reality.

Such judgements that imaginative intuition may be based on is the fact that something similar has happened before. There is also the failure of many social scientists to accept the persistent factor of chance which is more likely to be a factor in small samples. The persistence in their research may have made their encounters with certain types of behaviour and conclusions more likely. There is always the illusion of validity which comes from the 'magical' value attributed to written and printed results, which does not apply to the more easily forgettable but impressionable spoken word.

ONE OFF EVENTS INFLUENCING INDIVIDUALS

Research with even the most impelling of personal motives tends to become monotonous after the initial excitements of culture shock have worn off and the social scientist is left with the realities of daily recording of what they now recognise as the daily life of 'others'.

Every individual if questioned at length will be able to list the critical events in their lives and even if they are categorized into groups, they will still be seen as unique and immensely influential on their lives. Those who have survived wars, epidemic diseases, animal attacks and such horrendous events as the experience of concentration camps in Nazi Germany, Stalin's Russia or PolPot's Cambodia must be scarred for life by such experiences. In addition each individual will have experienced domestically the traumas of death and the degeneration of the elderly, the birth of children, sibling rivalry and the inevitable crises in personal relationships.

While on the credit side each individual will have achieved personal successes which will have distinguished him or her from their neighbours and peers at least in their own estimation by the small successes even achievements of which they alone may be aware. Looking at the personal lives of 'others' there must always be the inevitable recognition of the uniqueness of even what appears to be the dullest of lives as factory workers or subsistence farmers. There is very little similarity in even the simplest of activities carried out by a group of people even when there are few material differences between them.

Social scientists with the statistical requirements of 'hard' science lurking in the backs of their minds tend to avoid the factor that any behavioural event is unique almost by definition and the more important the factors being considered, the greater the uniqueness of everything related to these occurrences (Tversky and Kahneman, 2006).

There is also the factor that the researchers themselves may take events out of context and inflate their importance just because they are unusual from their cultural points of view. There is also the tendency for researchers to be attracted to events which according to their cultural understandings are unique but which may not be all that much according to the social situation being observed so we have Westerners paying more attention to witchcraft than agricultural and domestic practices. So the Western researcher may pay much attention to fortune-telling and rain-making because it is not what they will have experienced in their university environments. The Chinese and Indian researchers working in Europe or America will similarly be paying attention to the crudity of much Western social behaviour when it is compared to their own cultural understandings.

THE RESEARCHERS AND MYOPIC SAMPLING

A further bias on individual perceptions which may distort assessments comes from the inability of the social sciences to get detailed information from large populations. They use small samples not because they feel that they are more accurate but because of time and money factors, and indeed the convenience of dealing with twenty informants conveniently situated rather than two thousand living miles apart. There is little reason to suppose other than hope that the sample is a microcosm of the universe from which it is chosen since the categories used to discriminate samples are too general to reflect large scale social accuracies and differences (Kahneman and Tversky, 2006). The unjustified confidence in the replicability of samples has severe consequences for the estimation of probabilities when there is little likelihood of one sample replicating another no matter how carefully selected.

In the assessment of probabilities that certain behavioural events will occur, it seems that the thinking about such estimates is dominated by the latest information thought to be relevant rather than from the accumulation of related information (Lyon and Slovic, 1976).

There is also the dominance of lineal thinking and that it must be demonstrated in any results. There is no reason to suppose that lineal thinking has any general existence in the everyday lives of people whether they come from the highlands of Papua or from the university campus of Delhi, Harvard or Oxford. It is used for certain restricted decision makings but in the generalities of living it excludes too much to carry any general social weighting in social choices which have to combine innumerable ill-defined factors of much importance. Of course, it is possible that what may appear to be lateral thinking is more or less lineal thinking carried out instantaneously but this remains a supposition. People make decisions more or less instantaneously bring into consideration many more unconscious than conscious considerations.

There is also no reason to suppose that the framing of categories for data, contingencies and outcomes for one piece of research would apply to another done at a different time and different social environment. The base lines for any human behaviour have very little stability and even less when the social scientist is combining several sets of data (Tversky and Kahneman, 1982). The fact that these researchers may be ostensibly creatures of habit does not make them necessarily professionally consistent.

It has also been demonstrated that in probability estimates in which there will always be a personality factor, there is a similarity between this and the stereotypes of the roles involved of those researched (Kahneman and Tversky, 1973) and in prior expectations that medical diagnostic tests are infallible (Hammerton, 1973).

However, formal probability efforts may be there can only be as satisfactory as the definitions of what is going on and the aims and objects of these exercises. No matter how rigorously trained in logic the estimators may be, we do not know the states of their minds; what subconscious inserts may have occurred from peripheral and related matters of possible influence on their decisions. Someone estimating medical probabilities may have been the victim of a medical misdiagnosis or knows about people who have had such experiences, and so may well take a different approach than someone without such connections.

PARTICIPANTS INFLUENCING PROBABILITIES

As far as we can know from historical and so-called contemporary data and anthropological studies those who consult accepted experts as to their future probabilities as well as the experts themselves become part of what is suggested to be the solution. Both the fortune teller just as much as the economic forecaster in a major industrial enterprise have their reputations at stake in what they say about future probabilities. In no sense are they scientific blank slates onto which only pragmatically verifiable data is going to be written; they are part of what they propose.

The expert throws out a tentative solution which the patient or business manager accepts or argues for alternatives. In a divination ceremony in Mombasa (Kenya) in which a spirit was possessing a wife and speaking through her stated that it would withdraw if she was given a diamond ring and a white horse which the husband stated flatly was beyond his means. The solution negotiated through the medium was that the spirit-cum-wife would be satisfied with the sacrifice of a goat and the wife to be given a new dress. Such a situation is not much different to the economic adviser tailoring his probabilities to what he assesses would be acceptable to his employers or those to whom he is presenting his report.

Certainly in countries which do not have a medical system with wide coverage and adequate free resources, the physician is similarly going to assess their patients in terms of what they can afford to pay and treatment would be suggested to conform to such a rational or realistic possibilities. So we have medical solutions which are not courses of treatment but more or less one short attempt so that in such situations the solutions might just as well have been eschatological.

These professionals ask the client questions and from their own knowledge of social behaviour in general about their own particular specialisations, there are all the elements of a shared cultural background. The oracle at Delphi in ancient Greece, the diviner in contemporary Kenya and the economic forecaster in Mumbai are not producing solutions in anyway comparable to a diagnosis based on depersonalised laboratory data.

So the consulters are in an inter-relationship with the professionals they consult who are not constrained by the data as it might be in a scientifically based problem. The questions asked will provide the clues to an acceptable solution which the client will see as not only logical in terms of their shared background but also within their social and economic means.

There is a measure of social equality in the relationships between diviner and client despite the former's specialisation and reputation and this would extend to that of the economic or political adviser. However, where the adviser and the advised come from different cultures over east and west or northern and southern divides the problems escalate. The negotiations between the parties become much more difficult because the dimensions in which they can reasonably negotiate contain many unknown factors; both parties are to some extent socially uncomfortable. The white coat worn by physicians is an alienating symbol in most cultures and in China white is a colour associated with death and mourning. Whatever paraphernalia is worn by the Kenyan diviner or the Hindu saddhu it is not alien to the understandings of their clients just as the economic adviser and those advised are likely to wear mutually acceptable clothes.

There are also differences in the nature of the consultations between those in developing and developed societies. In the former most consultations are not behind closed doors although they may be in the case of quasi-traditional urban diviners. This keeps the questions and answers within the boundaries of communal acceptability. But in the urban-industrial setting the problems are more likely to be directly confrontational and have no communal aspects. The office in which discussions takes place is a prison-like social box.

In the Western scientifically based form of consultation, meetings take place in private and the range of adjustments is confined to a narrower social environment in which matters that are situated outside this inter-relationship are not considered to be of relevance. In the medical consultation the physician acts on the symptoms which the patient raises and factors outside this are not assumed to be known or necessary for any clinical decision to be reached. Certainly now there is a movement to involve patients in discussions about treatment should they so wish. However, physicians have for so long provided for themselves and maintained a high degree of professional isolation and this has discouraged any invasion of their expertise by the uneducated laity. In the United States the majority of patients prefer a passive role (Arora and McHorney, 2000), while in Sweden most patients preferred a shared approach to clinical decisions in primary care (Rosen *et al.*, 2001).

The theory that physicians and their patients except possibly with family doctors, can work together to reach decisions that fit in with the preferences of patients and the available options, is unlikely to have any universal acceptance. The social differences between patient and physician are too extreme to have any universal appeal which bridge the gap between the average physician and the average patient (Frosch and Kaplan, 1999). So it would seem that the production of probabilities in formal clinical situations remain professionally with physicians, except in the circumstances of terminal illness when it is the custom to involve relatives. However, in Pakistan families and physicians might make decisions in a high proportion of cases without feeling any need to give any primacy to the views of the patient (Moazam, 2000).

PEOPLE AND PROBABILITY—THE PERSONAL FACTOR

Social scientists by design seek information from people and situations who are the objects of their research interests. It is safe to say in the majority of cases these people have not asked for this attention. It is not that they are necessarily unwilling but their willingness to be studied is almost certainly passive rather than active. Informed consent is just a legal cover without much social meaning. They are participants but the parallels in their degree of involvement is more with the fieldwork on primates than as partners in joint projects; they are rarely named and almost invariably numbered.

So whether the data obtained can form a reasonable and rational base for estimating future probabilities often seems questionable. While the researchers may have their professional standards they are still involved as particular people with aims filtered through this factor of personality and the need for wide-ranging abilities. There can be no scientific methodological rigidity in the ways that they carry out their research work involving human behaviour or in how they show their results.

When they work on quantified data as in economics they are detached from much direct association with behaviour as would be the work on political opinions in any quantified form. Even with the agreement to participate by volunteers, this does not necessarily make for accuracy with or without their knowing the objectives of the research.

It would seem safer to assume that anything recorded by direct means is likely to be proportionately incorrect and that where indirect methods are used as in the use of security cameras, the hardness of such data is still filtered through personal interpretations. So any formulation of probabilities should be seen through some understandings of the very general handicaps of social science data collection. The nature of passive agreements and passive obstructions, the extent of community control, the ethical control of institutions as to what can be researched and the layers of situational agreement which must exist in any social universe within which research is carried out. Finally, we must look at the factors involving probabilities which are not quite so clearly related to human frailty.

22

Pathways to Probability

The pathways to any consideration of probability for something to happen in the future have certain similarities in all societies and at all levels within them, but to paraphrase Hartley's comment about the past, the future is a foreign country they do things differently there. It is a universal source of anxiety as much now as it has always been in the past.

An individual has a problem which he or she cannot solve within their own minds or with the social resources which they command. These include the private rituals which they have developed or the social and ritualistic processes which are available in their society.

If that fails then in a process of social escalation such individuals go to someone for a solution or at least the mitigation of their anxieties. The persons consulted are accepted as an expert by reputation or because they have been professionally certified as officially competent to deal with such difficulties. They include ordained ministers of religion, doctors and various types of diviners whether they be fortune tellers or economic and political forecasters.

In how these accepted experts deal with distress and anxiety there will usually be the same amalgam of professionally acquired knowledge as in the training of doctors and economists, the apprenticeship of all such experts which will have taken years of slow professional advancement. Finally, there is the acquisition of knowledge about the social environment in which they practice and about the people with whom, they are dealing. This is usually culturally restricted and there are always problems over the passage of such expertise from within one culture into another.

The local doctor or diviner have some acquired but limited knowledge about the background to those who consult them. The specialist who is consulted is more detached from such aids to diagnosis whether in a hospital or in a stock exchanges of Mumbai or Shanghai.

While institutions will always wish to plan their futures as accurately as possible as in the national development plans of many countries whether based on ideologies such as the Tanzanian Villagisation policy and the Five Year Plans of Soviet Russia or the annual budgets of democratic Western countries, but it is in health that the assessment of probabilities are overwhelmingly commonest.

For many if not most people health and well-being are not only indivisible but are also involved in economics, politics and religion. However the decisions in all these matters, just as much in modern medicine as in their ancient forms are probabilistic. There is considerable uncertainty in medical decision making which is the end of a process of thinking and consultative interrelationship. There is always uncertainty surrounding the processes by which such decisions are made.

It is not just that medical decision making whether by a clinician or a quasi-traditional herbalist, is always involved in the assessment of and attempts to reduce uncertainty. However, it is this an area of human behaviour for which much social science information is available as well as the 'hard' data provided by laboratories. This is a mass of information but the relationship of these two forms is not so much unacceptable as uncertain; a combination of professional needs and personal ambition.

The fact that there is this accumulation of Western oriented scientific data and enormous successes in reducing human distress, may overlook the fact that access to these treatment successes and what modern medicine aims to do, has only been available to minorities. So for the reduction of the more day-to-day processes of dealing with personal anxieties the majority are left to their own resources. They use traditional and quasi-traditional processes as well as what is often disguised as alternative medicine combined with the placebo effect by which the mind appears to solve at least some of its own problems.

While medicine certainly sees itself as providing a public service detached as far as possible from the situational requirements of morality, economics and politics, how it operates in particular circumstances depends on social demands. There is certainly a supply induced demand to which medical administrators and politicians have to pay attention in their budget proposals. There is the reality of epidemics and the switch to AIDS research as a response to the massive increase in this frightening disease. But there have always been fashions in scientific thinking (Kuhn, 1962) and more specifically in medical practice in particular areas and with particular physicians with their personal interests and specialities.

This happens in much the same way that quasi-traditional healers in developing countries and the practitioners of alternative medicine everywhere have responded to the escalation of anxieties by the expansion in their numbers in urban rather than rural areas. As we have seen everywhere as in Nigeria the estimated number of traditional healers runs into many thousands and in Lagos there were fifteen thousand and Kano had seven thousand (Harrison, 1974).

THE UNRELIABILITY OF PROFESSIONAL EXPERTISE

These experts are dealing with the possibility of similar symptoms reoccurring in the area of their specialities but in medicine it is in the interpretations that there are the variations which show up in second opinions perhaps not advertised because of the legal consequences. A tabulation of dissent even when there is laboratory data shows that there are often diagnostic disagreements (Kaplan and Frosch, 2005). There was a 42 per cent mean disagreement between specialists over coronary angiographies (Zir *et al.*, 1976).

In a more interesting example of variations in diagnoses, cardiologists were given the same angiogram at two different times; at the second assessment they disagreed with their own first judgements in 8 per cent to 37 per cent of the cases (Detre *et al.*, 1975). In another example of variability in the detection of prostate cancer agreement was only fair after adjustment for chance (Smith and Catalona, 1995). There are so many variations in the patterns of diagnoses that patients with the same problem going to different doctors will not just may get but will get different diagnoses or solutions.

In a study of the opinions of 220 physicians about the limiting of pediatric life support in six out of eight scenarios, the same level of intensive care was chosen by less than half of the sample (Randolph *et al.*, 1999). In a less important occasion in a study of sore-throats which the doctors thought were caused by streptococcal infections in 577 patients which were checked by laboratory tests; there was an overestimate of 33.2 per cent action leading to unnecessary use of antibiotics (McIsaac and Butler, 2000).

What it comes down to is 'somehow experienced surgeons are able to sift through a massive amount of information and properly select patients who are appropriate for surgery with quite reasonable peri-operative and long-term mortality rates (Fillinger, 2007). So clearly in medicine which is based on scientific research we can anticipate substantial variations in the opinions of experienced physicians and surgeons as to how to deal pragmatically with materially visible patient centred situations for which there can be laboratory based support.

In the area of psychology both the Western trained professional and the quasi-traditional diviner are not backed up by any laboratory based pragmatism. One has to presuppose that in this field there is likely to be a much higher degree of variation in diagnoses by these men and women specialists who have a much more personal interrelationship with those who come to them for consultations and moreover this will vary as much with the background of cultural as clinical understandings. A hypothetical case involving the treatment of aggression among physicians in Canada, Germany and the United States found variations of 61 per cent, 65 per cent and 86 per cent (Koeck *et al.*, 1998).

What is the difference between the practices of these scientifically trained professionals and the quasi-traditional specialists whom they in practice despise for the crudities of their understandings? The physicians are faced with the existence of massive amounts of information about which they have more or less accidental knowledge when we recognise the vast amount of updating medical literature which is available in English alone; it is a physical impossibility. The quasi-traditional diviners will similarly know that they have only partial knowledge of all the factors relevant to those that consult them. Probabilities in both situations are assessed in terms of the knowledge which they do have rather than what they might or should have.

DECISION MAKING AND THE LIMITATIONS OF RATIONALITY

Decision making involving social behaviour on which probabilities are based except in the case of 'hard' science experiments in which the materials are both limited and accurately defined and any variations in methodology, ideas and materials are long-term, is a question of making choices.

We dupe ourselves into thinking that our choices are rational as they inevitably involve a number of guesses (March, 1978) including uncertainty about the future consequences and guesses about future preferences, but this surely minimizes what is involved in the making of most decisions.

In this there are two types of attempted rationality. The descriptive one in which the researchers make a cohesive whole of the social behaviour which they have been studying and which they accept will in reality be a work of historical significance and based on whatever data they have been able to collect. Secondly, studies in which they are attempting to suggest what the future might be which except in the case of short-term probabilities, will usually be expressed in terms of broad generalities combined with a long mental list of possible often unwritten conditions which may undermine any such conclusions.

Of course, there are minimalist logics on the level of two plus two equals four in our private accountancies and in collecting hens' eggs from the bushes behind the house. It is always a question of what the figures in quantification actually represent and whether in fact they represent anything hard enough to form the basis for estimating probabilities and decisions based on those assessments. There is a professional need for such conclusions to be classed as rational rather than as a hope that they might be. These conclusions as to future probabilities are in effect the best we can do in the current circumstances which we are rarely going to admit to being inadequate.

At most we must accept that individuals make decisions on their own future behaviour on the basis of a limited range of information. In practice they limit the number of factors which are brought into active consideration as in the case of badly wanting a partner, buying a house or planting a crop. In such situations the number of factors used is limited by the need. Economists and the managers of household budgets consider the cost of objects and they have some idea of the self-imposed priorities which limit what is considered in their decision making.

Decision making can be accurately based when deciders are in possession of almost all the factors as in the switching off of life-support machines for someone who has been diagnosed as brain dead by two unrelated doctors. This is a rarely necessary decision but even then we do not know what were the ancillary factors which enabled the next of kin to reach such a decision relative to costs and inheritance which can be seen as inhumanly rational.

Perhaps decision making can only be made to appear rational by restricting the amount of data or possible factors that can be brought into consideration because we have to make it seem that we are being logical in our decision making and in what we propose to others as being probable. It is not just recent events in Western economic forecasting which has shown their chronic inability to make any accurate long term statements about what is likely to happen (Taleb, 2007).

Much of the data on the rationality of decision making comes from sitting down and thinking about how to deal with a problem which is common enough in economic decision making (Fehr and Tyran, 2008) for which there are accurately detailed occasions and analyses over the granting of mortgages.

If the logic of decision making involves and indeed requires the use of all the facts necessary to reach a rational decision then this can rarely be the case because of the variability and constant changes in human behaviour. The facts on which decisions are made are already past history and behaviourally out of date. There is usually the unwarranted assumption that future events will reduplicate what has already occurred which might be better described as no more than a hope.

Most events which the social scientists encounter seem to have an existential but circumscribed reality only momentarily fixed in time and space. They have caught the event by chance not by any assumption of necessarily independent reality. They are forced to accept in their minds these ephemeral events as having more than a momentary reality, but they find it inadequate for the scientific presumptions of their professionalism. It is this which requires the stable formulations of successfully proved hypotheses and the legitimizations of statistical logic.

Whatever has happened has long since past into history and its circumstances changed by new social environments and personal changes brought about by chance. Trying to tie down ephemeral events by procedures created by and satisfying for the social scientists themselves is creating an isolated form of social and psychological reality which almost inevitably has little relationship to any realities recognisable by those from whom the information was obtained. In practice it may be that a large proportion of social science productivity is for confirming their own professionalism.

Individuals whatever their social environment certainly think that they are acting rationally in what they assume to be their own self-defined interests. As a cognitive species they search for intelligence and rationality in the decision making of others in an attempt to rationalise, and this is perhaps a culture bound activity, the anomalies in the behaviour of others. Action is presumed to follow either from explicit calculations of the consequences in terms of objectives or from rules of behaviour that have evolved culturally. These thought processes are presumed to have once been rational rather than just sensible at that time and in those circumstances for reasons which are now obscure. Social scientists are always working from data which they have collected but of which they are usually a part and about which they should admit that they do not know enough.

THE FORMS OF RATIONALITY

Whatever the theories of rational decision making may be whether limited by what researchers see, hear or are able to locate in literature there is the simple fact that whatever human behaviour is being observed it will always be in the process of changing. A community from one week to the next will have separations, illnesses, conceptions, accidents, chance understandings and encounters as well as profits and losses at work and in business; it is an ephemeral social landscape.

Decisions are reached within the context of the illness of a particular person or business transaction and then factors outside this are not directly considered (Chatterjee *et al.*, 1999) as management has to choose the right extent of analysis in preparing for major decisions such as whether to consider family share holdings, possible civil disturbances, trades union power or what pressure can be brought to bear on the local government.

Game situations in which as in gambling the odds are rationally considered is often a factor as in the maintenance of reciprocal networks which are created in traditional communities under the guise of friendship. They are in fact a survival strategy since the number of possible contacts are always limited in relation to resources (Back and Flache, 2008).

There is adaptive rationality in which decision making is related to previous individual or community experiences by which they progressively adapt to the conditions under which they are living as with the Tikopia islanders tying their population size to the limits sustainable on that island. In comparison the failure of the Easter islanders to adapt their religious practices to their progressive deforestation of the island from which then there was no escape since they could no longer construct sea-going canoes, a sorry sequence of irrational choices. The persistent negative information about the ill effects of smoking and alcohol on health led to little voluntary adaptation. This has had to be combined with economic costs and prohibitive legislation in Britain before there was any drop in smoking rates and little in drinking. The couple in a bar who go outside to smoke in bitterly cold weather because it is prohibited inside are moving towards adaptive rationality.

Selective rationality would be the process of selection among individuals and communities by which they survive direct challenges such as the reaction to famine which has been shown to follow a rational progression as its severity becomes apparent. The use of their own reserves, turning to relatives, using up of reciprocities previously organised and finally the resort to what their surrounding natural environments can produce.

It seems obvious that probability estimates are unlikely to be substantially correct unless the objectives are narrowly defined and indeed confined in such a way as to prevent the inclusion of disruptive factors.

Finally, historical rationality in which existing situations are examined retrospectively to show that what happened was the result of a succession of rational choices. This is perhaps the easiest form of rationality because it is able to ignore what in effect was the contemporary environment at the time decisions were taken as there were always factors of chance which could not have been foreseen. The building of a bridge to carry a maximum load or a dam to have the maximum water pressure behind its wall and the planners would have carried out exercises in probability as to possible excesses. It would not have been rational to plan the World Trade Center towers to withstand the sideways blows of 120 ton aircraft but the nearby Empire State Building had been hit by a military aircraft and survived so the probability planning was faulty.

The D-day planning for the invasion of France by the Allies took two years but it went seriously wrong on Omaha beach with the failure of the naval bombardment to eliminate the German defences and no allowance was made for the unseasonal storm which blew up on the second day. So it would seem that even when objectives are supposed to be limited and circumscribed, this is not enough to exclude chance.

All these forms of rationality start from the assumption that the Western developed pattern of linear thinking has to be used and that there are no alternatives. They assume that the data on which decisions are made is defined or at least definable but they do not accept that all decision making is done by people who do not possess all the relevant facts which this form of rationality needs for such decisions. Further it would seem that most decision making is based on lateral rather than lineal thinking; the spread sheet approach by which we reach personal decisions in our appreciation of a painting and our dislike of certain people whom we meet for the first time. Even if this should be the case we have no assurance that individuals would be able to handle all this accumulation of data which rationality dictates that they should use (Greco *et al.*, 2002).

EXPERIMENTS INTO THE PRACTICE OF ASSESSING PROBABILITY

Experimental studies of prediction and probability do not mirror reality since they are both linear and finite. They present the people who are participating in the experiment with a finite set of facts usually in print so that those involved can be assumed to be highly literate.

This is an unreal situation as those involved are detached from the day-to-day realities of their own lives. They are thus required to make decisions in the abstract for which they have no more than impersonal interest except that they have agreed to participate in such experiments. "Given specific evidence, e.g. a personality sketch, the outcome under consideration, occupational level of achievement, can be ordered by the degree to which they are representative of that evidence" (Kahneman and Tversky, 1973). But then this study undercuts its own statistical validity by stating that the personality sketches on which these experiments were made were notoriously unreliable. They were out of date by the time they were used as those sketched would have had subsequent experiences. There was also the problem of the stereotypes which the sampled individuals would have carried into the experiment. In such experimental circumstances it would not seem rational to produce quantitative results as indeed they write "it is hardly believable that a accurate description of a fourteen years old child based on a single interview could justify the degree of infallibility implied by the predictions of our subjects". In no sense are such experiments tests of social reality in which individuals for personal reasons have chosen to make such choices which have no direct bearing on their lives.

An experiment cannot be directed with any accuracy as to what might happen under conditions of contemporary life. Their validity must depend on the degree to which conditions of the experiment can duplicate a contemporary situation which is equally valid for all those participating in the experiment which is in practice a virtual impossibility. In the crudity of such experimental work there is almost a paper and pen working out of the best probable possibilities. In 'real' life there are no such parallels to the military appreciation of the situation as a result of which some formal institutional action is taken often under hurried and stressful circumstances.

The attraction of experiments probably lie at least in part to the degree of suggested control which it gives to the social scientists involved so that it fits in with theoretical possibilities. It assumes that there are finite features in social behaviour which can be unravelled from such studies of human activities. The vast range of probabilities can be reduced to some sort of order which is always a professional illusion. Primarily their use is their demonstration of the researcher's efforts and ability to reduce data to an orderly presentation and in this experimental works are essential parts of any professional career.

Experiments are also attractive to social scientists because in terms of the time effort and economics of research they are more profitable from their sheer convenience. They are usually done from an existing office in the employing institution and those sampled are already part of the researcher's working environment. The cost of such experiments are probably covered by departmental budgets for office running costs and computer use and even the sorting out of data can often be done by volunteers.

Experiments are attempted short cuts involving as much hope as reality. Any assessments of probability in the conditions of any social environment would always be faced with a mass of concurrently active factors which only the individual can consider and utilise without any conscious knowledge of how such decisions are reached. No matter what their social status may be and intellectual level, there is always a massive area of fluctuating factors which are intuitively brought into consideration. Some of these factors may be the result of socialisation and immediate social environments. In the circumstances of everyday life there are constantly varying and variable factors and it is the static nature of social science experiments into probabilities which makes them unreal.

THE ABILITY TO PREDICT

While it may be generally accepted that individual lives are unstable but not uncontrollably so, the larger organisations or the military have an air of stability and competence which rests in their assumed ability to predict their own futures and to change appropriately. The reading of company reports and the professional behaviour of the military shows that their record is at best patchy. It is in fact a poor record despite the existence in all such organisations of professional planning staffs of whose creditability and professionalism are the subject of much advertising. The financial pages of the quality press frequently record that companies have not been able to conform to their advertised programmes or have disastrously miscalculated their economic chances for factors that they state they could not have foreseen or controlled.

Nevertheless there are often major bankruptcies as with the recent collapse of the American bank Lehmann Brothers. In Britain the greatest miscalculation was that the National Health Service would be paid for out of national insurance contributions but once treatment became free the demand increased enormously and freed the middle classes and the elderly from substantial financial burdens.

The ability to predict is not covered by the clarity of any predictions made which are rarely in the form that something will or will not happen and most organisations cover this inexactness of predictions by keeping substantial reserves. Thus the reputation of these professional predictors probably comes from the ambiguity of their conclusions and by providing a range of alternatives. In the end it is only remembered that they did state that something might happen and the provided alternatives are forgotten.

THE LACK OF HARD FACTS

Hard science starts from hard data which has been found by calculations under laboratory conditions. It is available for replication by any researcher wishing to challenge its conclusions. There could be human error and indeed deliberate fraud as well as in the way that the machinery of analysis functioned. As we have already detailed it was found in one American research project that the significant results were due to fluctuations in the city's electricity supply over which the laboratory had no control. Similarly in Kampala, Uganda where the Social Research Institute in the 60s had much of its data on punched cards, there were almost daily afternoon showers. This added some dampness to the cards which led to a percentage difference in the machine sorting of cards between morning and afternoon.

In most social science research projects there are no prime facts base lines from which changes can be assessed with some confidence. There are few substantiated demographic facts, test performances have no parallel to hard science laboratory work, questionnaires self-administered and the assessment of skills may be according to the standards of other cultures and created by foreign intellectuals (Lynn *et al.*, 2006). In practice it would be unwise to calculate any probabilities on the basis for which the provided data is assumed to be accurate.

Human behaviour can only rarely be subject to definition as in the diagnosis of a particular disease by a laboratory test, but the prognosis of this defined condition is always subject to situational factors so that recovery or not is a question of probabilities which can only be calculated retrospectively. Unlike inorganic materials human behaviour has no static qualities that can be calculated and even those are subject to change as in carbon dating. There are certainly sequences as in material and mental decay as well as an inevitable final death but not any calculable exactnesses between birth and death.

PROBABILITY AND THE KNOWN ELEMENT

Few people recognise or are even aware of the instability of their own ideas and even if they have kept diaries they are not often reread for comparative purposes. People overwhelmingly live in a personal world of self-created stability and would find it unsettling to have their own instabilities pointed out to them. The workings of the mind are highly adaptive changing to the situations in which it finds itself.

Social scientists as a result of their research and on-going reading, will commit what they find to paper and in this data acquires a stability which is detached from the social realities of which they themselves were a part. Social environments move on from the moment that they have been recorded. What has been written down with its detailed conclusions from both quantitative and qualitative approaches acquire a merit and a justification for their use which is probably unjustified?

Any attempts to detail the future starts with what is known and in a non-literate approach. The assessors forming their ideas of probability starting with their own on-going adaptation to reality as they reinterpret the current situation in accordance with their own appraisal of what they consider to have happened recently. This it is not only that the human memory is unreliable which leads many social scientists to place importance on written data which may have similar unreliabilities built into their formulations.

THE FACTOR OF FEAR

The contemporary Western social scientists are used to making their probability assessments in an environment in which they do not have to consider any direct consequences of what they write except in terms of their own careers. Unless their thinking is obviously part of what the government considers to be subversive to the stability of the state, even then they will be no more than a file which might make them unlikely to get employment with a government agency.

In that environment much social science research work is done independently of any direct government assistance. We have very little direct evidence that these results are read by power holders and influence them in their decisions. In the rare cases in which research does appear to have had an effect as in the Swedish sociologist's report on the effects of racial discrimination in the United States (Myrdal, 1944), this work coincided with a change in the political and social understanding by the power-holding white elite. Whether it would have been as widely publicised if it had been written by an American who would have been politically suspect is difficult to assess. In the McCarthy period of virulent anti-Communism he might have lost his job or find employment difficult but he would not have been in any danger.

There have been a number of single party states in recent history which would not accept any criticism or any comment which they could interpret as hostile to their ideological commitments. So it will have been the case that social scientists in China, Soviet Russia and the Communist states of eastern Europe who will have carried out supportive work for the state (Rigby, 1974) or remained silent because of the reality of possible lengthy imprisonment. Outsiders will not have had any opportunity to assess what is going on except indirectly through the analysis of information supplied by state organisations or those controlled by the state.

In Soviet Russia social scientists were used quite extensively in support of the Communist Party's programmes but there were not ideologically free agents and their assessments of probabilities would have been made to help adjustments to a fixed policy rather than to conclude that it was not likely to work. The wholesale social and economic disruption caused by the villagization programme of the Tanganyika African National Union was not pointed out by local social scientists, and it was even supported by Oxfam who must have had some real knowledge of what was going on.

Social scientists have often been able to comment on their national educational policies because their assessments of future probabilities were not seen as a threat to any existing political establishment and those in power would usually have benefited from whatever changes were suggested (Halpenny, 1974).

Most newly independent states have universities but their social scientists have kept silent about the probabilities over what has been going on under their noses out of a very real fear for their own safety (Gingyera-Pinycwa, 1974), while making comments about neighbouring states. Some have felt it necessary to explain why they do not write about their own countries (Mazrui, 1974). Visiting social science researchers do not write about their findings until they have reached the safety of their own countries but even then their assessments may be muted by considering the future relationships with their university or employers.

So we can see that the assessment of probabilities in many modern situations cannot be carried out within the broad academic freedoms which exist in Western states. Any social scientist who does not consider such very personal issues while working not only in secular one party states but in those dominated by religious issues in Iran, Pakistan and Saudi Arabia would be foolish indeed.

THE EXTREME EDGE OF PROBABILITY

Social scientists in their assessments of probabilities stay as close as they can to the data which they have collected themselves or about which they have obtained from other sources on which they may have little information about the circumstances in which it was collected. They play safe on the assumption that what is going to happen soon is going to be very like what is happening now. But time sneaks in and with it the inevitable increases in chance events.

There are of course certain probabilities, events that subsequently are part of actual happenings that are so extreme that no social scientists except ideologues committed to that form of thinking, is likely to give their professional credence to such probabilities. They are outside professional betting or imagination but are nevertheless part of the dialectics of change. They are so improbable in terms of contemporary thought that gambling companies would take your money with a laugh and give you fantastically long odds in anticipation of such an event occurring.

There are within any range of specialisations and a corresponding range of probabilities which are likely to happen sooner or later and trends which are likely to develop. There are corresponding indecisions as to when, where and how these are likely to occur. They know only too well that there are innumerable known and unknown chance factors that get between a probability and its likely expression.

Transcendental meditation in the Western world is a tolerated form of idiosyncratic behaviour particularly among middle-class intellectuals. In so far as there is any public opinion about this eccentricity, it is that if participants are paying for this they are simply being duped.

However, the Maharishi Yogi organisation assembled 4,000 meditators in Washington, the United States capital in June and July 1993 to demonstrate that they could significantly lower the rates of violent crime there during that period by increasing coherence and reducing stress in the collective consciousness of that large population (Hagelin *et al.*, 1999). Indeed that is what happened with a maximum decrease in violent (homicide, rape and aggravated assault) crimes coincident with the peak numbers of participators. This project was monitored by a large group of independent scientists. The meditators had no contact with outsiders since their sessions were in-house and these results were independent of temperature changes as hot weather usually raises violent crime rates. Forty-two other studies have shown similar reductions.

The point of such an improbable result for which no explanation has been provided other than that of the Maharishi Yogi Programme that collective meditation perhaps in relation to the numbers meditating can have an effect in quietening a surrounding neighbourhood which has no idea that such a collective activity is happening on their behalf. No administration acted on this data.

So we have some very unusual conclusions clearly outside any conventional range of probability with which social scientists might wish to be involved. The problem remains of how to explain such a substantial percentage change to Chiefs of Police who are committed to understanding simpler linear causes and effects. Probability must always remain on the fringes of accepted and acceptable current paradigms.

23

Conclusions

The future cannot be known to any degree of accuracy even when assessed by experts. They do the best they can but should they come up with an accurate and narrow forecast and this is probably due to accidents by which unknown and undefined factors come into coincidence. It seems likely that the narrower the range of the estimated probability, the greater the inaccuracy or the greater the incorporation of chance factors.

It is perhaps easier for probabilities to be worked out with some exactness in clinical medicine since these estimates start with base lines backed up with the laboratory examination of data. Even when a disease has cross-cultural incidence, this hard base line may well be modified by cultural factors.

Marketing studies, an applied social science division of all major companies, of the probable sales of a particular object have the base lines as what is being put on then market need not have the sales for which it was designed. The choice of a particular model of car involves a very large number of possible factors. The Ford Edsel had design failures and high fuel consumption and came on the market in the unexpected 1957 recession. Viagra was originally marketed as a cure for high blood pressure rather than for sexual dysfunction for which it was subsequently a huge success.

So there is a scale of probability in considering any future events; the narrower the issue for which a statement of probability is made, the greater the inevitability of inaccuracy. The broader the matter made subject to any estimate of probability, the greater the chances of an estimate which may indicate no more than the range of probabilities.

A reasonable example of the way in which probabilities can

be tied into what is known about some particular behaviour are the hypotheses connecting homosexual black men and AIDS infections (Gregorio *et al.*, 2006). This group of researchers studied 148 published research works and from this evidence made certain conclusions in relation to twelve hypotheses. Three hypotheses were not supported by scientific evidence; black men were not more likely than others to engage in high risk sexual behaviour, they were not less likely to disclose their homosexuality which may have increased their risk behaviour nor were they more likely to inject drugs so increasing their risk of HIV infections. Hypotheses which were supported by scientific evidence were that black men were more likely than others to contract sexually transmitted diseases facilitating the transmission of HIV and that they were less likely to know their HIV status.

But for the other hypotheses there were insufficient or conflicting evidence that black men had a some genetic susceptibility to HIV, less likely to be circumcised, have HIV positive infections for longer periods, that they were more likely to have sex with HIV positive partners, their sexual networks put them at greater risk of being infected and more likely to be at risk of being imprisoned.

This careful analysis of the data about a particular disease in relation to a particular American social group showed a range of probabilities and improbabilities on which social planners and medical services could work out their guidelines for future activities. On these hypotheses it seems likely that no further research would be able to provide any narrow directed application because of the wide range of connected factors. However, even such wide ranging research has so far missed out the individuality of behaviour or consider that blackness or whiteness are rather more social than biological classifications and that they would almost certainly have been status and religious commitment factors. We have seen that the numbers who classified themselves as Arabs diminished when they were taxed at a higher rate than Africans. Then there is also the underlying impossibility of getting accurate facts from activities which are in any public sense private and also the factors of the mind of which so very little can be found out except by what people are prepared to talk about or react to which reliability cannot usually be applied with any scientific confidence.

THE DIVISIVENESS OF SOCIAL SCIENCE THEORIES

While it is accepted that most theories are not right or wrong but more or less useful for the purposes at hand, but in their conceptualizations they have a built-in binary quality at least in the sense that those who promote or criticize a particular theory it is either right or wrong; it is a process that excludes.

It seems likely that no one theory can explain any particular behaviour however carefully it is defined and supported by adequate contemporary research. It is certainly going to be dated sooner or later as they all have an ephemeral quality underlined by Kuhn and are subject to the fashions of professional and public opinion.

There is another basic factor typified by the dictum' you cannot communicate' (Watzlawick *et al.*, 1967) as a background factor to the innumerable theories of communication which in practice subdivide and exclude from the simple wholeness with which events are taken into the mind of social science observers. Perhaps the social sciences should accept that any human activity can quite adequately be explained by a variety of co-existing theories in which there are no particular predominant understandings which are independent of fashion and personalities except by the ways into which researchers are professionally socialized. We are trained to or train ourselves to see human behaviour in particular ways and thus use particular theories to support this socialization. Few social scientists are likely to describe their own way of life as deviant. Whatever theory is accepted as explaining communication and the clarity with which it covers the material, any such viewpoint excludes as much even perhaps more than what it includes so successfully.

Human behaviour is too variable and varying to come under any particular form of theory so surely they should be seen as contributions to sectional understandings. What is there in positivism or structuralism which makes such theories right or wrong when the situations being considered have personal and situational elements apart from the constant appearance of chance events.

There is another factor which make theoretical understandings susceptible to criticism is that they are thoughts committed to writing, inanimate abstracts from the thinking of these theoreticians and simplified abstractions from the events to which they are being related. From time to time social scientists such as Malinowski have made theoretical statements from their personal accumulation of data. As the years pass the data on which these theories have been based become more and more intellectually detached from the human realities which such researchers originally encountered. Such ideas become dependent on notes and the vagaries of memory leading to humanly doubtful reinterpretations.

THE INSTABILITY OF ANY FIELD OF SOCIAL SCIENCE ENQUIRY

The researchers and the researched are always living in an unstable environment which comes in the first instance from the changes which occur in their own physiological and psychological understandings; the built-in personal instabilities which are part of the human condition. It is probably no more than a human affection to assume that there is anything static in how a Bengali farmer or a Birmingham intellectual views and experiences the world around them.

There are constant expected and unexpected changes in the primary inter-relationships which everyone has on a day-to-day basis. The hope for stability may be no more than a necessary human illusion but an illusion it is. Then in the secondary relationships in which different roles divide up individual experience and finally, the tertiary touch and go relationships. In this world of micro-relationships the social science researcher is trying to catch onto some recordable stabilities in social situations which are intrinsically in the constant process of inevitable as well as chance occasioned change. These difficulties are augmented by the social distance handicaps separating the intellectual researcher from those they are researching.

Then there are macro changes in the society surrounding everyone about which they can do little to mitigate their influences. Climatic change and uncertain weather in India, fluctuating copper prices on which Zambia bases its possibilities of development, changes in the value of currencies, civil war and oppression in the Sudan and Myanmar, new religious and political movements under charismatic personalities. Social environments in which primary groups exist are always changing.

Finally changes in the environment of which the Western world often considers that it is exempted by its scientific and intellectual superiority. Floods in Bangladesh, typhoons in Florida and Myanmar, prolonged droughts in Australia and Ethiopea, earthquakes in Pakistan and China, the Indonesian tsunami and locust hoards which can no longer be internationally controlled because the low flying aircraft while spraying chemicals are shot at.

Researchers stabilize social behaviour because that it is the only way that it can be recorded but it is in a constant state of vibrant change like flowing water made even more difficult by the slowness of attempts at accurate work which turns much if not most social science work into not much more than the recording of recent social history.

RATIONALITY AND ITS CULTURAL REALITIES

All societies and individuals unless they are bent on social and individual destruction such as the mass suicides of the whole community at Jonestown, Guyana or the Russian Skopsi men castrating themselves, are logical as far as their cultural and cognitive understandings go. The basic problem here is whose standards of rationality are we going to use and thus presumably impose in our assessments of cultural understandings of behaviour other than our own.

The distinctions between societies having traditional thinking patterns and modern so-called civilisations with rational ones cannot be maintained in any such categorical boxes. According to the standards of Western thinking, those of markedly less economically developed Papuan societies rely proportionately on magic. However, to state that modern societies do not have a large number of magical practices is manifestly absurd. Western religious thinking is festooned both publicly and privately with religious ideas and practices that are no more or less logical than those of the Papuans, certainly made more obvious by ethnic bias factors (Mimica, 1988).

So it may come down to three types of reasoning (Shweder, 1992) which have to be assessed in the cultural context in which each occurs. Firstly, irrationality in which individuals have failed to apply themselves to their cultures accepted and proper standards of reasoning; following spirit guidance he tries to cultivate at the wrong season or she leaves her baby outside at night which the Tanzanian Sukuma would consider to be just plain stupid. But what about the three schizophrenics who all thought that they were Jesus Christ (Rokeach, 1964) would find themselves quite acceptable to the same Sukuma as they would each acquire a small following without intellectual conflict since these people have a cognitive style which has developed into overriding rational dominances. Such ideas would parallel those held by French peasants prior to the Revolution who held that the Virgin Mary worshipped in their village was not the same as the Virgin Mary worshipped in neighbouring villages (Robb, 2007:124). It seems likely that this feeling may be just as common in contemporary worship.

There can be little doubt that in all societies both traditional and socially changing there ones have always been thinkers who were out of line with predominant rationalities and that they may well have been quite common in the dialectics of cultural change. Galileo was right scientifically but Al-Ghazali, a prominent Iraqi Muslim fourteenth century mystic and mathematician, well educated even by modern standards held that there could not be any such thing as laws of nature as this would bind the power of God; a common enough thought at that time which may have accounted for the decline in Islamic scientific thinking which had been well in advance of the West up to that time (Weinberg, 2008).

In any society depending on the status of the individual going against what is culturally accepted as rational is seen on a sliding scale from stupidity to dangerously going against the rules by which the power holders run their societies. We have already seen that comment on the methods of power is as it has always been dangerous for these deviant commentators whether in Islamic, communist or other secular dictatorships.

So we see that there are cultural rationalities in which most of the time most of the people apply rationality to primary events; planting in the correct way, wearing sensible clothes in the winter, watering cattle. Many perhaps a majority of contemporary Hindus would accept the rationality of widows burning themselves to death on the funeral pyres of their dead husbands. Some New Guinea societies have held the belief that woman do not conceive from sexual intercourse but because the ancestor spirits of their husbands have arranged for conception to occur. The Sukuma believe that a difficult birth is a sign that the child was adulterously conceived. Cultural rationalities are exactly what they are and only scientific rationality has successfully crossed these cultural boundaries and only then to a limited extent.

Finally, the non-rational in which the culturally accepted explanations for primary events using such concepts as ancestor malevolence and witchcraft may not apply to a white majority in Birmingham. Nevertheless the evil eye is an ongoing active concept among long-standing Pakistani immigrants in the suburbs of London. The majority in Banaras, Beijing and Bamako would fluctuate between divine intervention and luck.

It is not so much that we can assess probability on a dichotomy of rational and non-rational as if there was a some global single standard apart from Kuhn's hypothesis of fashionable ideas. Within a culture at a particular time there are strong ideas of rationality which apply differentially to human behaviour and these are subject to historical change whether in a Bengali village or in the university communities in Kolkata or Mumbai. Sulphuric acid and oxygen are partially immune to cultural change based on human variability.

So into the consideration of probabilities in human behaviour comes the rational about which it may be possible to have exact knowledge but in very limited circumstances because of innumerable lateral influences. This type of assessment is probably confined to primary events such as traffic accidents and venereal infections.

The problem is that in most matters other than perhaps in criminal motivations, Western cognitive thinking is quite prepared to let primary causation to be sufficient explanation. Most people want further explanations as to why they were hit by that motorcycle or why they were burgled. It does seem likely that even in Western societies this is an elite form of thinking and that there the vast majority wants to know more. This is shown in the enormous amount of money and effort which is put into fortune-telling.

For the rest of the world people are quite ready to accept the obvious that the branch broke when they sat on it and that they were hit by a car when crossing the road but they want to know more as to what was behind this primary cause. Here comes in the non-rational according to Western rational thought which is not the same as irrationality.

THE RESTRICTIONS ON SOCIAL SCIENCE UNDERSTANDINGS

Social scientists take their human as much as their theoretical understandings from the cultures into which they have been socialised from childhood as well as to what they have learnt in higher education. Unless they are studying some aspects of their own societies in which they would have some understanding, this would be an inadequate grounding for the study of other societies. There is always the semi-conscious disposition to see the behaviour of people in other cultures as deviants from the rightness of their own cultural behaviour. Thus when Japanese social scientists study some aspect of their own culture there is the basic understanding which would be denied to a non-Japanese. This would occur even if such strangers had an intellectual understanding of what the differences are likely to be. Both would find the behaviour in Benin or Bogota intellectually explicable but still oddly deviant since there may well be very little cultural and cognitive overlap.

Such theoretical understandings were found in work done in different social situations so that these people are experiencing these 'new' cultures through the commitment of culturally specific spectacles. This is less likely to cause difficulties over house-building, farming and working on a factory production line than would more obviously in public religious behaviour and private spirituality.

Social science studies often partially ignore the realities of the people themselves in their explanations of their thinking and behaviour. Spirit possession is often seen as a psychological issue since spirits cannot possess anyone. Such an approach ignores the fact that not only are many thousands possessed but their societies as a whole consider that it is quite normal for some to be possessed in this way. It seems likely that this approach comes from the secular frame of mind in which most contemporary social scientists see their work. Whereas earlier missionaries in Africa and Asia had no difficulty at all in eliding their conviction of the powers of the Devil with local ones about possession.

There are many studies of spirit possession because of its unusualness to the secular thinking of most social scientists. It is certainly better recorded than the more repetitive behaviour of cooking, eating and washing. Yet it is seen almost always as a form of abnormality rather than as a useful way of keeping individuals functioning adequately in their societies. Quasi-traditional societies are quite able to distinguish between the abnormal and normal in their mental processes (Claus, 1984). It appears to be slotted into abnormality because that is what it would be in the middle class suburbs of London and Los Angeles.

SOCIAL SCIENCE AS THE WEAK LINK IN THE ASSESSMENT OF PROBABILITIES

In our perceptions and understandings of human behaviour the weak link to any understanding are the social scientists themselves as there is nothing that humans do or think that is necessarily exact and repeatable. They are not recording machines and they are always as variable and varying recorders of the behaviour which they think they are observing in a detached and professional manner. They are able to provide data for which they are professionally qualified to collect and comment on, but at the same time they are always part of what they observe. This information is always to some extent attached to them in a personal way while there is always the illusion of detachment.

Of course, we have cameras and recording machines which appear to provide hard data but photographs tell us little by way of explanation and tapes record only in a single sense. Biomedicine has machines providing information which is finite and short of deliberate deception and mechanical failures, they do not lie about DNA and the presence of a virus but again this data is provided out of their social contexts.

Thus the social sciences are always looking at human behaviour which inevitably has an individual form and it is being seen from an equally inevitable personal viewpoint. 'All of us including doctors have our own 'view from somewhere'. Scientists will develop individual perspectives on what they choose to look at but are rather more able to reconcile particularities through the conventions of inter-subjective agreement, to create what they call 'an objective account'. This has the air of a 'view from nowhere', (Sweeney, 2006).

In the social sciences as much as in medicine there is Miller's pyramid of assessable competences (Miller, 1990) which means that there is always going to be information and approaches which have been missed out as a result of professional inadequacies.

The social scientists do not have however much they aspire to have, any hard data from which they can draw hard conclusions. Human behaviour cannot provide binding situations in which there can be dichotomous answers such as can be applied to 'hard' scientific data. Probably if they are professionally honest with themselves, they can conclude no more than the famous statement alleged to have been made by the Hollywood director Sam Goldwyn "I can give you a definite maybe".

The social scientists approaching an enquiry which links public religious behaviour and private spirituality with health and well-being, are having to deal with a range of ill-defined themes which are being connected in their professional thinking. The correlations which they find need not necessarily apply to these poorly defined concepts. Even if they are studying a relatively straightforward issue of farming, this is just as much tied into other factors which have no direct relationship to agriculture. Social scientists overwhelmingly are secularists in their appreciation of human behaviour while an equally predominant number of the people they observe see their activities from a non-secular viewpoints.

Their approach to research is a three part mixture of what they have ostensibly decided to study which is itself a creation of their intellectual and social needs. Then there are the consequences of the teaching that they have received and the influences of particular teachers who may belong to recognisable schools of thought, an amalgam combined with the endless series of chance events which will complicate any simplicities implicit in categorizations. Finally, there will always be the basic as well as the changing personality of the researchers themselves so overall there can be nothing static about the observers and the observed.

Certainly chance is the most difficult of all research factors when it involves who they meet under what circumstances, the life experiences of all who become part of research; casual conversations, unexpectedly coming across a ceremony or familial crisis, the accidents of finding an article in a journal and the results of a computer search. Then research is further complicated by the limitations imposed by time as researchers may recognise that more information is needed but it is beyond their reach with the resources available.

THE OVERVALUING OF FACTUAL INFORMATION

It is understandable that in attempting to assess any human behaviour from the past on a scale from the planting of seeds or cooking a meal to that which involves the transcendent, there should be a reliance on what is written and associated material objects because after all that is all there is from which to gain understanding although much of this data is skewed to high status activities.

But as we reach contemporary life we should surely accept that what social scientists collect as facts or what they collect from written records are almost inevitably subject to serious methodological misgivings as to their quantifiable accuracy. Further there is the drawback that they can almost always tell us very little of the social and psychological environment in which these events occurred. The relative simplicity of the factual information available often leads to a conclusion about the simplicity of the behaviour of the less educated rather than that it should be treated as just as complicated as that of an Indian philosopher or academic.

It would seem that social scientists in their use of facts and making certain observations into facts must know that these are no more than segments of social realities and that a large proportion remains unknown. This must qualify all their professional conclusions and assessments of probability. There is also the overvaluing of what has been personally observed and recorded for which often enough researchers have had no special training or personal aptitudes.

There are always the limitations imposed not only by finance since few pay for their own research but the handicap of time which for any project in its personal relationship is always very limited. Then there is the frequent choice of large samples with which there are peripheral contacts in preference for the more difficult in depth relationship with a limited number of informants. Further the sense both of secular but intellectual superiority which accompanies research which handicaps social scientists from appreciating the human realities of lives other than their own. Finally, the feeling that anything written has a self-attributable reality of greater value in social understandings than what is known from inter-personal discourse.

THE SEARCH FOR REGULARITIES

The commonest attribution for any human behaviour is that it has regularity but this is an assumption which has often enough been proved to be a convenient illusion created by researchers. People themselves overestimate the regularities of their own behaviour as particularly in the Western world there is the quantification and timing of most activities in so far as they can be observed and controlled. When it comes to recording in response to a questionnaire, the relative frequency of an activity, this will provide results which relate to how respondents feel that they should reply at that time in the presence or absence of a researcher. Any correlation with what actually may have happened must be more a matter of professional hope than a provable reality.

Most of the world's population for most of their lives may have some pattern of potential regularity in their minds but the reality of their lives and their own individuality prevents any consistency. We often single out the compulsively regular as an exception when the majority are less consistent when the factors of chance cause irregularities in timing, attendance and practice. It may well be that such observable regularities as are found to exist are no more than primary and that the reasons for them are as complex as every behavioural event must be.

Regularity is what social scientists may hope to find and in fact are able to do so by excluding what they know to be intrinsically irregular as must be for almost all human inter-relationships. Regularity is much easier to process and to fit into the categorisations with which researchers are provided by their own socialisations or which they themselves create for their own needs. There is a tendency for certain cognitive processes to drift in the direction of information about which it is easier to be specific (Garner, 1966).

In any mass of human activity there will be the appearance of chaos until it is approached through the groupings in which the people themselves categorize their own social activities or on which social scientists impose their own categorizations. These are dictated according to social theory or by way of the system through which they record their own observations. The numbered pages of a notebook or the mechanically numbered sequence of camera pictures create their own categorizations. The commonplace use of sampling also creates artificial unity out of necessarily dissimilar activities.

The problem with attempting to foresee probabilities is that there are just too many loose factors which are either ill-defined or not defined at all because in any particular circumstance they are just unknown. Attempts at probability are a necessary part of orderly or to be realistic bureaucratic government but they have just as great a possibility of accuracy or indeed inaccuracy as personal or private planning.

A staunch Confucian scholar Zeng Guofan known for his rectitude and determination in a political system aiming successfully at orderliness over several centuries remarked during the turmoil of the Taiping rebellion that fate (i.e. chance) determined 70 per cent of any situation and that only 30 per cent came under human control. Another hard working scholar Guo Song Tao who specialized in foreign affairs asked that his obituary should end with the comment that he did not believe in gods but in luck (Smith, R.J. 1991:267).

It is no part of Western thinking much less its approach to public affairs to suggest that the efforts of professionals to make accurate statements of probability are no more accurate than they were centuries ago before the advent of the European Enlightenment.

THE ILLUSION OF DEFINABLE BOUNDARIES

The 'hard' sciences define themselves into exact and limited areas in which of course there can be chance events but it is a narrowed approach in which there are professional colleagues working on the same topic so that surprises are likely to come to the half prepared mind and a few and far between unexpected occurrences.

With the social sciences research can never be bounded except by artificial delimitations and in fact what they investigate can be made retrospectively logical while chance may have been the predominant factor. Whatever is the object of study defined as a village, an institution, a profession or the reactions to addiction, disaster or marriage, there will always be social and psychological leakages over whatever boundaries have been defined. The Muslim youth shuffling down the main street of a Swahili town said that he was imitating the walk of the Western film gunfighter. The Maasai women with their coloured bead necklaces and the men with thin spears made in Birmingham. Hindu highly coloured religious pictures were originally a German import as an offshoot of their success in coloured dyes.

Even with experiments we cannot know what predispositions are brought into the test. A written text no longer has any direct connection with its originators and has become and becomes by interpretation part of the lives of whoever reads it or indeed possesses it (Ricoeur, 1971).

In the absence of any exact definitions of what they propose to research and indeed do come to research as planned, must be an undisclosed rarity or it may be that an area is chosen as a random number from a list of possible choices. If social science and medical literature constantly refer to the objects of their work as coming from systematic randomisation we can see that individuals in their social environments have been and are examples of chance.

The social science researchers start their work in a state of unknowing except for the stereotypes which they have picked up in teaching and reading and what they have picked up from previous reports on their subject and area. While this may tell them that in a patrilineal society the mother's brother is an important source of affection, it does not prepare them for their absence or the creation of numerous entirely fictional mother's brothers among Tanzanian migrant workers.

Social science teaching has to concentrate on common behaviour and cannot really teach the individuality of human behaviour and in fact the demeaning aspect of grouping people in research as having a methodological priority over their individuality and the distinctiveness of their social environments.

THE INSTITUTIONAL BIAS IN SOCIAL SCIENCE RESEARCH

The factors dictating what is researched is rarely the untrammelled choice of the researchers who are tied to the need to get financial support as much as anyone else in the market for employment. This support is provided by institutions who interpret public need and no doubt the interests of their committee members as to whom their funds should go and to do what, where and when. Apart from the fashions in scientific interests, little research is going to be supported which is too far outside the existing thinking of the academic establishment and the mass media. In this sense research is in support of vague conformities.

There is also the fact that a majority of researchers are caught within the support and conveniences of their own institutional membership. Experimental work using conveniently located students and a high density housing estate or Indian Reservation just a few minutes drive away from the university. People who are located in a fixed locality and in convenient numbers will always attract researchers. The sick cared for at home are more difficult to study than those in hospitals. To provide funds for research which is so reasonably located and which fits in with public concerns is a sensible not necessarily rational use of limited funds.

This is not the predominant way in which people behave and in which they are socially involved in their primary groups and it is only in psychotherapy that the researchers are in such a relationship but who still see the 'other' from a one-sided point of view. So social scientists are often involved in assessing human behaviour from within an institutionalised viewpoint. We are perhaps overawed by the complexities of organisational life at the expense of researching the varied and seemingly rather chaotic primary inter-relationships.

THE DOMINANCE OF CHANCE

From the moment that social scientists enter any research interest they are confronted with what are in fact chance events often disguised by some fictions that they were pragmatically chosen; where they live and with whom they talk as well as what they see and hear are dictated by chance. Even the relationships with particular informants who are so essential to research are to all intents and purposes chosen by chance. What they then know may be based on the pragmatics of theoretical methodologies, but the key pivots from which conclusions come to be drawn are as likely as not to come from chance.

There are always chance factors that make what happens circumstantial. A community member whether in Mumbai or

Manchester can state that under ideal conditions this is what ought to happen, but in this situation this is what occurred. Some researchers are lucky in what they see and hear and others are not because they had an accident, became ill or just took a day off to go for fishing.

Researchers, the researched and the situations in which they inter-relate will always be constantly modified by chance events which cannot be foreseen. These may form the basis of more important dialectics than might come from the straightforward differences between the social understandings and personality differences between the researchers and the researched.

Everyone approaching social science research starts with acquiring perceptions of methodology; that such research requires an ordered approach to their research work. This is not only required by academic institutions, donors and examiners but is regarded as possible and attainable from the received experience and teaching of their professional superiors.

This approach is neither rational or reasonable as human behaviour is too disorganised to fit into the requirements of any ordered methodology because the human units are all basically dissimilar and their social experience in different environments is invariably individualised.

Thus almost all social science research contains fundamental chance factors which cannot be foreseen and which cannot be allowed for in both hypotheses or research findings except to lead to statements that such factors will always prevent factual conclusions since consistency does not exist.

There are chance factors which cannot be pragmatically allowed for in all social science research work. But which will necessarily occur. The choice of research topic is governed by the chance coincidence of personal need, institutional opportunities and support. The choice of a research area is based on the chance coincidences of convenience, time, political environment and finance. The choice of informants and the availability of information can never be based on pragmatic preconditions but upon chance encounters and in the case of informants a measure of acceptable relationships. Whether the researchers have access to and experience of key events depends upon the chances of being with the right people at the right time. The composition of any sample and their cooperation is a matter of chance so in effect chance is a dominant and inexplicable factor of any work which involves human behaviour.

UNCERTAINTY

It is not only difficult to find fact in relation to human behaviour but there is always the factor of chance about which in its variety and occasional appearance we can do little but guess and hope that it will not come in to upset any assessment of probability. Although it may be possible to define risk which insurance and business companies have done for some time (Knight, 1921) in as broad sense as possible to cover their costs, there is a fine distinction between risk as set of measured uncertainties related to the length of life and certain diseases and uncertainty based on limited knowledge (Hubbard, 2007).

It is only for a limited range of activities that there is sufficient exact data to make it of value for the assessment of economic probabilities. It is common knowledge that such forward looking evaluations are as likely to be radically wrong as strikingly right. Economists can cover their errors when calculating the risks for individuals, they are often caught out in mass disasters over earthquakes, terrorist attacks in Mumbai and New York and downturns in national and international economies. They invariably shut the gate after the horse has got out.

Social scientists particularly when they are working on applied projects cannot do this because the conditions of their employment probably relates to the implementation of policies which have already been decided on and for which their conclusions are without the social and political power to affect what might happen.

It would seem that much social activity is consciously or unconsciously designed to offset the inevitability of uncertainty where people are more dependent on their own resources while in developed states it is accepted that there are bureaucratic provisions to cope with uncertainties. The division between uncertainties with which individuals and primary groups are expected to cope with any situations in which the state or international aid agencies step in, which has resulted in more accurate assessment of some probabilities.

The effectiveness of social welfare and insurance systems depends more on the back-up depth of their financial resources than the accuracy of any forecasts that social scientists may make about probabilities. Nevertheless they will only be able to offset a small proportion of everyday uncertainties which are as common in slums as suburbs. There are always uncertainties over personal relationships in homes as well as in politics which Winston Churchill typified with his comment that "a day was a long time in politics". Most activities and certainly important ones are dependent on the weather in which science provides some seventy per cent accuracy.

Whether uncertainty is objective and based on national issues or subjective and related to norms and intuition, it is a matter of constant concern in the day-to-day lives of everyone. The work on probabilities carried out by social scientists to some extent obscures this uncertainty by their assumption in their professional title that it is a science which it is not.

FACTORS IN PROBABILITIES

There seems little doubt that probabilities as to what might or might not happen in the future is handicapped by two factors no matter how carefully the statistical chances are calculated or the data categorised. In the 'hard' sciences it is often possible for the researcher to state with confidence that there will be certain consequences but in the social sciences it must be rare indeed for any researcher to state with confidence that an event narrowly defined in advance has occurred. Social scientists can state that they have identified a trend which is likely to continue but not that it will necessarily continue.

Firstly, here are innumerable factors which might be involved in any probable or possible human activity. We just do not know what may or may not influence any human action however well defined it may be. The influence of any such unknown chance events is almost certainly beyond calculation and are beyond methodological certainty in the social environmental and psychological reactions relating to any individual, institution or group. This influence statistically might be 5 per cent, 0.5 per cent or 0.005 per cent; we just do not know nor can we know whether even the smallest of percentages may tip the balance in favour of particular behaviour or cumulatively become significant.

The second point is that binary and lineal thinking and its

scientifically validated methodologies are capable enough to work out the probable consequences of isolated, definable and, therefore, rather more simple acts. They are not adequate for dealing with multiple and indeed unknown factors. Hard science is tied to lineal considerations but human behaviour is holistic in the Eastern sense of understandings in which there are continuous influences rather than isolatable events. This may not be any easier to assess but it may possibly fit more easily into the complexities of influence than discrete events. Nevertheless science has been operating for some time under the discretionary-chance paradigm in which small discrete units of behaviour will have probable but not statistically determinable occurrences (Kaellis, 2006).

THE LIMITATIONS OF RATIONALITY

A matter of greater importance is the recognition of the limitations of accuracy related to rational behaviour. In this context, there are widely accepted rationalities in primary activities in any culture, institution and family. Behaviour which is so clearly against what that society considers to be rational that it and its consequences can be isolated in a scientifically acceptable manner. Even this has its problems since most of its, if not all cultures have the concept of madness but it is always in a form which is culturally explicable.

The companion of an Ethiopean student who dropped out of his London university course in theology replied to an offer of help that it would be useless as he was mad in an Ethiopean way. The current continuing wave of Muslim suicide bombers in Iraq, Pakistan, Afghanistan, Britain and the United States is rational enough since these men believe that their acts will involve their instant admittance to paradise.

Whether these factors are discrete or holistic can come within the understandings of science and its rationalities. What prevents any enlargement of the use of scientifically valid arguments and data is the presence in all societies and at all collective and individual levels of non-rational ideas for which there can be no proof or disproof. 'These presuppositions may have been banished from the grammar of Positivism since the Enlightenment, they have certainly not been banished from the mind either individually or collectively' (Shweder, 1992).

In this respect we have the major influences of the Eastern

religions, Islam and numerous Christian denominations whether seen in regular public worship or in pilgrimages. In addition there are many private forms of spirituality whether in urban or rural situations which have not been recorded in writing but which make up the personal rationalities of people whether in London or Ludhiana.

There are four types of non-rational ideas for which there can be no empirical proofs and which are tied into human creativeness and behaviour. Firstly, synthetic hypotheses which state that there are laws of nature which are a fixed feature in all human behaviour but there is so much variation in this that the possibility of any constant restrictions on or enablements of behaviour have yet to be discovered.

Secondly, there are hypotheses which humans have created and which have provided their own proofs. This is not just individual and institutional religious dogmas; the medical theory of humours persisted in Western thinking for centuries and still remains in much Eastern medical practices. The social basis of such thinking occurs conspicuously in Darwin's theory of the survival of the fittest with existing humans as evidence of this.

Thirdly, statements about the existence of God or gods, spirits and so on for which the only evidence is personal experience. The fact that prayer has been correlated to certain minimalist physiological improvements and to substantial contributions to mental health is not in itself evidence of divine causation. It remains a probability causing a persistent and seemingly irreducible amount of human activity. Certainly people have many ideas which they believe to be true and seemingly base or think they base their behaviour on these improvable convictions.

Finally, statements about the nature of the world in general such as creationism, the transmigration of souls, *karma* and individual resurrection. Overall this means that there are somewhat limited grounds for using the rationalities in human behaviour as the grounds for certain assessable probabilities.

The point must surely be that we do have a limited amount of positive data on human behaviour which is tied into lineal scientific conceptions and from which can come some reasonably acceptable probabilities. Beyond this in all societies and in all individual minds there are non-rational motivating ideas in plenty and however non-rational they may be in the understandings of uncommitted social scientists, they are believed by many to be real and they are real in their consequences (Thomas, W.I. and D.S. Thomas, 1925: 572).

However, detached social scientists may aspire to be personally and professionally in their approach to research and in their interpretations of the information which they have collected both processes will be at least in part reflecting the character and life experiences of the researchers themselves. No work concerning human behaviour can ever have the circumscribed clarity of the laboratory examination of material through the use of impersonal machinery.

So we are left with two factors which relate to any probability assessments since exact causalities are infrequent and fail to explain the wider circumstances in which any behavioural event occurs. There are of course some circumstances in which a set of events are more likely to occur than others such as the occasions in which members of the Jehovah's Witnesses Christian sect refuse blood transfusions so that their set of beliefs lead to infrequent deaths. In other cases there are vague possibilities such as the refusal of Christian Scientists to use modern medicines which has been estimated to have shortened the lives of some 5 per cent of such believers. So we have overall situations in which there are innumerable correlations which can be made between sets of events however they have been defined, but there is limited evidence as to what brings these sets of events together.

Firstly, there are the likelihoods of coincidence. For every single factor both known and unknown there are probabilities which are not necessarily connected either vertically or horizontally. Towards the end of Second World War the Germans launched 'flying bombs' in the direction of London. It was widely believed that these bombs fell proportionately on the high density poor areas but although the machinery was the same, fuel levels and air flow on their flight paths were not, so where they landed was entirely accidental. This is a comparatively simple mechanical exercise in which there were no human factors involved except the choice of the timing of their launching (Clarke, 1946).

Secondly, there is the ever-present factor of chance. Events are taken out of context and inserted into significance out of the far more common events in daily lives in which no coincidences occur. It is easy enough to retrospectively make coincidences which have no logical connection into lineal causality but they are in fact no more than chance events in which the only causal link is the person making the connection.

There seems little doubt that chance is a major delimiting factor in the ability of social sciences to provide scientifically valid data. Further that the available methodologies cannot insure accuracy because of the conscious and unconscious instability of the people involved and the social environments in which all behaviour occurs. The assessment of probabilities made by social scientists whatever their professional field and skills is not likely to be effective beyond the informed accuracy of foretelling trends and that anything beyond this is foredoomed to inaccuracy.

Bibliography

(The numbers in bold faces give the text page on which each reference is cited)

Aarts, F. and Aarts, J.(1982). *English syntactic structures: Functions and categories in sentence analysis*. Pergamon Press. Oxford.

Abrahams, R.(1981). *The Nyamwezi today*. Cambridge University Press. Cambridge.

Adam, A.(1973). 'Genetic diseases among Jews' *Israeli Journal Medical Science*. 9:1383-92.

Adam, A. *et al*.(1967). 'Frequencies of protan deutan alleles in some Israeli communities and a note on the selection-relaxation hypothesis'. *American Journal Physical Anthropology*. 26: 297-305.

Alther, L.(1975).'The snake handlers'. *New Society*. 34:532-5.

Altorki, S.(1982). 'The anthropologist in the field. A case of 'indigenous' anthropology from Saudi Arabia' in H.Fahim.(ed). *Indigenous anthropology in non-Western countries*. Carolina University Press. Durham. North Carolina. 167-175.

Angell, M.(2009). 'Drug companies and doctors, A story of corruption'. *New York Review of Books*. 15 January.8-12.

Ankerl, G.(2000). *Coexisting contemporary civilisations. Arabo-Muslim, Bharati, Chinese and Western*. INU Press. Geneva.

Aphek, E.K. and Y.Tobin.(1983). 'On image building and establishing credibility in the language of fortune telling'. *Eastern Anthropologist*. 36(4):287-308.

— — (1986). 'The semiology of cartomancy. The interface of visibility and textuality'. *American Journal Semiotics*. 4(1-2): 73-98.

— — (1989). *The semiotics of fortune telling*. Benjamini. Amsterdam.

Arora, N.K. and C.A,.McHorney. (2000). 'Patient preferences for medical decision making. Who really wants to participate'. *Medical Care*. 36:335-41, **267**.

Asad, T.(1986). 'The concept of cultural translation in British social anthropology'. in J.Clifford and G.E, Marcus.(eds). *Writing culture. The poetics and politics of ethnography*. 141-164. University of California Press. Berkeley, **179**.

Atakan, Z. *et al.* (1990). 'Can psychiatrists predict the one-year outcome of schizophrenia?' *Social Psychiatry Psychiatric Epidemiology*. 25(3):117-24, **7**.

Austin, J.H. (1977). *Chase, Chance and Creativity. The lucky art of novelty*. Columbia University Press. New York, **191**.

Back, I and A. Flache. (2008). 'The adaptive rationality of interpersonal commitment'. *Rationality and Society*. 20(1): 65-83, **276**.

Bagchi, P.O. (1950). *India and China; a thousand years of Sino-Indian cultural relations*. China Press. Bombay, **236**.

Baker, M.S. (2007). 'Creating order from chaos. Mass casualty and disaster response'. *Military Medicine*. 122(3): 232-243, **108**.

Banton, M. (1964): 'Anthropological perspectives in sociology'. *British Journal Sociology*. 15;95-112.

Basu, S. and R.G. Schroeder. (1977). 'Incorporating judgments in sales forecasting; Application of the Delphi method at American Hoist and Derrick'. *Interfaces*. 7(3):18-27, **246**.

Batibo, H. (1985). *Le keSukuma, langue Bantu de Tanzania*. Editions Recherche sur les Civilisations. Paris, **121**.

Baumeister, R.F. and M.R. Leary (1995). 'The need to belong. Desire for interpersonal attachments as a fundamental human motivation'. *Psychological Bulletin*. 117(3):497-529, **220**.

Becker, J. (1996). *Hungry ghosts. Mao's secret famine*. Holt. New York, **106**.

Belik, S.L. *et al.* (2007). 'Traumatic events and suicidal behaviour. Results from a national mental health survey'. *Journal Nervous and Mental Disease*. 195(4):342-9, **216**.

Bennett, D.J. (1998). *Randomness*. Harvard University Press. Cambridge. Mass, **233**.

Berlin, B. *et al.* (1973). 'General principles of classification and nomenclature in folk biology'. *American Anthropologist*. 75(1):214-242, **52**.

Beveridge, W.L.B. (1957). *The art of scientific investigation*. Heinneman. London, **155**.

Billar, F.C. and A.C. Liefbroen. (2007).'Should I stay or should I go? The impact of age norms on leaving home'. *Demography*. 44(1): 181-198, **156**.

Bird, S.M. *et al*. (2003). 'Performance indicators; good, bad and ugly'. *Journal Royal Statistical Society*. 168 Part 1:1-27, **98**.

Birks, J.B. (ed). (1962). *Rutherford at Manchester*. Heyford, **12**.

Blackwood, E. (1984). 'Sexuality and gender in certain Native American tribes: the case of cross-gender females'. *Signs*. 10:27-42, **53**.

Bloom, B.S. *et al*. (1956). 'The taxonomy and illustrative materials' in Bloom, B.S. (ed). *Taxonomies of educational objectives, the classification of educational good*. Handbook .1. Cognitive domains. 62-197, **257**.

Bogardus, E.S. (1933). 'A social distance scale'. *Sociology and Social Research*. 12:265-271, **20**.

Bowen, L. (1964). *Return to laughter. Doubleday*. New York, **134, 138**.

Boyd, R. (1999). *The coming of the Spirit of pestilence. Introduced infectious diseases and population decline among Northwest Coast Indians*. University of Washington Press. Seattle, **160**.

Bradshaw, A and G.Fitchett. (2003). 'God why did this happen to me; three perspectives on theodicy'. *Journal Pastoral Care Counselling*. 57(2):179-189, **149**.

Briggs, J. (1970). 'Kapluna's daughter' . in P. Golde. (ed). *Women in the field. Anthropological experience*. Aldine. Chicago. 19-44, **77, 147**.

Brown, J. (2007). *The canonization of al- Bukhari and Muslim. The formation and function of the Sunni hadith canon*. Brill. Leiden, **99**.

Budd, M, (1989). *Wittgenstein's philosophy of psychology*. Routledge. London, **82**.

Bushnak, A.A. (1978). *The Hajj transport system*. Hajj Studies. London, **104**.

Campbell, D.T and Fiske, D.W. (1959). 'Convergent and discriminant validation of the multi- trait multi-method matrix'. *Psychological Bulletin*. 56:81-105, **21, 85**.

Carrier, N.H. and A.M. Farrag. (1959). 'The reduction of errors in census populations for statistically underdeveloped countries'. *Population Studies*.12(3):240-285, **156**.

Casanueva, C.E. and S.L. Martin. (2007). 'Intimate partner violence during pregnancy and mothers' child abuse potential'. *Journal Interpersonal Violence*. 22(5):566-584, **51**.

Casteneda, C. (1968). *The teachings of Don Yuan. A Yaqui way of knowledge. Barnes and Noble*. New York, **24**.

Chagnon, N.A. (1977). *Yanomano, the fierce people*. Holt Rinehart and Winston. New York, **77-8**.

Chang. I. (1997). *The rape of Nanking. The forgotten holocaust of World War II*. Basic Book. New York, **105, 216-7**.

Chatterjee, S. *et al.* (1999). 'Argumentation rationality of management decisions'. *Organisation Science*.10(5):672-690, **275**.

Choudhry, N.K. *et al.* (2002). 'Relationships between authors of clinical practice guides and the pharmaceutical industry'. *Journal American Medical Association*. 287:612-617, **151**.

Cicero (1920). De divatione. In *Collected works*. A.S.Pease.(ed). University of Illinois Press. Urbana, **283**.

Clarke, A.D. and Clarke, A.M. (1984). 'Constancy and change in the growth of human characteristics'. *Journal Child Psychology Psychiatry*. 25(2):191-210, **4**.

Clarke, R.D.(1946). 'An application of the Poisson distribution'. *Journal Institute of Actuaries*. 72:481, **305**.

Claus, P.J. (1984). 'Medical anthropology and the ethnography of spirit possession *Contributions to Asian Studies* 18(1):60-72, **293**.

Cohen, J. (1964). *Behaviour in uncertainty and its social implications*. Allen and Unwin. London, **227**.

Cory, H. (1953). *Sukuma law and custom*. Oxford University Press. London, **171**.

Curtin, P.D. *et al.* (1984). *Cross-cultural trade in world History*. Cambridge University Press. Cambridge, **236**.

D'Andrade, R.G.(1965). 'Trait psychology and componential analysis'. *American Anthropologist*.67:215-228.

—— (1970). 'Cognitive structures and judgment' Research Workshop on Cognitive Organisation and Psychological Processes. Huntington Beach. California.

—— (1981). 'The cultural part of cognition'. *Cognitive Science*.5:179-195, **56**.

D'Andrade, R.G and A.K.Romney.(1964). 'Summary of participants' discussion'. *American Anthropologist*.66(3): 230-242, **28**.

Daniel, C. (1966). *The story of the Eyam plague*. Privately printed. Eyam, **45**.

Dawkins, R. (2006). *The God delusion*. Bantam. London, **31**.

Detre, K.M. *et al.* (1975). 'Observer agreement in evaluating coronary angiograms'. *Circulation*.52:979-86, **271**.

Diamond, J. (2005). *Collapse. How societies choose to fail or survive.* Allan Lane. London, **106**.

Douglas, M. (1966). *Purity and danger*. Routledge and Kegan Paul. London, **150**.

Dua, V.(1979). 'A woman's encounter with Arya Samaj and Untouchables.' In M.N.Srinivas et al.(eds). *The field workers and the field*. Oxford University Press. Delhi.115-126, **134**, **169**.

Dumont, L. (1970). *Homo hierarchus*. Chicago University Press. Chicago, **171**.

Duranti,, A.(1993).'Truth and Intentionality, An ethnographic critique'. *Cultural Anthropology*. 8(2): 214-245, **92**.

Durkheim, E. (1961). *Elementary forms of religious life*. Collier. New York, **214**.

Eaker, E.D. *et al.* (2007). 'Marital status, marital strains and risk of coronary heart disease or total mortality'. *Psychosomatic Medicine*. 69:509-513, **260**.

Ecks, S. and W.S. Sax. (2005). 'The ills of marginality. New perspectives on health in South Asia'. *Anthropology and Medicine*. 12(3):199-210, **112**.

Editor. (2004). 'On the nature of scientific interests'. *British Medical Journal*. 328: 1459, **61**.

Ekman, R. and M.O'Sullivan.(1991). 'Who can catch a liar'. *American Psychologist*. 46: 913-20, **5**.

Elliott, E. & L.D. Kiel. (1996). Introduction to Elliott, E. and Kiel, L.D.(eds). *Chaos theory in the social sciences. Foundations and Applications*. University of Michigan Press. Ann Arbor. 1-15, **103**.

Elwin, V. (1947). *The Muria and their ghotul*. Oxford University Press. Bombay, **104**.

—— (1988). *The tribal world of Verrier Elwin*. An autobiography. Oxford University Press. Delhi, **148**.

Ermenc, B.(2003). 'Comparison of the clinical and post-mortem diagnoses of the causes of death'. *Forensic Science International*. 114(2):117-119.

Evans-Pritchard, E.P. (1937). *Witchcraft, oracles and magic among the Azande*. Oxford University Press. Oxford, **121**.

—— (1939). Nuer time reckoning. *Africa*.12, **40**.

—— (1967). *The Nuer religion*. Clarendon Press. Oxford, **24**, **30**.

Fahim, H.(1979), 'Field research in a Nubian village; the experience of an Egyptian anthropologist ' in G.M.Foster *et al* (eds). *Long-*

term field research in social anthropology. Academic Press. New York, **186**.

Farooq, Q.M. and Mallah, M.B. (1966). 'Behavioural pattern of social and religious water contact activities in Egypt-49 Bilharziasis Project Area'. *World Health Organisation Bulletin*. 35:377-87, **64**.

Fehr, E. and J-R.Tyran. (2008). 'Limited rationality and strategic interaction. The impact of the strategic environment on nominal inertia'. *Econometrica*. 76(2):353-394, **274**.

Fillinger, M. (2007). 'Who should we operate on and how do we decide; predicting rupture and survival in patients with aortic aneurysm'. *Semin Vascular Surgery*. 20(2):121-7, **272**.

Firth, S. (1972). 'From wife to anthropologist ' in S.T.Kimball and J.B.Watson.(eds). *Cross-cultural boundaries. The anthropological experience*. 10-32. Chandler. San Franscisco, **205**.

Fischer, D.H. (19700). *Historians' fallacies. Towards a logic of historical thought*. Harper Torch Books. New York, **158**.

Fisher, F.M. (1966). *The identification problem in econometrics*. McGraw-Hill. New York, **76**.

Flynn, J. (2007). *What is intelligence*. Cambridge University Press. Cambridge, **18**.

Flyvbjerg, B. (2007). 'Five misunderstandings about case study research' in C. Seale *et al*. (eds). *Qualitative research structures*. Sage. London. 420-434, **11**.

Foshee, V.A. *et al*. (2007). 'Typologies of adolescent dating violence. Identifying typologies of adolescent dating violence perpetrations'. *Journal Interpersonal Violence*. 22(5):488-519, **21**.

Fox, R. (2004). *The participant observer. Memoir of a translantic life. Transaction*. New Brunswick, **151**.

Freedman, T.G. (1998). 'Why don't they come to Pike Street to ask us. Black American women's health concerns'. *Social Science Medicine*. 47(7): 941-7, **261**.

Freeman, D. (1983). *Margaret Mead and Samoa. The making and unmaking of an anthropological myth*. Harvard University Press. Cambridge. Mass, **23, 152**.

Frosch, D.L. and R.M. Kaplan. (1999). 'Shared decision making in clinical medicine; past research and future directions'. *American Journal Preventative Medicine* 17:285-94, **267**.

Garner, W.R. (1966). ' To perceive is to know'. *American Psychologist*. 21:11-19, **296**.

Geertz, C. (1972). 'The wet and the dry. Traditional agriculture in Bali and Morocco'. *Human Ecology*. 1:23-37, **34**.

— — (1972). 'Deep play. Notes on the Balinese cockfight'. *Daedalus*. 101: 1-37, **48**.

— — (1973). *The interpretation of cultures*. Hutchinson. London, **248**.

— — (1975). 'On the nature of anthropological understanding'. *American Scientist*. 63:47-53, **159**.

Gessler, M.C. *et al*. (1995). 'Traditional healer in Tanzania. Sociocultural profiles and three short portraits'. *Journal Ethnopharmacology*. 48(3):145-60, **149**.

Gingyera-Pinycwa, A.G.G. (1974). 'The African political scientist and decision making'. Universities Social Sciences Council Conference. Kampala. Paper 43, **283**.

Goffman , E. (1969). *The presentation of self in everyday life*. Penguin. Harmondsworth, **146**.

Goodall, J. (1986). *The chimpanzees of Gombe. Patterns of behaviour*. Belknap Press. Harvard, **43**.

Goodman, F.O. (1972). *Speaking in tongues. A cross-cultural study of glossolalia*. Chicago University Press. Chicago, **53**.

Goodstein, D.L. (2002). 'Scientific misconduct'. *Academe*. Jan-Feb., **23**, **150**.

Gore, C. (1998). 'Ritual, performance and media in urban contemporary shrine configurations in Benin City, Nigeria'. In F. Hughes-Freeland. (ed). *Ritual, performance, media*. 66-84. Routledge. London, **195**.

Gorer, G. (1938). *Himalayan village*. Joseph. London, **30**.

— — (1957). *Exploring the English character*. Criterion. New York, **30**.

Greco, S. *et al*. (2002). *Rule based decision support in multi-criteria choice and ranking. Symbolic and quantitative approaches to reasoning with uncertainty*. Volume.3:29-47. Springer. Berlin, **277**.

Green, R.H. (1981). 'Magendo in the political economy of Uganda; pathology, parallel system or dominant sub-mode of production'. Discussion Paper 164. Institute of Development Studies. University of Sussex. Brighton, **151**.

Gregorio, A. *et al*. (2006). 'Greater risk for HIV infections of black men who have sex with men; a critical literature review'. *American Journal Public Health*. 96(6): 1007-1019, **286**.

Griffith, L.Z. *et al*. (2007). 'Low-back pain in occupational studies. Meta-analysis using Delphic consensus methods'. *Journal Clinical Epidemiology*. 60:625-633, **51**.

Grinker, R.R. (2000). *In the arms of Africa. The life of Colin.* M. Turnbull. St Martin's Press. New York, **198**.

Gronewold, S. (1972). 'Did Frank Hamilton Cushing go native' in S. T. Kimball and J.B.Watson,(eds). *Cross-cultural boundaries. The anthropological experience*. Chandler. San Francisco. 33-50, **146**.

Groopman, J. (2007). *How doctors think.* Houghton Mifflin. New York, **51**.

Gulliver, P. (1957). *Interim report on land and population in the Arusha chiefdom*. Tanzania National Archives. Dar es Salaam, **77**.

Gunther, M. (1977). *The luck factor*. MacMillan. New York, **80**.

Guppy, N. (1955). *Wai Wai. Through the forest north of the Amazon.* Murray. London.

Guttman, L. (1944). 'A basis for scaling quantitative data'. *American Sociological Review*. 9:134-150, **20**.

Haas, S.A. (2007). 'The long-term effects of poor childhood health; an assessment and application of retrospective reports'. *Demography*. 44(1):113-135, **155**.

Hagelin, J.S. *et al*. (1999). 'Effects of group transcendental Meditation Program on preventing violence in Washington, DC. Results of the National Demonstration Project June-July.1993'. *Social Indicators Research*. 47(2):153-201, **284**.

Halford, G.S. *et al*. (2005). 'How many variables can humans process'. *Psychological Science* 16(1):70-6, **6**.

Halpenny, P. (1974). 'Economic determinants and educational policies; the irrelevance of experts.' Universities Social Science Council Conference.Kampala. Paper 44, **283**.

Hamil-Luker, J. and A.M.O'Rand. (2007). 'Gender differences in the link between childhood socio-economic conditions and heart attack risk in adulthood'. *Demography*. 44(1):137-158, **155**.

Hammer, M.R. *et al*. (2003). 'Measuring inter-cultural sensitivity. The intercultural development inventory'. *International Journal Intercultural Relations*. 27(4):421-3, **221**.

Hammerton, N. (1973). 'A case of radical probability estimates'. *Journal Experimental Psychology*. 101:252-254, **265**.

Harris, G.G. (1978). *Casting out anger*. Cambridge University Press. Cambridge, **162**.

Harrison, I.E. (1974). 'Traditional healers. A neglected source of health manpower'. *Rural Africana*. 26:5-16, **195**, **271**.

Hartley, C.P. (1953). *The go-between*. Hamish Hamilton. London, **156**.

Harvey, D.L. and M. Reed. (1996). 'Social science in the study of complex systems'. In L.D.Kiel and E.Elliott.(eds). *Chaos theory in the social sciences. Foundations and Applications*. University of Michigan Press. Ann Harbor. 295-323, **232**.

Heikki, H. (2007). *The fear of losing out. Tobacco industry strategies in Finland*. 1975- 2001. Tampere University Press, **47**.

Hennigh, L. (1981). 'The anthropologist as key informant inside a rural Oregon town' in D.A.Messerschmidt.(ed). *The anthropologist at home in North America*. Cambridge University Press. Cambridge, **135**.

Hill, D.C. and Hood, R.W. (1999). *Measures of religiosity*. Religious Education Press. Birmingham. Alabama, **20**.

Holmes, C.H. and R.H.Rahe.(1967). 'The Social Readjustment Rating Scale'. *Journal Psychosomatic Research*. 11: 213-218, **127**.

Hong, Y. *et al*. (2007). 'Internet use among Chinese college students. Implications for sex education and HIV prevention'. *Cyberpsychology and Behaviour*. 10(2):161-169, **130**.

Honkonen, T. *et al*. (2007). 'Employment predictors for discharged schizophrenic patients'. *Social Psychiatry Psychiatric Epidemiology*. 42(5):372-80, **156**.

Howard, J. (1989). *Margaret Mead. A life*. Libri. New York.

Hubbard, D. (2007). *How to measure anything. Finding the value of intangibles in business*. Wiley. Chichester, **301**.

Humphreys, R.A. (1970). *The tea-room trade. Impersonal sex in a public place*. Duckworth. London, **104**.

Hyman, M.M. *et al*. (1980). *Drinkers, drinking and alcohol-related mortality and hospitalizations*. Rutgers Center of Alcohol Studies. New Brunswick, **47**.

Ibn Khaldun. (1967). *Muqaddimah*. Trans F.Rosenthal. Princeton University Press. Princeton. New Jersey, **13**.

Iller, K. (2006). *Communication theories. Perspectives, Processes and Context*. McGraw Hill. Boston.

Ioannidis, J.P.A. (2005). 'Why most published research findings are false'. *Public Library of Science Medicine*. 2(8), **19**.

Jabara, R. *et al*. (2007).'Risk characteristics of Arab and Israeli women with coronary heart disease in Jerusalem'. *Israeli Medical Association Journal*. 9(4):316-20, **156**.

Jaffe, D.H. *et al*. (2007). 'The protective effect of marriage on mortality in a dynamic society'. *Annals Epidemiology*. 12(7): 540-7, **128**.

Jahoda, G. (1968). *The psychology of superstition*. Allan Lane. London, **31**.

Jenkins, R.A. (1995). 'Religion and HIV: Implications for research and intervention'. *Journal Social Issues*. 1(2): 131-144, **20**.

Jules-Rosetts, B. (1978). 'The veil of objectivity. ; prophecies, divination and social enquiry'. *American Anthropologist*. 80:549-570, **30**.

Kaellis, E. (2006). 'About hypotheses and paradigms exploring the discretionary chance paradigm'. *Medical Hypotheses*.66(1): 188-192, **303**.

Kahneman, D. and A.Tversky. (1973). 'On the psychology of prediction,' *Psychological Review*. 80:237-251, **265**, **278**.

—— (2006). 'Subjective probability. A judgment of representativeness'. 32-47. in D.Kahneman *et al*. (eds.). *Judgment under uncertainty; heuristics and biases*. Cambridge University Press. Cambridge, **264**.

Kalmijn, M. *et al*. (2007). 'Income dynamics in couples and the dissolution of marriage and cohabitation'. *Demography*. 44(1): 159-179, **125**.

Kaplan, R.M. and D.L. Frosch. (2005).' Decision making in medicine and health.' *Annual Review Clinical Psychology*. 1:525-56, **271**.

Katchadourian, H. (1974). 'A comparative study of mental illness among the Christians and Moslems of Lebanon'. *International Journal Social Psychiatry*. 20(1- 2):56-67, **15**.

Katz, A.W. (2002). 'Fathers facing their daughters' emerging sexuality'. *Psychoanalytic Study Childhood*. 57:270-93, **124**.

Kawlu Ma Nawng. (1942). *The history of the Kachins of the Hukawng Valley*. J.L.Leyden (trans). Privately printed. Bombay.

Kean, L.T.M. *et al*. (2006). 'Post traumatic stress disorder. Etiology, epidemiology and treatment'. *Annual Review Clinical Psychology*. 2:161-197, **133**.

Kendrick, M.A. (1979). 'Viral hepatitis in American missionaries abroad'. *Journal Infectious Diseases*.129:227-9.

Kennedy, D. (2006). 'Retraction'. *Science*. 311(57810):606-7, **36**.

Kettering, C. (1977). Quoted in J.H. Austin.(1977). *Chase, Chance and Creativity. The lucky art of novelty*. Columbia University Press. New York, **192**.

Khokhlov, N. (1983). 'Remote biofeedback in voluntary control of heart rate'. *PSI Research*. 2(3):66-92, **81**.

Kiasch, I. *et al*. (2002). 'The Emperor's New drugs. An analysis of anti-depressant medication data submitted to the U S Food and Drug Administration'. *Prevention and Treatment*.15 July, **23**.

Kilduff, M. and R. Javers.(1978). *The suicide cult*. Bantam. New York, **45**.

King, M. *et al.* (1995). 'The Royal Free Hospital Interview for religious and spiritual beliefs; development and standardisation'. *Psychological Medicine*. 25:1125- 1134.

Knight, F.H. (1921). *Risk, uncertainty and profit*. Hart, Schaffner and Marx. Boston, **301**.

Koeck, C.M. *et al.* (1998). 'Using a hypothetical case to measure differences in treatment of aggressiveness among physicians in Canada, Germany and the United States'. *Wien klin wochenschr*. 110(22):783-8, **272**.

Koenig, H.G. *et al.* (2003). 'Religion, spirituality and health service use by older hospitalized patients'. *Journal Religion and Health*. 42(40):301-314, **17**.

Kondo, D.K. (1990). *Crafting selves. Power, gender and discourses of identity in a Japanese workplace*. University of Chicago. Chicago, **174, 206**.

Kuhn, T.S. (1962). *The structure of scientific revolutions*. University of Chicago Press. Chicago, **10-1, 58, 271, 287, 291**.

Kumar, N. (1988). *The artisans of Banaras. Popular culture and identity*. Princeton University Press. Princeton. New Jersey, **68, 104, 148**.

— — (1992). *Friends, brothers and informants. Fieldwork memories of Banaras*. University of Chicago Press. Chicago, **205**.

Ladd, J. (1957). *The structure of a moral code. A philosophical analysis of ethical discourse applied to the ethics of the Navaho Indians*. Harvard University Press. Cambridge. Mass, **70**.

Landewe, R.G. and van der Heljde, D.M. (2003). 'Principles of assessment from a clinical perspective'. *Best Practice Res Clinical Rheumetology*. 17(3):365-79, **124**.

Lang, S. (1998). *Men as Women, Women as Men: Changing gender in Native American cultures*. J.L.Vantine(trans). University of Texas Press. Austin, **53**.

Lansing, J.S. (1987). 'Balinese water temples and the management of irrigation'. *American Anthropologist*. 89(2):326-341, **34**.

— — (1991). *Priest and programmes*. Technologies. Princeton University Press, **34**.

Lasaga, J.I. (1980). 'Death in Jonestown. Techniques of political control by a paranoid leader'. *Suicide Life-Threatening Behaviour*. 10:210-3, **107**.

Leighton, A.H. (1969). 'Cultural relativity and the identification of psychiatric disorders'. in W.Caudill and T.Lin.(eds.). *Mental health in Asia and the Pacific*. East-West Center Press. Honolulu, **254.**

Lewis, C.S.(1955). *Surprised by joy. The shape of my early life.* Harvcourt, Brace and World. New York, **158.**

Lewis, O.(1979). *The children of Sanchez.* Random House. New York, **24, 104.**

Libby, R. (1976). 'Man versus model of men. Some conflicting evidence'. *Organizational Behaviour and Human Performance.* 16:1-12, **69.**

Le inhardt, G. (1961). *Divinity and Experience. The religion of the Dinka.* Clarendon Press. Oxford, **24, 162.**

—— (1967). 'Modes of thought' in E.Evans-Pritchard *et al.* (eds). *The institutions of primitive society*. 95-107. Blackwell. Oxford.

Likert, R. (1932). 'A technique for the measurement of attitudes'. *Archives of Psychology,* 140, **20.**

Livingstone, D. (1857). *Missionary travels in South Africa.* John Murray. London, **8, 229.**

Long, C.W. (1849). 'An account of the first use of sulphnuric ether by inhalation as an anaesthetic in surgical operations'. *South Medical Journal*. 5:705.

Loo, B.P. and K.L.Tsui. (2007). 'Factors affecting the likelihood of reporting road crashes resulting in medical treatment to the police'. *Injury Prevention.* 13(3): 186-9, **188.**

Loukaitou-Sideris, A and J.E.Eck. (2007). 'Crime prevention and active living'. *American Journal Health Promotion.* 21(4supp):380-9, **187.**

Lyman, J.M. *et al.* (2004). 'A comparison of three sources of data on child homicide'. *Death Studies.* 28(7):659-69, **6.**

Lynn, D.J. *et al.* (2006). 'Relationship between self-assessed skills, test performances and demographic variables in psychiatry residents'. *Adv Health Sciences. Education Theory Practice.* 11(1): 51-60, **18.**

Lyon, D. and P. Slovic. (1976), 'The dominance of accurate and the neglect of base rates in probability estimation'. *Acta Psychologica.* 40: 287-298, **264.**

Maddison, D. and Viola, A.(1968). 'The health of widows in the year following bereavement'. *Journal Psychosomatic Research.* 12:297-306, **17.**

Madzimbamuto, F. and Madamumbe, T.(2004). 'Asphysxia during stadium stampede'. *Central African Journal Medicine.* 50(7-8): 69-79, **5.**

Malinowski, B. (1961). *The Argonauts of the Western Pacific.* Dutton. New York., **107.**

— — (1967). *A diary in the strict sense of the term.* Harcourt Brace and World. New York, **24, 133, 146.**

Malk, J. (2000). *Telling and foretelling. African divination and art in wider perspective.* Smithsonian Institute. Washington, **247.**

March, J.G. (1978). 'Bounded rationality, ambiguity and the engineering of choice'. *Bell Journal Economics.* 9:587-608, **273.**

Marsh, A.A. *et al.* (2003). 'Non-verbal 'accents'. Cultural differences in facial expressions of emotion'. *Psychological Science.* 14(4): 371-376, **132.**

Martin, B.(1992).'Scientific fraud and the power structure of science.'. *Prometheus.* 10(1):83-98, **24.**

Mascarenhas-Keyes, S.(1987). 'The native anthropologist; constraints and strategies in research' in A.Jackson (ed). *Anthropology at home.* 180-195. Tavistock. London, **170.**

Mayaram, S.(1996). 'Speech, silence and the making of Partition violence in Mewat' in S.Amin and D.Chakrabarty. (eds). *Subaltern Studies.ix. Writings on South Asian History and Society.* Oxford University Press. Delhi. 126-163, **167.**

Mazrui, A. (1974). 'Africa, my conscience and I'. *Transition.* 46:Oct/ Dec., **283.**

McClelland, J.L. *et al.* (1986). 'The appeal of Parallel Distributive Processing.' in D.E.Rumelhart *et al.*(eds). *Parallel Distributive Processing. Explorations in the microstructure of cognition.* MIT. Cambridge.Mass. Vol 1:3-44, **94.**

McGlynn, E.A. *et al.* (2003). 'The quality of health care delivered to adults in the United States'. *New England Journal Medicine.* 348:2635-45, **251.**

McIsaac, W.J. and C.C. Butler.(2000).'Dopes clinical error contribute to unnecessary anti-biotic use'. *Medical Decision Making.* 20(1):33-8, **272.**

McKeown-Eyssen, G.E. *et al.* (2000). 'Reproductability of the University of Toronto self-administered questionnaire used to access environmental sensitivity'. *American Journal Epidemiology.* 151(12):1216-22, **237.**

McKusick, V.A.(1973). 'Genetic studies in American in-bred

populations with particular reference to the Old Order Amish'. *Israeli Journal Medical Science*. 9:1276-84, **96**.

McLay, J. and S. Ross. (2008). 'Medication errors caused by junior doctors'. *British Medical Journal*. 336:456, **90**.

Mead, M. (1928). *Coming of age in Samoa*. Morrow Quill. New York, **25, 119, 152**.

— — (1956). *New lives for old. Cultural transformation.1928-1953*. Manus. Gollanz. London, **40, 48, 146**.

— — (1962). *Male and female*. Penguin. London, **119**.

Meadows, S. (1994).'Cognitive development.' in A.M.Coleman.(ed). *Companion Enclopedia of Psychology*. Routledge. Volume 2, **93**.

Meehl, P.E. (1970). *Nuisance variables and the ex post facto design. Minnesota Studies in the Philosophy of Science*. Vol 4, **16**.

— — (1977). 'Specific etiology and other forms of strong inference. Some quantitative meanings '. *Journal Medicine and Philosophy*. 2:33-53, **85**.

— — (1978). 'Theoretical risks and tabular asterisks'. *Journal Consulting and Clinical Psychology*. 46:806-834, **85**.

Mehta, S. (2004). *Maximum City. Bombay lost and found*. Headline. London, **65**.

Mercer, J. and I.C.Talbot. (1985). 'Clinical diagnoses; a post-mortem assessment of accuracy in the 1980s'. *Post-Graduate Medical Journal*. 61:713-716, **90**.

Meyers, M.A. (2007). *Happy accidents. Serendipity in modern medical breakthroughs*. Arcade. New York, **62**.

Miller, G.E. (1990) 'The assessment of clinical skills and competent performance'. *Academy Medicine*. 65:563-7, **294**.

Milstein, T.(2005). 'Transformation abroad. Sojourning and the perceived enhancement of self-efficacy'. *International Journal Intercultural Relations*. 29:217-238, **28, 220**.

Mimica, J. (1988). *Intimations of Infinity. The cultural meanings of the Iqwaye counting and number system*. Berg. New York, **289**.

Mkenda, F.L.M. (2005). *Mazoezi ya Kiroho ya Mtakatifu Inyasi was Loyola*. Paulines Press. Nairobi, **173**.

Moazam, F.(2000). 'Families, patients and physicians in medical decision making; a Pakistani perspective'. *Hastings Center Reports*. 30(6): 28-37, **267**.

Moreland, R.L. and Beach, S.R.(1990). 'Exposure effects in the classroom. The development of affinity among students'. *Journal Experimental Social Psychology*. 28:255-76, **5**.

Mueser, K.T. and H. Berenbaum.(1990). 'Psychodynamic treatment of schizophrenia.; is there a future'. *Psychological Medicine*. 20(1): 253-262, **61**.

Murphy, A.H. and R.L.Winkler. (1992). 'Diagnostic verification of probability forecasts'. *International Journal of Forecasting*. 7;435-455, **229**.

Musa, A.Y. (2008). *Hadith as scripture. Discussions on the authority of prophetic traditions in Islam*. Palgrave. New York.

Myhre, K.C. (2006). 'Divination and experience. Exploration of a Chagga epistemology'. *Journal Royal Anthropological Institute*. (ns).12:313-330, **34**.

Myers, D.G. (2002). *Intuition; its powers and perils*. Yale University Press. New Haven, **5**.

Myrdal, G. (1944). *An American dilemma. The negro problem and American democracy*. Harper and Bros. New York, **282**.

Needham, J. (1954). *Science and Civilisation in China*. Cambridge University Press. Cambridge. Volume 1, **236**.

Newbold, P. and C.W.J. Granger.(1974). 'Experience with forecasting univariate time-series and the combination of forecasts'. *Journal Royal Statistical Society*. Series.A. 137:131-165, **244**.

Offer, D. *et al*. (2000). 'The altering of reported experiences'. *Journal American Academy Child Adolescent Psychiatry*. 39(6):735-742, **237**.

Opler, M.E. (1936) 'Some points of comparison and contrast between the treatment of functional disorders by Apache shamans and modern psychiatric practice'. *American Journal Psychiatry*. 92:1371-1387, **254**.

Osgood, C.E. *et al*. (1975). *Cross-cultural universals of affective meaning*. Illinois University Press. Urbana, **20**.

Ortendahl, M.(2007). 'Predicting lapse when stopping smoking in pregnant and non-pregnant women'. *Journal Obstetrics and Gynaecology*. 27(2): 138-43, **217**.

Pagani, L.S. *et al*. (2008). 'The case of unexpected pathways towards high school drop-outs'. *Journal Social Issues*. 64(5): 175-194, **14**.

Parkin, D.J. (1971). 'Language choice in two Kampala housing estates' in W.H.Whiteley.(ed). *Language use and social change. Problems of multilingualism with special reference to Eastern Africa*. 347-363. Oxford University Press. Oxford, **179**.

Parsons, T. (1968). *The structure of social action*. Vol 1. Free Press. New York.

Peek, P.M. (1991). *African divination systems*. Indiana University Press. Bloomington, **199**.

Peires, J.B.(1989). *The dead will arise: Nonqaeuse and the Great Cattle Killing movement 1857-7*. Raven Press. Johannesburg, **107.**

Perkins, G.D. *et al.* (2007). 'Discrepancies between clinical and post-mortem diagnoses in critically ill patients. An observational study'. *Critical Care*. 11:R48.

Phillips, D.L. (1967). 'Mental health status, social participation and happiness'. *Journal Health and Social Behaviour*. 8:285-296, **128.**

Popper, K.(1964). Quoted by M.Banton. 'Anthropological perspectives' *British Journal Sociology*. 15:95-112. 99, **6.**

— — (1974). Autobiography in P.A. Schilpp. (ed). *The Philosophy of Karl Popper*. Open Court. LaSalle. Illinois, **81.**

Postal, S. (1965). 'Body image and identity; a comparison of Kwakuitl and Hopi'. *American Anthropologist*. 67:455-462, **162.**

Powdermaker, H. (1966). *Stranger and friend. The way of an anthropologist*. Secker and Warburg. London, **78, 139, 198.**

Qadeer, I.(2006). 'Gender and health. Beyond numbers'. in S. deSouza.(ed). *Women's health in Goa*. Concept. New Delhi. 3-33, **18.**

Rakow, D. and Bull, C.(2003).'Same patient, different advices. A study into why doctors vary'. *Archives Diseases Childhood*. 88(6):497-502, **125.**

Randolph, A.G. *et al.* (1999). 'Variability in physician opinion on *limiting pediatric life support. Pediatrics*.103(4):46, **271.**

Rao, R. (1938). Preface to 'Kanthapura'. New Directions. New York, **180.**

Rappaport, R.A. (1979). *Ecology, meaning and religion*. North Atlantic Books. Berkeley, **80.**

— — (1999). *Ritual and religion in the making of humanity*. Cambridge University Press. Cambridge, **214.**

Rea, S.L. *et al.* (2005). 'A stress-sensitive reporter predicts longevity in isogenic populations of Caenorhabditis elegans.' *Nat Genet*. 37(8):894-8, **4.**

Read, K.E.(1967). 'Morality and the concept of reason among the Gahuku-Gama' in J.Middleton.(ed). *Myth and Cosmos*. 185-229. Natural History Press. New York, **162.**

Remus, W.E. and L.O. Jenicke. (1978). 'Unit and random linear models in decision making'. Multivariate Behavioral Research. 13:215-221, **69.**

Rescher, N. (1995). *Luck. The brilliant randomness of everyday life*. University of Pittsburgh Press. Pittsburg, **221-2.**

Reulbach, U. *et al.* (2007). 'Late onset schizophrenia in child survivors of the Holocaust'. *Journal Nervous and Mental Disease.* 195(4):315-9, **217**.

Rey, S.M. *et al.* (1999). 'Parental satisfaction and outcomes; a four year study in a child and adolescent mental health service'. *Australian and New Zealand Journal Psychiatry.* 32(1):22-8, **260**.

Reynolds, V. (2005). *The chimpanzees of Budongo forest. Ecology, behaviour and conservation.* Oxford University Press. Oxford, **43**.

Reynolds.V. and Tanner, R. (1995). *The social ecology of religion.* Oxford University Press. Oxford, **122**.

Ricoeur, P. (1971). 'The model of the text. Meaningful action considered as a text'. *Social Research.* 38(3):529-62, **180, 298**.

Rigby, P. (1974). 'The sociologist in decision making or the logic of false dichotomies'. Universities Social Science Council Conference. Kampala. Paper 19, **282**.

Robb, G. (2007). *The discovery of France.* Picador. London, **194, 236, 290**.

Roberts, D.F. and Tanner, R.E.S. (1959). ' A demographic study in an area of low fertility in north-east Tanganyika'. *Population.* 13(1), **97**.

— — (1967). 'Some problems of colour blindness'. *Journal Indian Anthropological Society.* 2:33-51, **54**.

Rokeach, M. (1964). *The three Christs of Ypsilanti.* Knopf. New York, **290**.

Rosen, P. *et al.* (2001). 'Patient views on choice and participation in primary health care'. *Health Policy.* 55:121-28, **267**.

Rowe, R.G. and G. Wright. (2001). 'Expert opinions in forecasting. The role of the Delphi technique' in J.S.Armstrong.(ed). *The principles of forecasting. A handbook for researchers and practitioners.* Kluwer Academic Publisher. Boston, **246**.

Rudski, J. (2003). 'What does a 'superstitious' person believe. Impressions of participants'. *Journal General Psychology.* 130(4), **19**.

Rumelhart, D.E. *et al.* (1986). 'A general framework for Parallel Distributive Processing'. in Rumelhart, D.E. *et al.* (1986). *Parallel Distributive Processing. Explorations in the microstructure of cognition.* MIT Press. Cambridge. Mass, **82, 93**.

Schubert, A. *et al.* (1999). 'Consistency, inter-rated reliability and validity of 8441 consecutive mock diagnoses'. *Anaesthesiology.* 91(1):288-98, **260**.

Scurletis, T.D. *et al.* (1969).'Trends in illegitimacy and associated mortality in North Carolina.1957-66'. *North Carolina Medical Journal*. 10: 214-21, **15**.

Segal, E.S. (1999). 'Gender transformation in cross-cultural perspective'. International Interdisciplinary Congress on Women. Tromso, **53**.

Seth, V. (1994). *A suitable boy*. Amazon. London.

Sharpe, L. *et al.* (2003). 'Testing for the integrity of blinding in clinical trials; how valid are forced choice paradigms'. *Psychotherapy Psychosomatics*. 72(3):128-131, **132**.

Shibutani, T. (1966). *Improved news. A sociological study of rumour*. Indianapolis, **199**.

Shi Meifen.(1989). *Peasant Daily*. 1/2, **58**.

Shoemaker, S.(1970). 'Persons and their pasts'. *American Philosophical Quarterly*. 7(4):269-285, **237**.

Shojania, K.G. *et al.* (2007). 'How quickly do systematic reviews go out of date? A survival analysis'. Annals Internal Medicine. 147:224-33, **38**.

Shweder, R.A. (1975). 'How relevant is an individual difference theory of personality'. Journal Personality. 43:455-484.

— — (1992). 'Anthropology in romantic rebellion against the Enlightenment or there's more to thinking than reason and evidence'. In R.A. Shweder and R.A. Levine (eds.). *Culture theory: Essays on mind, self and emotion*. Cambridge University Press. Cambridge. 27-66, **289, 303**.

Shweder, R.A. and E.J. Bourne. (1992). 'Does the concept of self vary cross- culturally' in R.A. Shweder and E.J. Bourne.(eds). *Culture theory. Essays in mind, self and emotion*. 158-199. Cambridge University Press. Cambridge, **171**.

Smith, D.S. and W.J. Catalona. (1995). 'Inter-examiner variability of digital rectal examination in detecting prostate cancer'. *Urology*. 45(1);70-74, **271**.

Smith, M. (1954). *Baba of Kano. A woman of the Muslim faith*. Faber and Faber. London.

Smith, R.J. (1983). *Japanese society. Tradition, self and the social order.* Cambridge University Press. Cambridge.

— — (1991). *Fortune teller and philosopher. Divination in traditional Chinese society.* Westview. Boulder, **297**.

Spero, M.H. (1980). *Judaism and psychology. Halakhic perspectives.* Yeshiva University Press. New York, **99**.

Spiro, M.E. (1971). *Buddhism and Society. A great tradition and its Burmese vicissitudes*. Allen and Unwin. London, **71**.

Srinivas, M.N. (1979). 'The field worker and the field. A village in Karnataka'. in M.N. Srinivas *et al.* (eds). *The field worker and the field*. Oxford University Press. Delhi, **134, 205**.

Suzuki, T. (1978). *Japanese and the Japanese*. Trans. A. Miura. Kodansha. Tokyo, **174**.

Sweeney, K. (2006). 'Personal knowledge'. *British Medical Journal*. 332:129, **293**.

Taleb, N.N. (2007). *The Black Swan. The impact of the highly improbable*. Allen Lane. London, **227, 256, 274**.

Tanner, R.E.S. (1964). 'Conflict within small European communities in Tanganyika'. *Human Organisation*. 23(4):319-327, **150**.

—— (1964).'Cousin marriage in the Afro-Arab community in Mombasa, Kenya'. *Africa*.34(2):127-138.

—— (1966). 'European leadership in small communities in Tanganyika prior to Independence'. *Race*. 7(3):289-302, **150**.

—— (1969). 'The theory and practice of Sukuma spirit mediumship'. In J. Beattie and J. Middleton.(eds), *Spirit Mediumship and Society in Africa*. Routledge and Kegan Paul. London. 273-289, **63**.

—— (1970a). *Homicide in Uganda.1964*. Scandinavian Institute of African Studies. Uppsala, **199**.

—— (1970b). *An East African prison*. Scandinavian Institute of African Studies. Uppsala, **207**.

—— (1978). 'Rumour and the Buganda Emergency.1966'. *Journal Modern African Studies*. 16:329-338, **199**.

—— (1979).'Word and Spirit in contemporary African religious practice and thought'. *Journal Religion in Africa*. 9(2):123-135, **175**.

—— (1993).'East African ethical ideas and translation'. *Anthropos*. 88:29-37, **167, 175**.

—— (1997).'Cognitive development, socialisation and cognitive mutations. A critique and elaboration of Boyer's Naturalness of Religion. A case study of the Sukuma of Tanzania'. *Journal Social Sciences*. 1(2):91-98.

—— (2001). 'Some reflections on being the subject of research into memory. An academic critique of methodology applied to a single person'. *Quality and Quantity. International Journal of Methodology*. 36(1):83-93, **142, 239**.

—— (2001). 'Informants and Researchers. Cooperation, self-interest and reciprocity. An examination of changing relationships.' *Journal Social Sciences*. 5(4):279-290.

—— (2007). 'Alternative methodologies for research work with children. Parallel Distributive Processing as a new possibility or another dead end.' *Quality and Quantity*. 41:319-332, **94**.

Temkin, N.R. *et al*. (1999). 'Detecting significant change in neuropsychological test performance; as comparison of four models'. *Journal International Neuropsychology Society*. 5(4):357-69, **261**.

Thomas, W.I. and D.S. Thomas (1925). *The child in America*. Knopf. New York, **305**.

Thumboo, J. *et al*. (2003). 'Quality of life in an urban Asian population; the impact of ethnicity and socio-economic status'. *Social Science and Medicine*. 56(8): 1761-1772, **187**.

Thurstone, L.L. (1928). 'The theory of attitude measurement'. *Psychological Bulletin*. 36:222-241, **20**.

Turnbull, C. (1961). *The Forest people*. Chatto & Windus. London, **117**.

—— (1973). *The mountain people*. Simon & Schuster. New York, **78, 117, 141**.

Turner, E. (2006). *Heart of lightness*. Berghahn. New York, **147**.

Turner, E.H. (2008). 'Selective publication of anti-depressant trials and its influence on apparent efficacy'. *New England Journal Medicine*. 17 January.

Turner, T.S. (2001). Letter re Yanomano. *New York Review of Books*. 26 April:09, **77**.

Turner, V. (1967). *The forest of symbols. Aspects of Ndembu ritual*. Cornell University Press. Ithaca, **66, 137, 207, 254**.

Tversky, A. and D. Kahneman.(1982). 'The framing of decisions and the psychology of choice' in R.M.Hogarth.(ed). *Question framing and response inconsistency*. 3-20. Jossey-Bass. San Francisco, **191, 265**.

—— (2006). 'Judgement under uncertainty; heuristics and biases'. in D. Kahneman *et al*.(eds.). *Judgment under uncertainty; heuristics and biases*.3-22. Cambridge University Press. Cambridge, **263**.

Van Riper, M. (1997). 'Death of a sibling. Five sisters, five stories'. *Pediatric Nursing*.23(6): 587-595, **126**.

Varadachar, B.D. (1979). 'The bottom view up. Some cognitive categories' in M.N. Srinivas et al.(eds). *The field worker and the field*. Oxford University Press. Delhi, 127-140, **145**.

Wahlberg, A. (2007). 'A quackery with a difference. New medical pluralism and the problem of dangerous practitioners in the United Kingdom'. *Social Science and Medicine*. 65:2307-2316, **254**.

Watanabe, S. (1969). *Knowing and Guessing*. Wiley. New York, **53**.

Watkins, T. (2007). Obituary. *Daily Telegraph*. 10 September, **217**.

Watzlawick, P. *et al*.(1967). The pragmatics of human communication. Norton. New York, **287**.

Weber, M. (1946). *Essays in Sociology*. Oxford University Press. New York, **228**.

Weinberg, S. (2008). 'Without God'. *New York Review Books*. 25 Sept: 73-76, **290**.

Weiss, R.S. (1973). *The experience of motional and social isolation*. MIT Conference Memoranda.13, **219**.

Whyte, W.F. (1951). *Street corner society*. Chicago University Press. Chicago, **104**.

Williams, C. and S.W. Vines.(1999). 'Broken past, fragile futures. ; personal stories of high-risk adolescent mothers'. *Journal Social Pediatric Nursing*. 4(1):15-23, **261**.

Williams, W.H. and L. Goodman.(1971). 'A simple method for the construction of empirical confidence limits to economic forecasts'. *Journal American Statistical Association*. 66:752-4, **244**.

Wolfgang, M.E.(1958). *Patterns in criminal homicide*. Philadelphia, **199**.

Wolmer, R.N. (2001). *Thinking with your soul. Spiritual intelligence and why it matters*. Harmony Books. New York, **173**.

Wolpert, L.(2006). *Six impossible things before breakfast. The evolutionary origins of belief*. Faber and Faber. London, **35**.

Wuthnow, R. and W. Cadge. (2004). 'Buddhists and Buddhism in the United States. The scope of influence'. *Journal Scientific Study of Religion*. 43(3):363-380, **87**.

Xu, E. *et al*. (2007). 'The association between amount of cigarettes smoked and overweight central obesity among Chinese adults in Nansing China'. *Asia Pacific Journal Clinical Nutrition*. 16(2):240-7, **256**.

Yang, K-P. (2006).'The spiritual intelligence of nurses in Taiwan'. *Journal Nursing Research*. 14(1): 24-35, **173**.

Yank, V. *et al*. (2007). 'Financial ties and concordance between results and conclusions in meta-analyses; a retrospective cohort study'. *British Medical Journal*. 8 December. 335:1167-9, **57**.

Yeo, B.H. *et al*. (2007). 'Factors influencing breastfeeding rates in south-western Sydney'. *Journal Pediatrics Child Health*. 43(4).249-55, **187**.

Young, M.(2004). Malinowski. B. *The odyssey of an anthropologist*. Yale University Press.

Zajonc, R.B. (1998).'Emotion' in D. Gilbert *et al*. (eds). *Handbook of Social Psychology*. McGraw-Hill. New York, **5**.

Zautra, A. *et al*. (1977). 'The dimensions of life quality in a community' *American Journal of Community Psychology*. 5:85-98, **128**.

— — (1983). 'Surveying the quality of life in the community'. In R.A. Bell *et al*. (eds). *Assessing health and Human Service Needs. Concepts, Methods and Applications*. Human Sciences Press. New York, **128**.

Zeltlyn, D. (1990). Professor Garfinkel visits the soothsayer; ethnomethodology and Mambila divination'. *Man (ns)*. 25:654-66, **30**.

Zir, L.M. *et al*. (1976). 'Inter-observer variability in coronary angiography'. *Circulation*. 53:627-32, **271**.

Index